T0271657

MURDER IN THE GULAG

Also by John Sweeney

NON-FICTION

Killer in the Kremlin: The Explosive Account of
Putin's Reign of Terror
Hunting Ghislaine
North Korea Undercover: Inside the World's Most Secret State
The Church of Fear: Inside the Weird World of Scientology
Big Daddy: Lukashenka, Tyrant of Belarus
Rooney's Gold
Purple Homicide, Fear and Loathing on Knutsford Heath
Trading With the Enemy: Britain's Arming of Iraq
The Life and Evil Times of Nicolae Ceausescu
Murder on the Malta Express: Who Killed Daphne Caruana Galizia?
(with Carlo Bonini and Manuel Delia)

FICTION

The Useful Idiot
Road
Cold
Elephant Moon

MURDER IN THE GULAG

The Life and Death of Alexei Navalny

John Sweeney

HEADLINE PRESS

First published in 2024 by Headline Press
An imprint of Headline Publishing Group

2

Cataloguing in Publication Data is available from the British Library

Hardback ISBN: 978 1 0354 2228 9
Trade Paperback ISBN: 978 1 0354 2229 6

Typeset in 13/16pt Bembo MT Pro by Jouve (UK), Milton Keynes

Printed and bound in Great Britain by Clays Ltd, Elcograf S.p.A.

Headline's policy is to use papers that are natural, renewable and recyclable
products and made from wood grown in well-managed forests and other
controlled sources. The logging and manufacturing processes are expected
to conform to the environmental regulations of the country of origin.

Headline Publishing Group
An Hachette UK Company
Carmelite House
50 Victoria Embankment
London EC4Y 0DZ

www.headline.co.uk
www.hachette.co.uk

'Air raid sirens across the country
It feels like everyone is brought out
For execution
But only one person gets targeted
Usually the one at the edge
This time not you;
All clear'

Victoria Amelina, Ukrainian human
rights investigator, 1986–2023

'I didn't kill him. I shot him, bullets and the fall killed him.'
Vincent, the hitman played by Tom Cruise
in the film noir *Collateral*, 2004

'I don't understand this position. First of all, it's boring. Second of
all, forgive me if this sounds pompous, but it's better to die standing
up than to stay alive on your knees.'
Alexei Navalny, explaining why he refused
to be intimidated by the power and
corruption of the Kremlin

CONTENTS

Author's note

Throughout this book, I have taken the liberty of fiddling with original translations because I've got an O level in Russian, I'm a professional writer and where the original feels clunky and offends my lah-de-dah Gunner Graham's English-English. For international readers who can work out the source of that particular cultural reference, if we chance to meet I will buy them a beer.

Introduction

Terminator 2: Judgment Day was Alexei Navalny's favourite movie so he was laid to rest to the schmaltzy melody that saw Arnold Schwarzenegger's Terminator T-800 meet his bad metal maker in a steel mill, giving a final thumbs-up to John Connor, the symbol of humanity's hope. Navalny's last joke was, of course, targeted at Vladimir Putin's neurosis that, in Arnie's catchphrase: 'I'll be back.'

The question that haunts the killer in the Kremlin – haunts, too, the future of the largest country on earth – is whether the snuffing out of Navalny's courage, charisma and honesty will stick in Russia's craw and bring on Putin's overthrow; that, in a kind of way, Navalny, his face half-metal, half-human, one cyborg red eye blink-blink-blinking, will one day stomp across Red Square towards the high red walls of the citadel of the tsar in blood. As a 'fuck you!' from beyond the grave, it was rather cool.

And: on brand.

Snuffed out Navalny most definitely was. It's hard to check facts in Russia because if you do it properly you end up dead. If you doubt my word, you will get a lick with the rough edge of my tongue. Anna Politkovskaya, Natalia Estemirova,

Boris Nemtsov and Navalny all challenged the Kremlin's magical untruths to me in person. Now, they are no more: in sequence, poisoned, then shot; shot; shot; poisoned, twice, then murdered, precise method as yet unknown. You will see an exhaustive list of the people Putin has killed and the most likely method at the end of this book. By the way, I'm not worried about being sued by the psychopath president. He uses different methods to secure satisfaction.

But get this: the word 'disinformation' doesn't begin to properly convey the power of the Kremlin to generate doubt and uncertainty across the bright and darkened lands of the earth. How do you react to evil if you are not sure what, exactly, has happened? Or who did what? Schrödinger's Cat is a thought experiment in quantum physics setting out that tiny particles can exist in two places at once until they are observed. Imagine a cat in a box with something that could kill it. Open the box: the cat is both dead and alive. The Kremlin has repurposed Schrödinger's Cat with evil intent, so that not knowing, not understanding, is the natural condition of the enemies of the Russian dark state. Vladimir Putin has built the greatest fog machine in history.

The point of *Murder in the Gulag* is to blow away that fog. This book isn't a whodunnit. Putin hated the Russian who mocked him like no one else, hated him so much he would never, ever mention him by name. Navalny joked with me when I interviewed him in Moscow in 2018 that he was like 'He Who Must Not Be Named' in the Harry Potter books, that 'I am Lord Voldemort.' Putin had Navalny murdered.

It is, though, a howdunnit. How, exactly, did they kill him? Navalny was a man of extraordinarily good health considering that he had been beaten up countless times, poisoned twice, and, once he returned to Russia in 2021, suffered two years more of torture in Putin's gulag, including three hundred days in isolation. In his first prison colony, IK-2 Pokrov, about sixty miles from Moscow, he was woken up eight times a night. This was torture by sleep deprivation.

Navalny was moved to an even nastier prison, IK-6, in the village of Melekhovo. He described the cooler therein, a seven foot by nine 'concrete doghouse . . . I have a beach version – very hot and almost no air. The window is tiny, because of the thickness of the walls air does not go – even the cobwebs do not move. There is no ventilation. At night you lie there and feel like a fish on the shore.'

His last home was IK-3, the 'Polar Wolf' prison colony in the middle of a very cold fridge-freezer. One day this bouncy and full of fun 47-year-old was filmed on a video link from IK-3, taking the piss out of the duty judge down the line, teasing her to use some of her vast salary to top up his own bank account. The camera panned out to catch his IK-3 jailers standing next to him laughing at the prisoner's wit. The next day Navalny is dead.

Nothing official in Russia is true; or stays true for long. The poisoning of the well of information in the Western world through bots and counter-facts and internet rumours, dark fairy stories boosted on social media sites, is no accident but one of the most successful exports of the dark Russian state. Everything Putin does in the West, he's tried out back home before. He has been corroding truth since his very first days in power, when Boris Yeltsin – once the hope of a new, democratic Russia but by the summer of 1999 a senile alcoholic controlled by some of his own wretchedly corrupt family – appointed his creepy secret police boss acting prime minister. Within days, blocks of flats in Moscow and southern Russia were blown up by

'Chechen terrorists', according to the official version of events. But the evidence is overwhelming that the true culprits were the FSB: the new name for the KGB. For more on Vladimir Putin's original sin in power, that he blew up Russia, read my book, *Killer in the Kremlin*.

Within hours of Navalny's death, a whole variety of causes of death had hit the internet. The official version was that he had suffered some kind of natural death, but when his 69-year-old mother, Lyudmila Navalnaya, asked for the body of her son, the authorities fired back, launching a new criminal investigation into Oleg Navalny, Alexei's younger brother, who had been jailed for three and a half years on trumped-up charges, only getting out of prison in 2018. Oleg is believed to be in hiding, but the message was clear enough to Navalny's mother: shut up or you won't see your son's body, or even maybe your other son, again, ever.

To get your head round Putin's Russia, watch *The Godfather*.

Navalny's death brought forth tributes from around the world, but, more to the point, hundreds of people were arrested in Russia for daring to mark the passing of their hero. One noted exception to this outpouring of grief was Vladimir Putin. The day the news broke, he was hanging out in Chelyabinsk, in the Urals. Ordinarily a miserable git when he takes part in official ceremonies, Putin, parked a safe distance from any potentially infectious mortals, was full of fun, laughing, teasing and high as a kite. And why not? He'd just had the leader of the opposition murdered.

Putin's PR man Dmitry Peskov denied allegations that the Russian state was connected to Navalny's death. Of course he did. Peskov sports a ginger mullet and looks like a zombie version of a Rotherham United manager from the

1970s. He called Yulia Navalnaya's accusations that Putin had her husband killed 'unfounded and vulgar', to which Navalnaya said: 'I do not give a damn how the press secretary of a murderer comments on my words.'

The boy Navalny had a picture of Schwarzenegger on his bedroom wall. 'My main hero was, and still is, Arnold Schwarzenegger,' he told Russian *Esquire* in 2011. Navalny's love for the *Terminator 2* cyborg is striking because we all know that *Terminator 1* was a bad 'un. Like *Terminator 2*, Navalny was an awkward sod but that comes with the territory if you have the balls to stand up to Putin. He was also charismatic, very; tall and blue-eyed, a natural leader whose love of the absurd saved him from turning into a full-blown messiah. He had started out as a lawyer representing clients who had been wronged by Russia's corruption engine. In politics, he started out as a liberal in the Yabloko party but became frustrated with its lack of traction with ordinary Russians. Then began his hugely controversial flirtation with the far right. He turned up for the annual 'Russia March' three years in a row from 2007, albeit with a Jewish friend who waved a huge Star of David sign. He did make two short videos that are obnoxiously racist, implying that Chechens are 'cockroaches' and playing on fears of immigration. The details are not good. On these videos, Navalny came across as a bit of a fascist. But, at Yale on a fellowship, one of his closest friends was the first black British mayor of a big city. Navalny's defence is that to challenge Putin's fascism effectively, he had to play along with some strange bedfellows.

From around 2011 he put aside his earlier dark nonsense, never repeated it – but never apologised for it – and became the most popular champion of a democratic Russia that would blow away the stink of Putinesque corruption and follow the rule of law.

After he had left the far right behind, he got into fresh trouble by infuriating the Ukrainians. Firstly, in 2011, he adopted the Kremlin's patter: 'Of course, it would be great if now we lived in one country with Ukraine and Belarus, but I think that sooner or later it will happen anyway.' When Russia seized Crimea in the spring of 2014, a huge number of Russians thought this was a good thing. Put on the spot by the head of the Ekho Moskvy station, Alexey Venediktov, that October, Navalny tried to fudge a way through.

'Is Crimea ours?' asked Venediktov.

'Crimea belongs to the people who live in Crimea,' Navalny hedged.

'You will not escape answering. Is Crimea ours? Is Crimea Russian?'

'Crimea, of course, now de facto belongs to Russia. I believe that, despite the fact that Crimea was seized in blatant violation of all international norms, nevertheless, the reality is that Crimea is now part of the Russian Federation. And let's not fool ourselves. And I strongly advise Ukrainians not to deceive themselves either. It will remain part of Russia and will never become part of Ukraine in the foreseeable future.'

Venediktov twisted the knife. If Navalny was in the Kremlin, would he return Crimea to Ukraine?

'Is Crimea a sausage sandwich, or something that you can take and give it back?'

Navalny, for oh so many Ukrainians, was another Russian imperialist seeking to keep their country on its knees. To be fair, Navalny's north star had always been dethroning

Putin from the Kremlin. Siding with the lawful owners of Ukraine would not help him win votes in Russia, if ever he would be allowed to stand in a fair ballot against Putin. He never was. In February 2023, when he was back in Putin's gulag, he issued the following statement: 'What are Ukraine's borders? They are the same as Russia's, internationally recognised and defined in 1991. Russia also recognised these borders back then, and it must recognise them today as well. There is nothing to discuss here.'

In plain language, he meant that Crimea is Ukrainian, full stop. He called for Russia to get out of Ukraine, for the proper investigation of war crimes and for Russia to pay reparations by using its gold from oil and gas.

'Are all Russians inherently imperialistic? This is bullshit. For example, Belarus is also involved in the war against Ukraine. Does this mean that the Belarusians also have an imperial mindset? No, they merely also have a dictator in power. There will always be people with imperial views in Russia, just like in any other country with historical preconditions for this, but they are far from the majority. Such people should be defeated in elections, just as both right-wing and left-wing radicals get defeated in developed countries.'

It is extremely hard to come to a settled judgement on the weight of Russian opinion polls. My take is that if you say what you really think in twenty-first-century Russia, you are likely to jump out of a window very soon afterwards. The polls suggest Putin's 'special military operation' – Russia's war against Ukraine – is popular. Navalny said that it wasn't. He continued: 'The real reasons for this war are the political and economic problems within Russia, Putin's desire to hold on to power at any cost. He wants to go down in history as "the Conqueror Tsar."'

Too little, too late, say many Ukrainians. 'Russian democracy ends where the Ukrainian question begins', as they like to say in Kyiv.

As I write this introduction, I am conscious that my Ukrainian pals won't like it that I am standing up for Navalny. My friend Vlad Demchenko, who arrested me for being a Russian spy on day two of the big war, raged, is raging and will rage some more. He is fighting for Ukraine on the front line and is a hero. He has lost too many wonderful Ukrainian comrades to give someone like Navalny the benefit of the doubt. They believe that Russia is a perpetual monster factory. I was in Kyiv in February 2022 when I saw the aftermath of the Russian missile strike against the TV tower and saw the people from the morgue pick up the bodies of an old man and a mother and her five-year-old child with my own eyes. There have been too many times when I find it hard to disagree with them.

But I do not think that Navalny, for all his faults, was a monster. All I can say is that from London, where I write this the night before another operation on my knee, buggered up after I fell on black ice in Kyiv, the fact that Navalny was killed in Putin's gulag proves Ukraine's reason for fighting to the death. From London, telling Navalny's story, warts and all, helps Ukraine.

In *Navalny*, the extraordinary 2022 Oscar-winning documentary about him, director Daniel Roher asks: 'When you were a kid, did you have any political awareness? Was this a political family?'

Navalny replied: 'Yes, my family talks about politics all the time. They start to talk much more after the Chernobyl disaster because, actually, my father and his family, they are from Chernobyl, from a small village, I would say, ten kilometres away from the nuclear station. Everyone knows that there was an explosion of a nuclear station, but news keeping silence and so all this nuclear and radioactive dust was on these fields and they were forced to go to plant potatoes, just to prevent rumours, just to explain population that everything is fine.

"Everything is okay! Go and work in the fields!" And with the first appearance of Putin on the screen, I just felt it. I have this same feeling like I am watching TV and I am watching political lizard and he's looking into my eyes and lying to me.'

The monster in this book is not Navalny, but Russia's lizard king.

Navalny's father was born in Soviet Ukraine and young Alexei spent his first nine summers in his grandmother's village, Zalyssia, before the Chernobyl nuclear disaster forced the authorities to move the whole community to New Zalyssia, near Borodyanka, to the north of Kyiv. Come the big war in 2022, the Russian occupiers murdered one of his second cousins simply because he was called Navalny. You can make the argument that Navalny, in defying the Kremlin the way he did, lived up to his Ukrainian roots.

To me, Navalny symbolised the idea of a Russia without fascism, free and democratic. Von Stauffenberg dared to try to kill Hitler but he also did something else: he kept the idea of another Germany alive in 1944. Navalny dared to stand up to Putin and kept the idea of another Russia alive in 2024. That Von Stauffenberg had worn a Nazi uniform is beside the point.

Or let's take *Terminator 2* head on. At the end of the movie, we hear Sarah Connor, the mother of the human saviour, John, acknowledge that there is hope because a machine could learn to love her son. That a Russian nationalist like Navalny could end up calling for Putin's killing machine to get out of Ukraine and for Russia to respect the 1991 boundaries, that Crimea is Ukrainian, is no small thing.

The Kremlin watches what Kyiv says and so does its useful idiots. Tucker Carlson was at one time the most watched cable news presenter in the States until he was sacked from Fox News. The Murdoch empire that owns the network were happy running Carlson's conspiracy theory that Joe Biden had stolen the 2020 election from Donald Trump thanks to voting machines that had generated a false result. They didn't like paying the maker of the machines, Dominion Voting Systems, $787.5 million in a lawsuit so that is why many people think Fox sacked him. On 9 February, Carlson, now freelance, interviewed Vladimir Putin in Moscow. What you got was a sometimes surreal but most often extremely boring encounter in which the Russian president lectured the far-right American television personality on abstruse bits of Russian history that set out his junk case that Ukraine belonged to Russia. Putin talked rubbish but Carlson let him get away with it. Carlson's patsy questions bored even Putin, who later said he 'didn't get complete satisfaction . . . I honestly thought he would be aggressive and ask so-called sharp questions. And I wasn't just ready for that, I wanted it, because it would have given me the opportunity to respond sharply in kind . . . But he chose a different tactic.'

Putin, always keen to sniff out an adversary's weakness, even referred to Carlson's pitiful attempt to join the Company. Bringing up his own conspiracy theory, Putin asserted that Ukraine's 2014 revolution was staged.

'With the backing of whom?' Carlson asked.

'With the backing of CIA, of course.'

A frisky Putin then jabbed: 'The organisation you wanted to join back in the day, as I understand. Maybe we should thank God they didn't let you in.'

It didn't sound like a compliment and it wasn't.

When I doorstepped Putin in 2014 in a mammoth museum in Siberia, I asked him about the shooting down of MH17 when 298 innocent people were shot out of the sky by a Russian missile. Putin lied and blamed the Ukrainians for not talking to the separatists in the east, a formula he later used on President Macron of France a few days before the big war. A few hours later, a silent goon punched me in the stomach. That was, in its own, funny peculiar way, a compliment from the Kremlin. Violence means they are taking you seriously.

The interview lasted two hours but Carlson failed to mention the fate of Russia's most famous political prisoner once. Is it possible that Putin banked Carlson's lack of interest in Navalny and steeled him to have him murdered a week later? I believe it is.

On his return to the States, Carlson gave an interview to Chris Cuomo, the former CNN star, who challenged him about his omission.

Cuomo: 'You didn't ask him about Navalny. You said all leaders kill. But don't you feel that if you are gonna go and sit with someone like that you have to hold them to account for things that matter? He may have murdered somebody, a lot of people?'

Carlson: 'The Ukrainians say that he didn't kill him.'

Cuomo: 'That guy looks good one minute. Next minute, he's dead.'

Carlson: 'The Ukrainian government said no, he died of natural causes.'

It is true that the Sphynx of Kyiv, Ukrainian military intelligence chief Kyrylo Budanov, was quoted as telling reporters on Sunday that 'I may disappoint you, but we know he died from a blood clot,' adding that it was 'more or less confirmed.'

Carlson continued: 'Now, what is actually going on there? I can't even guess. OK, Navalny died in the middle of the Munich Security Conference. Also, in the middle of the debate over Ukraine funding in the United States, and his death was within hours used by the president of the United States to justify another 60 billion. So those are just facts. I haven't the faintest idea. Here's what I learned – and I'm hardly a Russia expert – is that this is an extremely complicated political environment. Extremely. Like: next level. These are the people who dominate world chess. And so their politics are incomprehensible to me. So what's actually happening? I mean, I've been in a lot of countries and covered a lot of stuff abroad. And the one thing I've learned is you actually don't really know what's going on.'

I struggle with this. I struggle with how someone as fluent as Carlson could be so wittingly ignorant of the succession of people critical of Putin who have ended up dead. I struggle with knowing the torture Navalny suffered in the Russian gulag, that his lawyer was so shocked on seeing her client's face gone grey, but that Carlson, given a two-hour slot with the man responsible for the killings of so many, with the man ultimately responsible for creating Navalny's airless isolation cell, could not be bothered to mention his name.

It is as if Tucker Carlson is Moscow's creature.

★

Hard to imagine it now, but Navalny almost toppled Putin's regime. His big moment came in 2012 when Putin switched his patsy, Dmitry Medvedev – 'Al Capone's lawyer' – out of the Kremlin so he could get back in again, turning the constitution into so much used toilet paper. People who believed in Navalny's idea of 'Another Russia', one that stood for democracy and the rule of law, hit the streets in their hundreds of thousands. Navalny called Putin's political vehicle 'The Party of Crooks and Thieves', Putin a thief – in Russian: 'Путин вор'/'Putin vor' – and he became a kind of rock star. One time, the police arrested him, twisting his arm behind his back so he howled in pain, before locking him in a police van. That video was seen millions of times.

I first interviewed him via Zoom in 2016 when I was in Lake Baikal, Siberia. I held chips in the air, waiting for seagulls to pounce, the gag being that we were focusing on an investigation Navalny had made about Russia's then fabulously corrupt Prosecutor General, Yuri Chaika – and 'chaika' in Russia means 'seagull'. Fair cop: BBC *Newsnight* couldn't stump up the cash for me to fly to Siberia so we used Southend-on-Sea with the tide out as a stand-in. Hardly anyone could tell the difference.

On Zoom, Navalny was scathing about Londongrad as a sluice for Russian dirty money, and he blasted Putin as 'the tsar of corruption'. His words tolled as clear as a bell, and you knew that every syllable was a potential death sentence. It isn't a surprise that the Kremlin had him killed in February 2024; the surprise is that he lived for so long. But even as I type this, I mourn him and cannot quite believe that this great force of nature has been silenced for good.

Navalny was wary of – or didn't have much time for – most of the Western media press corps in Russia. Of course, he wanted to be on the popular Russian media, to reach everyone, but he was banned from all the state TV channels. He could get on a few independent stations like TV Rain, but they were closely associated with the opposition and watched by very few. If he was on Western TV all the time, he would start to look like an old-fashioned dissident and it would be easy for the Kremlin to pass him off as a Western puppet. There may have been another factor because, I suspect, he felt the Western media stationed in Moscow were more or less compromised by working to the Kremlin's rule book. Perhaps I was different because I really didn't do that; was based in London; had first called Putin a 'war criminal' in the *Observer* in 2000, long before it was fashionable, after I had gone undercover to Chechnya; and had doorstepped Putin in person over the shooting down of MH17. But, still, I got the impression that he felt he was wasting his time when he talked to me so I was pleased when, in March 2024, Roman Borisovich, a former insurance boss in Moscow, who was one of Navalny's earliest supporters of his Anti-Corruption Foundation, forwarded an old Navalny email about me: 'Sweeney is a cool dude, it was interesting for me to talk to him, and the subject was good. But it was not a *"coup d'état"*, just another telly piece. You are paying too much attention to this, like most people who don't often speak to the media. I would like to be interviewed by Channel One or *Komsomol Pravda*, but they are not asking. And BBC and CNN are not what I want.'

As you can tell from the flavour of that email to Borisovich, he could be annoying, very. The first time Navalny and I met in the flesh was at the European Court of Human Rights in Strasbourg in January 2018 where his lawyers were suing Russia for stopping him standing against Putin.

Hearing concluded, he had five minutes to talk to me for a BBC *Panorama* programme we were making about him called 'Taking on Putin'. Cameraman Seamas McCracken was fixing mics on lapels when I explained that Seamas was from Northern Ireland. Seamas stopped work. Navalny was greatly amused as precious seconds slipped away while I apologised and said that Seamas was from the north of the island of Ireland. Only when Navalny was happy that Seamas was happy did the interview lurch onwards and I got my sound bite. But what sticks in the mind was not my Irish pal sticking up for his rights, but Navalny's amusement at my difficulty. Seamas described the two of us meeting in these terms: 'It was like watching two big dogs sniff each other's bottoms.'

Filming in Moscow for 'Taking on Putin' in 2018 was heavy. I was taken aback by the barbarity of how the Russian secret police dealt with Team Navalny. I was doorstepped twice by Russian media, falsely accused of desecrating a shrine to Boris Nemtsov, the liberal heart-throb and former deputy prime minister who was shot dead 100 metres from the Kremlin. Then I was detained in a police station with Seamas, our passports leaked online so they had to be cancelled, followed by goons 24/7, and our fixer was declared a terrorist and had to leave the country for good. But we had it easy compared to Team Navalny. In Moscow, he and his supporters were under continuing attack. One chap was tasered, then stabbed and left to bleed to death in the snow. A senior member of his team had been hit over the head with an iron bar, another beaten black and blue by silent thugs. This opened my eyes to the machinery of Russian fascism as never before.

And yet Navalny was not cowed. What you got was the

real thing: sardonic, amused, amusing, him punching words out at the little man in the Kremlin. 'Is Russia a police state?' I asked him. 'Absolutely,' he replied.

Frustrated by Putin blocking his democratic path to oust him, Navalny made brilliant videos for YouTube detailing the monstrous scale of corruption in Russia watched by millions. They were both forensic and hugely entertaining. His last two films stand out. The first was *Navalny*, the Oscar-winning documentary, about how Team Navalny tracked down the Kremlin's poisoners, the goons who had almost killed him. Recovering in Germany, he was joined by the digital Sherlock Holmes of our time, Christo Grozev; his faithful Tonto, Leonid Volkov; and his investigations boss, Maria Pevchikh. Grozev bought phone numbers and flight manifests on the dark web and, hey presto, he got matches. The movie culminates in an astonishing scene where Navalny, playing a Kremlin high-up, called one of the poisoners. The hapless goon coughed up to the mechanism of assassination, that they lined the seams of the codpiece of his underpants with Novichok, while Grozev, listening in, puts his hands over his mouth because he dare not laugh out loud at the stupidity of the secret policeman. *Putin's Palace* appeared immediately after Navalny returned to Russia. That film got 125 million views on YouTube and set out in fine detail how his oligarchs paid for a naff palace by the Black Sea with golden toilet roll holders, how Putin the thief had robbed Russia blind.

To outsiders, the great puzzle of Navalny's life is why, having recovered from a monstrous murder attempt, he went back to Russia daring Putin to murder him. Which is exactly what Putin proceeded to do. One of the goals of this book is to explain what made Navalny go home. A show trial followed, the only thing real being the moment when Navalny, from his glass-walled dock, cradled his hands into the shape of a heart for his wife, Yulia.

When Navalny returned to Russia, he took a bet that Vladimir Putin would not dare to kill the man who was on the blackest of black lists. Navalny lost the bet. The other evening I had a vodka Martini, shaken not stirred, with a former officer in a Western intelligence service who told me: 'You've got to ask yourself, why was Navalny allowed to live for so long? I believe that part of the answer is that he was used by the oligarchs in the games they played, far above his head, against each other. They used him to embarrass their enemies and so, for at least some of the very powerful men who had Putin's ear, he was more useful alive, not dead. That was his insurance policy. But there came a moment when he was no longer useful.'

Navalny, to my friend, was a kind of gladiator, a brave warrior who would fight his heart out, never quite realising that he was not much more than a puppet controlled by higher forms of being. Perhaps there is some truth to this view of him as a plaything of the oligarchs, but I do not think it is the whole story.

For me, Navalny was killed in large part because of the West's appeasement of Putin that, even today, despite all the killings of innocent men, women and children in Ukraine, our leaders are afraid to stand up to the monster in the Kremlin, to properly enforce sanctions, to effectively arm Ukraine, to cut Russia off from the international financial system. The West is doing none of the above and is in danger of not just betraying Ukraine but its own security.

Murder in the Gulag is, then, three books in one: a murder mystery, trying to understand how a flawed Russian hero, a knight in dented armour, came to be killed; a study of the strange death of democratic Russia; and an analysis of the West's failure to defend itself against the psychopath who murdered that democracy. Since the paperback of *Killer in the Kremlin* was published in February 2023, two more big Russian beasts have been murdered: Yevgeny Prigozhin, blown out of the sky in his jet after his failed mutiny, and Navalny. Proof, if proof were needed, of concept. But *Killer* was written in the good times, immediately after the Battle of Kyiv in the early summer of 2022, when the Russian army was a bit of a joke. The story has moved on and got much, much darker. For a long time, even though he was immured in a concrete dog kennel, Putin had feared Navalny more than he hated him, he feared the real-world consequences of having him murdered. As the Russian killing machine grinds westwards, as the prospect of a Trump second term becomes more likely, as the West fails to deliver sufficient materiel to Ukraine, Putin is becoming stronger by the day. On Valentine's Day this year, the lizard king decided to kill the man he dared not name, gambling that he could get away with it.

Alexei Navalny was, then, a canary down a coal mine. When the canary is snuffed out, mourning is not enough. We need to act and act fast, otherwise it will be our funeral next.

That is why telling Navalny's story is so important.

That is why this book tries to get inside Navalny's head.

That is why I want to you to read *Murder in the Gulag*.

CHAPTER ONE

The Boy from Chernobyl

No alarms, no newspaper announcement, nothing on the telly: only a command to go out into the fields and plant potatoes to secure the crop for later in the year. And that was odd because Zalyssia, the home village of Navalny's grandmother, his father's mother, was less than twenty miles from the heart of the world's biggest nuclear accident. Navalny's mother was Russian but his father had been brought up in Soviet Ukraine, in the shadow of the red-and-white chimneys of the Chernobyl nuclear power plant, and that is where the boy Navalny spent his first nine summers. Vladimir Putin once said that the end of the Soviet Union was the 'greatest geopolitical catastrophe of the twentieth century'. Navalny knew Putin or anyone who thought like him to be an idiot from the age of ten.

What was supposed to be a safety test at the number four reactor at the Chernobyl nuclear power plant in April 1986 was the sickest of jokes. The RMBK reactor was the Soviet solution to big oil prices. But it had a series of horrible design flaws. It couldn't tell its operators what was really happening in its guts. Operators could turn a valve by moving a helm-sized wheel and not know whether this would make things more or less dangerous. And the designers' safety test could lead to a disastrous chain reaction which boiled the nuclear kettles. That had happened eleven years before in 1975 in Soviet Leningrad, now St Petersburg, when Putin was just starting his career inside the KGB in his home city. The secretive Soviet state covered up the huge leak of radiation. The exposed population were not told of the danger. The accident was not reported in the media. The Ministry of Medium Machine Building blamed the accident on poor construction, not terrible design. The commission investigating the incident made several recommendations. None were implemented. No one complained because no one knew. Welcome to the Soviet Union.

So, in April 1986, the moment the reactor technicians at Chernobyl pushed the AZ-5 button to lower the rods into the reactor, they thought they were ending the test. In fact, they were setting off a chain reaction which blew up the nuclear kettle, ripping open the concrete roof to expose the core and dumping tons of horribly irradiated graphite around the site. People in the plant town of Pripyat saw an extraordinarily beautiful jet of dark blue light power heavenwards from the broken plant, and then an orange glow, not realising that this ionising radiation and the massive core leak would lead to something like 9,000 deaths by cancer for people in Ukraine, Belarus and Russia in the years to come.

Years later, Navalny, when the few rare days officialdom allowed, would return to Zalyssia's empty streets inside the Chernobyl exclusion zone to look at its abandoned classrooms, to see the overgrown playgrounds he had run around in, to return to his grandmother's abandoned home and gawp in awe at what the Soviet Union had done to ruin it all.

Chernobyl, the compelling HBO TV drama series which

aired in 2019, was based on the personal stories of survivors brought together by the Nobel Prize-winning writer, Svetlana Alexievich, and a long, hard look at what had actually gone wrong. The authorities had pinned the blame on a martinet, Anatoly Dyatlov, the prickly, emotionally unsympathetic deputy chief engineer at the power station, for sticking with the safety test when things started to go wrong. Dyatlov was scapegoated and imprisoned. But the HBO series set out the evidence that it was the design of the reactor and, behind that, the closed mind of the Soviet system, not an individual, that had failed so badly. Putin's supporters hated *Chernobyl*, decrying the miniseries as Western propaganda.

Navalny knew they were talking poppycock and said so on YouTube: 'What happened in Chernobyl was really a monstrous catastrophe, in which guilt lay precisely with the constant lie, the disgusting, ugly lie told by these people, all these Soviet bosses sitting in Moscow and Kyiv. I get a bit emotional speaking about this because in a sense this is the story of my family. All the relatives from my father's side are from Chernobyl. I know perfectly well from my relatives about this whole story of endless lies. The power station blew up, but nevertheless they were silent, and drove them out there to plant . . . potatoes for the collective farm. Here they were digging with their own hands, with the radioactive dust falling and receiving a huge dose of radiation.'

Russia 24, one of the state's main propaganda channels, dedicated a whole package to knocking *Chernobyl*: 'The only things missing are the bears and accordions!' said TV anchor Stanislav Natanzon, pointing to images of twenty-first-century storm windows on a building in what was supposed to be 1986 Pripyat: proof of fabrication. The viewer only saw the anachronistic windows fleetingly. Natanzon also debunked the notion to Russia 24 viewers that the Soviet system would not allow fair comment: 'The scientist Valery Legasov not only led the government's response to the Chernobyl disaster, he was also openly critical of its management of the nuclear industry.'

Nearly right. Legasov had indeed written an article critical of safety conditions in the Soviet nuclear industry in 1987 for the country's most read paper, the *Komsomolskaya Pravda*. He set out the evidence that the design of the RMBK reactor was dangerous and needed to be improved, dramatically. But it wasn't published. Only after Legasov killed himself in protest at the state's cover-up in 1988 did the article, and his argument that all the RMBK reactors should be modified immediately, see the light of day.

Chernobyl made the case for liberal democracy in radiation burns, but Putin was too narrow-minded to get it. At the time of the disaster in 1986, he was a Cold War warrior, working as a low-level KGB officer, enforcing Soviet power by using all his secret policeman's tricks in Dresden, East Germany. When the Soviet Union fell apart five years later, Putin believed that the CIA, MI6 and the other Western intelligence agencies had plotted to undermine the country he had lived in and served his whole life. Locked in the cement of a Soviet secret policeman's thinking from the 1970s, he didn't understand that the three things that killed his country were not Western spies but the chronic failure of a planned economy to keep up with free markets; the catastrophic failure of the Soviet armed forces to conquer hearts and minds in Afghanistan; and a failure of a system of government that had turned a civil power station into a nuclear bomb. Navalny's understanding of Chernobyl was based in truth, that the system was wrong and beyond repair; Putin lived inside the dross of magical thinking. He still does.

Chernobyl scarred Navalny like Voldemort scarred Harry Potter, the scar so deep he could never root it out. From the age of ten, Navalny saw how a state that lied to its people was a thing of evil, that, in politics, in power, you must tell the truth to people. After seeing what moronic, lying power did to his childhood idyll, he spent the rest of his life not lying to people.

But it was also clear from friends and relatives during those first summer holidays in Ukraine and the rest of the year in Russia that there was also something special about the boy: his calm, his lack of fear, his way of thinking things through for himself. He was tall, blond and blue-eyed, boasting classic Slav good looks. But he was also different, very.

Alexei Navalny was born on 4 June 1976 in the military town of Butyn, about thirty miles from Moscow. Anatoly, his father, was an officer in the Soviet Army, his mother moving around with her husband as he was posted to different bases, most of them not that far from Moscow. Navalny has always said that his most vivid childhood memories were connected with Ukraine: 'The Uzh River, flowing into Pripyat, a high steep slope and swallow nests. And so I keep trying to get this swallow, I put my hand in the nest, but I can't get it.'

Before the Chernobyl disaster, almost three thousand people lived in Zalyssia, home to a collective farm and a flax mill. Now it's a ghost town. When Navalny tried to become the mayor of Moscow in 2013, one visiting journalist, Irina Guk, described 'looted houses, a twisted, rusty kindergarten playground, a "supermarket" sign overgrown with wild grapes. Only the memorial to the villagers who died during the Second World War looks well kept. There are several Navalny names on it . . .'

Alexei's grandfather, Ivan Tarasovich, was a carpenter and, like his wife Tatyana Danilovna, worked on the local collective farm in the village. They had their own small-holding too, a cow, a couple of pigs, a dozen chickens. It was a rural idyll until the Chernobyl disaster struck. To begin with, there was only a ten-kilometre exclusion zone around the plant which did not take in Zalyssia. It was only when people properly understood the extreme risk from radiation caused by the exposed reactor core that, more than a week after the disaster, the exclusion zone was tripled to thirty kilometres from the plant, taking in the Navalnys' home village.

Navalny told Russian *Esquire* magazine that he had spent every summer with his grandmother in Zalyssia and if the accident had happened in June, not April, 1986, then he would have been there: 'In order not to cause panic, all the collective farmers, and our relatives too, were sent to grow potatoes, dig in radioactive dust. Only later did they begin to resettle them. It was a real universal catastrophe in which I and my family were victims.'

The whole community was moved to a specially built new community called New Zalyssia, just north of Borody-anka, to the north-west of Kyiv. Only one old lady stayed behind. Reporter Irina Guk was given a conducted tour by Rosalia Otroshko, the only resident of the abandoned vil-lage: 'The grandmother no longer remembers her age and, in some way incomprehensible to modern man, survives into her eighties in a wooden house without light, water or heat. She is obviously confused by her memories of the Nav-alnys, so we enter the hut she indicated without much hope.

Later, however, relatives identified this house in photographs by green wooden shutters with carvings, which the opposition figure's grandfather Ivan Tarasovich made with his own hands.'

Natalya Ilyinichna Semenyuk was in her sixties when reporter Guk caught up with her in 2012 in New Zalyssia: 'We lived cheek by jowl, nursed the children together. Alyosha [Alexei's nickname] was brought to us probably when he was five months old. His mother, Lyuda, was studying then, and he lived with us for up to two years. And then he came for the whole summer,' she recalled.

The reporter described a rural idyll: nuts drying in the oven, beans and apples glistening in basins on the floor. A short woman, Semenyuk described herself as a dwarf next to Alyosha. 'When he arrived, he spoke Russian for a month, and then he picked up our local dialect' – a mixture of Ukrainian and Belarusian. 'The boy was curious, he asked questions and talked about everything. He helped to look after the cow, he picked cherries, like all the boys in the village; he fished and swam. He wasn't picky about food: he ate bread with water and sugar, our pies with poppy seeds, dumplings.'

Semenyuk realised that Navalny and his parents had to be careful about what they said, now that Navalny was a leading member of the opposition: 'They're afraid to talk at all . . . Luda [Navalny's mother] once admitted that they live like they're on a powder keg.' Natalya stops short. 'Politics is a dirty business.'

Twelve years and a big war on, for this book, my fixer Sasha Aleksandrenko went to New Zalyssia, in March 2024, to see if she could find more people who remembered young Navalny. The new settlement is celebrated by a classic piece of Soviet ironmongery, spelling out its name in red metal piping, with the date, 1986, but no reference to the dark logic behind its foundation. Navalny's closest family were nervous of journalists but Sasha found three women who remembered him very well.

And two who pointed to a war crime triggered by the Navalny name.

Galyna Denysivna looks to be in her late seventies or early eighties, grey hair kept tidily beneath a blue bonnet, a blue coat helping ward off the cold. She was a schoolteacher in old Zalyssia: 'Yes, I know Navalny's family. They don't talk to journalists. In today's times, it's too dangerous, you should understand. I moved to New Zalyssia in 1986. Before the Chernobyl tragedy, our house was across the garden from the Navalny family. They didn't grow anything there but had some land. I knew the father of Alyosha; he was the youngest of three brothers. We were classmates with the middle one, Vasyl. I don't know where Alexei was born, but I know that his father, after serving in the army, stayed in Moscow. I don't remember Alexei as a young boy, but I remember his visit as an adult. We are still neighbours with Alexei's cousin; we are all familiar with each other. I watched his movies about Putin and was following his progress and career. It was important for me. It seems they're all mad in that country [Russia], and I'm waiting for this insanity to stop. I really believed that Alyosha would change something there with the help of the opposition. But nothing is left of the opposition now. They've been murdered, poisoned, shot.'

'How did you hear about Navalny's death?'

'I was watching TV when my colleague called me with the heartbreaking news. I couldn't resist feeling pain and sorrow hearing about his death. We are kind people here, you know, with hearts. If you don't have compassion, how can you even call yourself a human?'

Tetiana Ivanivna is sixty-two years old, a plump woman in a mustard cardigan and pink headscarf. She recalls that awful night when their world changed for ever: 'We didn't hear the nuclear station exploding. We could only see the light from the huge fire. But we didn't really understand what had happened. Back then, moving from your beloved home was like living through a silent war. You couldn't see any threat around you, you can't hear or observe anything, but you need to take your children and leave your house, for ever. Old Zalyssia was a beautiful place with unbelievable nature and good job opportunities. Our river Uzh was always clean and transparent. The forest was full of berries and mushrooms. I could say it was heaven on Earth. It's so lucky to grow up in such a place.'

'Do you remember Alexei?'

'Of course. We didn't communicate much because he was a little boy, but one of his distant relatives, who was murdered by Russians during the occupation, was my class-mate, Ilya Navalny.'

Raisa Okroshko is in her sixties, dark hair covered in a leopard-print scarf, her face full of character, looking a little worriedly at Sasha's phone camera: 'Yes, I knew Navalny. I remember him as a child. It's hard to say anything special about him. He was just a boy on his bicycle like every boy in the village those days. Playing with friends, swimming in the river. No one paid much attention to him. We couldn't even imagine that he would become a fighter against Putin or something like this. He came almost every summer to his grandparents before the Chernobyl tragedy. After we were evacuated to New Zalyssia, he came a couple of times to see his relatives and to visit the cemetery in the old village. Some relatives, his cousin and aunt, still live there.

'You know, half of the village had the same surname: Navalny. It turned out bad for one of us villagers, Ilya Navalny. When he tried to cross the checkpoint during the occupation, he was shot immediately after the Nazis saw his surname in the passport.'

The Nazis in Raisa's telling were not the ones who came to Ukraine in 1941 but 2022.

Raisa may have got some of the details wrong, but not the essence of the story. In April 2022, after the Russian killing machine had pulled back from the north of Kyiv and abandoned its attempt to take the capital, the Ukrainian authorities started digging up mass graves. The *Moscow Times* reported that in one mass grave in Bucha, they found, along with 400 other bodies, the corpse of Alexei Navalny's second cousin, Ilya, sixty-one. By the way, please note that this wasn't the kind of mass grave where the 1939–45 Nazis dug a trench, shot people and then covered up the dead with the earth. The bodies had mostly been picked up by Ukrainian council workers, trying to follow some of the precepts of civilised society, and buried en masse because the Russian occupiers would not allow funerals or, indeed, Ukrainians to gather for any purpose.

'Ilya was Alexei's distant relative – they have a common great-grandfather,' Pavlo Navalny, the village head of New Zalyssia, who is also Navalny's third cousin, told the BBC's Ukrainian service. Locals had told the BBC before the full-scale invasion that 'half of our village is full of Navalnys', with the village registrar finding at least eleven residents with the same last name.

The fullest account of the killing of Ilya Navalny appeared in an investigation by Amnesty International into mass murder in the Kyiv area, published in 2022. Olexiy Sholudenko, a neighbour, said that on the morning of 12 March, Ilya had gone with a friend to the local clinic to charge his phone. As an old man, clearly in his sixties, the Russian occupying force would have seen him as a low-level threat and this errand would have been permitted. Sholudenko continued that he and his wife cooked outside – there was no electricity in the area – and invited their neighbour Ilya to lunch in their apartment in their shared block of flats, five storeys high, on Yablunska Street. After lunch, some Russian troops arrived and started shouting and firing their weapons. Everyone went downstairs to hide in the basement. After things had gone quiet, one of the residents went out at around 5pm and saw Ilya Navalny lying dead on the ground. One neighbour found that Ilya's door was open, suggesting that he may have gone down from his flat to check on his car which had been damaged in the shooting. In the morning three neighbours examined the body: he had been shot twice in the back and once in the head. His woollen cap was soaked with blood. On the ground were pages torn from his passport. His neighbours suspected he had been killed because of his name.

From his gulag cell, Alexei Navalny was able to post a message on social media condemning Ilya's killers as 'Putin's butchers'. He wrote: 'A passport with the surname Navalny lies next to the dead body on the ground. This is one of the people killed in the Ukrainian village of Bucha. Ilya Ivanovich Navalny. Everything indicates that they killed him because of his last name. I don't know if he is related to me. He is from the same village as my father.' The statement continued: 'All circumstances indicate that he was killed because of his last name. That's why the passport was thrown next to him.' Navalny reissued his call for Russians to 'protest where you can and however you can . . . Inaction is the worst and its consequence is death.'

Raisa reflected on the killing of Alexei Navalny in February 2024: 'When we heard about Alexei's death, we felt sorry. It was painful to hear that news.' Thinking about the many Ukrainians who saw him as just another Russian imperialist, she said: 'Many asked "Why?" We understand why a lot of people on social media were referring to the "Crimea sandwich" remark, making jokes or cheering his death. But for us, first of all, it was the death of a human being. He grew up in front of our eyes, and his grandparents were very hard-working people. This family was respected by the community. A lot of my friends still think he shouldn't have come back from Germany. His relatives refuse to talk; some say Navalny himself told them not to say anything because it can be used against the family. He was a boy from our community; we claimed him as Ukrainian.'

In my book – which this is – the views of the Ukrainians who knew the real Alexei Navalny bite. They knew the flaws but they also understood that he was a good man, killed before his time, killed because, the world over but far more so in Russia, politics is a dirty business.

CHAPTER TWO

Biting the Apple

It's hard to get across just how weird it was for people of Navalny's generation to lose the country they had been brought up in. All the stuff of their young lives turned, in a knife-slash of time on 26 December 1991, into old-fashioned junk. The Soviet Union was dead; long live a new Russia. Later on, Navalny mused about this in his blog, how strange it was for his people who were brought up in the fag-end of Communism for their realities to be changed about them. Growing up, they had sung patriotic songs at their Young Communist summer camps, but changing the lyrics, mocking the icons of a dying era. Not everything the Soviet Union did was wrong and Navalny was acutely aware of that, how it was right and proper to respect the Second World War generation that beat the Nazis. But also, seeping under the electric fences of the KGB, another reality was pressing in, that Stalin had ordered the German Communists to ally with the Nazis against the Social Democrats in 1931 and so helped Hitler to power; that Stalin's famine in 1933 had murdered millions of people, most of them Ukrainian; that the Soviet Union had sealed 'the midnight of the century' when it signed the Nazi–Soviet Pact in 1939;

that the Soviet Union could not feed or clothe or house its people at anything like the level of the West; that peoples who were forced to live in the Soviet bed with their Russian masters longed for freedom.

Out with the Soviet old; bring in the free market Russian new. That was what it looked like. But underneath the bonnet, not so much. And all the while, the old believers in a strong, imperial Russian world lurked in deep water, crocodiles biding their time.

The fall of the Soviet Union delivered real change. The old nonsense of Communism did start to die, but far more slowly than appreciated back then. Ordinary Russians for the first time in their lives could read honest newspapers, watch good telly, go abroad, buy fancy foreign cars, own their own homes. The *idea* of a free market was embraced, but a system without the functioning machinery of the rule of law was bound to struggle. The rhetoric of a free market masked the reality of a bloody anarchy where the people who came out on top were the most cunning, the most pitiless and the greediest. Russia turned into an oligarchy, the country's resources carved up and seized by a few rich men, but an oligarchy with democratic lipstick.

Under Yeltsin, democracy became a dirty word. I remember a trip to Moscow in the early 1990s when I went for a drink in the John Bull pub and watched a Russian businessman sob openly in the bar, watched over by his bewildered and frightened minder. It was hard to work out what was going on, but my educated guess was that someone had threatened to kill the man and, fearing assassination, he was spending as much time as possible in a pub known to be frequented by foreigners, weeping all the while.

The problem was that political power was in the wrong

hands. As the nineties wore on, Boris Yeltsin morphed from being an inspirational and courageous leader, willing to stand up on a tank to defend Russia's infant democracy, into a senile alcoholic, guarded by some of his hopelessly corrupt family. The president of Russia needed to be fighting like a tiger to stand up for the rule of law, to defend democratic principles, to strengthen Russia's fragile open society. Instead, he took the pith.

One story sums up Yeltsin's demise. In September 1994, Irish officials got a call saying that Yeltsin was flying back from San Francisco and would have to do a fuelling stop in Shannon airport in the west of Ireland, before continuing to Moscow. Taoiseach – Gaelic for prime minister – Albert Reynolds was in Australia, but he cut short his visit, hurried home, touching down in Shannon shortly before the plane carrying the president of Russia.

Thirty-one official vehicles waited on the runway to carry the honoured guest to a formal reception at Dromoland Castle. The Irish Defence Forces called up an honour guard from the 12th Infantry Battalion and a band to salute the great man. The official delegation – including Reynolds, the Russian ambassador to Ireland (Nikolai Kozyrev), Bertie Ahern (then Minister for Finance and prime minister to be), Brian Cowen (the Minister for Transport, Energy and Communications) and Willie O'Dea (Minister of State) – went to the runway to wait. And wait. And wait.

Airport officials reported that the plane was circling over Shannon. Eventually, after an hour, it landed. However, when the plane's door opened, there was still no sign of the Russian president. An Aeroflot official informed Ambassador Kozyrev that Yeltsin was unwell and that the vice premier, Oleg Soskovets, would meet with the Irish delegation. Kozyrev was able to board the plane but was not allowed to see Yeltsin. Alexander Korzhakov, Yeltsin's body-guard, told Kozyrev that Yeltsin was 'very tired'. Kozyrev returned to the runway and informed Reynolds that Yeltsin would not be making an appearance due to poor health. Reynolds replied, 'Well now, if he is sick, there is nothing we can do about it. I am willing to talk to the Russian president's representative, but Mr Yeltsin, my guest, is on Irish soil, and I cannot miss the opportunity to go on board the aeroplane for five minutes, shake the president's hand and wish him a speedy recovery.'

The Russians said *nyet*. The jet refuelled and it took off again. The *Irish Times* ran a cartoon on its front page the next day which depicted a bottle of vodka bouncing down the aircraft steps while an onlooker states: 'At last a message from President Yeltsin.' The term 'circling over Shannon' became a euphemism in Ireland to describe the condition of a person who has had too much to drink, along with sto-cious, langered and rat-arsed.

That's the funny version of Yeltsin being unsuited for power. Here is a second story – this one, not so funny. Grig-ory Yavlinsky, who will figure shortly in Navalny's story, was an economist and the leader of the liberal Yabloko party who, for a time in the early to mid-nineties, was a mover and shaker in and then out of Yeltsin's Kremlin. In late 1994, Yavlinsky opposed the stupid and disastrous war in Chechnya started by Yeltsin's generals. Yavlinsky's courage angered bad people. His 23-year-old son, Mikhail, was kidnapped. Mikhail played the piano beautifully and had dreams of making a living as a professional pianist. The kidnappers maimed him, cutting the webbing between his fingers, then let the boy go with a note telling Yavlinsky to get out of politics. The *Moscow Times* reported that the Yavlinskys appealed to the government for help. After an inadequate police investigation got nowhere, Yeltsin's Kremlin said no to federal protection.

'[Yavlinsky] was told to hire his own bodyguards, or to otherwise look to his family's safety. So he hid his children,' said Yevgenia Dillendorf, a Yabloko press secretary, according to the *Moscow Times*. His maimed son and a younger brother were sent to London where the British authorities kept an eye on them. The *Moscow Times* reflected: 'In 1994, Yabloko's voice was raised loudly in democratic opposition to Yeltsin's rule – and especially to his terrible decision to invade and carpet-bomb Chechnya. So Mikhail Yavlinsky's assailants could have been Kremlin-directed, or could simply have been freelancing nationalists. If nationalists, they were sophisticated enough to target his son – and the fingers. Which begs the question of why the Yeltsin government refused to protect the Yavlinskys.'

Yeltsin in the Kremlin was a joke but, for a better, brighter Russia, not a funny one.

While the Soviet Union went to hell in a handcart and Russia began its short experiment with democracy, Navalny finished school, attended university, fell in love and started out in life. After just missing a slot at Moscow State University – Russia's Oxbridge – Navalny studied law at the Peoples' Friendship University, where a lot of his fellow students were from the Global South. After that, he did a second degree in securities and exchanges at the Financial University, graduating in 2001. To keep the wolf from the door, he worked while he was a student. Whatever business and legal ideals Navalny was being taught at college, his first contact with Russian capitalism was nasty, brutish and short.

While working at Aeroflot Bank in 1997, 'he wrote all sorts of complaints like: "Immediately pay back our billion,"' but that year the bank lost its licence to practise. These and other early experiences of the Russian market being dominated by alpha predators formed in him an aversion to corruption and that, once Vladimir Putin was installed in the Kremlin as Yeltsin's anointed successor, could only spell trouble.

But becoming the great enemy of the tsar in blood was all in the future. In 1998 Navalny went on holiday to Turkey where he met a beautiful young Muscovite, Yulia Abrosimova, and fell in love.

Yulia was his rock and he hers. 'I didn't marry a promising lawyer, and I didn't marry an opposition leader. I married a young man named Alexei,' she told TV Rain, a Russian opposition TV channel that worked in Russia in 2013; now it is in exile, based in Amsterdam. 'I married a man with whom it was clear from the very beginning that sharp turns were possible, so nothing unexpected happened to me.'

The interviewer sniffed a fox. Sharp turns?

'He has always been very active,' Navalnaya replied, then shot the fox: 'with a very active citizenship.'

They married in 2000 and, as is the way in Russia and Ukraine, had a child almost immediately. Navalnaya gave birth to a daughter, Daria, in 2001 and a son Zakhar in 2008. A bright and formidable woman in her own right, Yulia went out of her way to stay in her husband's shadow. She did not develop her own career but played the loyal politician's wife, helping out with the Navalny family business. His father and mother run a basket-weaving factory in the Moscow region which Putin has allowed to continue, more or less. A gesture of humanity? Or just another mind game? As ever with the master of the Kremlin, it's hard to tell, but it is prudent to exclude kindness as his reigning motive.

Given that Navalny's father, Anatoly, was irradiated out of his family home by the stupidity of the Soviet mindset, it should come as little surprise that he hated Communism. Lyudmila once said that when Anatoly got started on the Commies ruining everything, she would close the windows so the neighbours wouldn't shop him to the secret police. The Navalny family looked for another path for Russia and found it in Yabloko, the liberal party.

This should not be confused with Russia's Liberal Democratic Party, a vehicle for stooges of the Kremlin, led from its creation by its founder Vladimir Zhirinovsky until his death in 2022. Zhirinovsky was a fool's bladder on a fascist stick, using his cruel wit to malign opponents of Vladimir Putin, further the Kremlin's far-right agenda and consign his immortal soul to darkness. I met him once and reader, do not be surprised, we ended up shouting at each other.

Yabloko's leader from the mid-nineties through to 2018 was Yavlinsky. He was born in Lviv in Soviet Ukraine to Jewish parents, a young boxing champ with a beautiful mind. He was Soviet Ukraine's youth boxing champion in 1967 and 1968, studied economics, was spotted as a rising star and tasked to set universal standards in the coal industry. He got stuck in, seeing an opportunity, as he wrote in his autobiography, to see the world hidden behind the propaganda posters. In the 1970s he went down coal mines to understand the conditions Soviet colliers had to deal with and was almost killed when the shaft he was in collapsed. Together with three workers, he spent ten hours waist-deep in ice-cold water, waiting for help. They were rescued but he was the only one to survive; the other three died in hospital. Yavlinsky wrote brave papers describing the dire conditions of the Soviet mine workers. This being the Soviet Union, his reports went unregarded by the bosses and unread by ordinary people and so his heroic efforts to document a horribly abused workforce had no consequence.

When the Soviet Union collapsed, Yavlinsky set out sober, sensible reforms which would lead to a properly policed free market. His ideas were passed over in favour of a plan roughly summarised as 'Let's Make the Oligarchs Get Rich Quick' which led to massive wealth inequality.

A big test for Russian democracy came in 1996 when Yeltsin stood for re-election. When the Communists looked like toppling Yeltsin, a few rich men ganged together to use their money and their nous to get their drunken old fool back into the Kremlin. Navalny persuaded his father and mother that Yeltsin was the least bad option and they voted for him over the Communists, fearing a return to the Soviet dark days. Down the track, Navalny regretted this judgement because it undermined democracy, but by then it was too late.

Yeltsin won the 1996 election but the big question for the oligarchs was who would replace him? For a time, Team Yeltsin considered plumping for Boris Nemtsov as the man to take over in the Kremlin. Nemtsov was a brilliant, funny, enormously handsome former nuclear physicist who had a gift for hand-cranking phrases full of wit and fun and insight. He popularised the term 'oligarch' for Russia's mega-rich.

Yeltsin had appointed Nemtsov the governor of Nizhny Novgorod Oblast in 1991 and the great Russian public fell in love with him. Looking around for a successor, in March 1997, Yeltsin made Nemtsov first deputy prime minister of

Russia and introduced him to President Bill Clinton as his chosen one. That summer, opinion polls said one in two Russians fancied him as the next president. But in August 1998, the Russian economy hit the skids, the rouble crashed and everyone close to Yeltsin was dog meat. The oligarchs dumped Nemtsov, and Yeltsin ended up with a different character entirely, a creepy secret policeman with a marked resemblance to Gollum from *Lord of the Rings*. The story of Putin's rise and rise is a toxic cocktail of power-grabbing perhaps best told by Brecht in his play about Hitler, *The Resistible Rise of Arturo Ui*, but I had a go in *Killer in the Kremlin*.

Meanwhile, Navalny and his beloved Yulia joined Yabloko and worked in the liberal trenches, trying to stop Putin and his synthetic power machine, the United Russia party, from doing an impression of the Borg – the alien cybernetic organisms linked in a hive mind from *Star Trek* – taking over the Russian world. They failed and the consequences of that failure led Navalny into darkness, so the story of what went wrong with Yabloko deserves study.

The liberal party was, according to Navalny to his Russian biographer, Konstantin Voronkov, 'the only consistently democratic party that talked about ideas and that didn't trade them for money or offices'. Not corrupt but a 'total mess', its meetings often a waste of time, too many in the party indulging in tokenism, lacking the deadly seriousness required to take on and overtake the Kremlin party limousine. From my encounters with Navalny, I can imagine how irritable and irritated he would have been with people whom he felt didn't cut the mustard.

All politics is local. Navalny, a political animal from top to toe, intuitively understood this. From early on, he wasn't just a backroom boy for Yabloko but got stuck into community activism. In 2004, he was the chief of staff of Yabloko's Moscow office. In that year, Muscovites were becoming fed up with what they perceived to be the blatant corruption of city mayor Yury Luzhkov. His wife, Yelena Baturina, became Russia's first woman billionaire. She remains fabulously wealthy and is thought to be living in Austria, and to still have property in London. From 1992 to 2010, Luzhkov signed the orders for major redevelopments across the city. But in the process, beautiful old buildings got knocked down to make way for modern rubbish and the ability of the press and parliament to fight back weakened when Putin became the master of the Kremlin. When locals banded together to organise a movement to defend historic places, the Committee to Protect Muscovites, Navalny was on hand to organise things. When asked by a *Kommersant* reporter whether Yabloko was trying to use public activists for its own purposes, Navalny replied that 'the movement will be non-political, moreover, open to cooperation with all parties, including United Russia.' But he went on to concede: 'It is unlikely that any party will support this initiative: we are the only ones who are not afraid of Luzhkov.' That's the first time, I believe, his name appeared in print and the ballsiness of his statement is on brand.

The Committee and its brave functionary took on some very powerful opponents. One of the best known was Vladimir Pozner, a Russian-American, as bald as a billiard ball and routinely dressed in a black turtle-neck jumper, famous in the West for defending the Soviet Union in beautifully modulated English. Pozner's family had fled Paris after the fall of France in 1940, making it to the United States where he became fluent in English. A primary school pal of Pozner remembered him for 'his capacities for one, having extraordinarily attractive fantasies and two, for getting the rest of us to believe them.' At the height of McCarthyism, Pozner's father was accused by the FBI of being a Soviet spy. Secret Venona papers, decoded by the Americans and eventually released in 1996, subsequently proved exactly that. The Pozner family returned to Russia in 1952 and young Vladimir became a propagandist for the Soviet state. In 2004, now an international celebrity based in Moscow, Pozner developed a plan to build a media school above a much-loved building – and it was that scheme that caught the Committee's ire. The project got shelved; others succeeded but the Committee was able to cast a shadow over their legitimacy.

Navalny, a lawyer with a second degree in financial wizardry, was a bloodhound, sniffing out procedural swerves and dodges like truffles and presenting them to the courts, the authorities, but best of all the public. Later he told his Boswell, Voronkov, that the Committee had done a bit of good, and that although it was tough, managing both bureaucratic and physical challenges, Luzhkov's City Hall was afraid of them.

In 2005, Navalny came up with another wheeze, again outside the umbrella of the party he worked for. He started the Democratic Alternative movement or DA! with Maria Gaidar, the daughter of one of Yeltsin's better prime ministers, organising debates in Moscow, injecting fresh blood into politics when Putin and his creatures were doing their level best to suck the life out of it. Not enough credit has ever been given to Navalny as a great entertainer, someone who could get bums on seats. True political debate is a blood sport, watching who survives, the lion or the Christian.

Navalny and his co-host were extremely good at booking gladiators and Navalny, naturally witty, tall and commanding, was a great MC.

Navalny's admirably exhaustive American biographer, David Herszenhorn, tracked down DA!'s mission statement which is written in pure Navalnyese: 'We believe that people with active citizenship can really change lives for the better through legal and nonviolent means. Nobody will do it for them. This is our alternative to extremism, idleness, whining and complaints.' As ever with anything to do with Navalny, there was an insurance policy: 'Members of DA! are good, active and purposeful people. We are not fanatics and not city madmen; we study and work. We are not building a revolutionary group and do not want to overthrow anyone. We just want to live in a free and democratic country and force the government to do what it is instructed to do.'

The context is that in 2005, the same year that DA! was set up, the Orange Revolution had occurred in Kyiv, overthrowing a pro-Putin patsy. Back in Moscow, the DA! felt it necessary to set out where they stood on that kind of thing: 'The Ukrainian revolution was "made" by ordinary Ukrainians, not by technologists.' Political technologists were beloved of Putin when they worked for him and demonised when they didn't. The phrase is hard to translate into English-English but something like 'backroom fixers' with a flavour of shenanigans will do.

The DA! insurance policy continued: 'Anyone who was in Kyiv in those days, and did not watch what was happening on Russian TV channels, understands perfectly well that without conscious citizens, political technologies would have turned into a farce (as happened with the Kremlin PR people). The government understands that the main threat to it is active citizens who are not silent when they see corruption, incompetence, gagging of independent journalists and arbitrariness. Therefore, it is interested in our passivity, and imposes on the Russians a cynical attitude towards manifestations of civic activity. No, we are not revolutionaries, and we are not going to overthrow anyone.'

The DA! debates became the stuff of legend, exploring themes such as 'Where are the fascists?' and 'Where are the honest journalists?' and pitting someone from Yabloko's youth wing against a spokesperson from Nashi, the proto-fascist Putinist version of the Hitler Youth. But this kind of success attracted the wrong kind of attention. The 2007 debate series kicked off with the daring title, 'Putin's Plan or Putin's Clan?' The politico booked to defend Putin dropped out at the last minute. He was replaced but the whole evening was soured by a group of drunk Putin supporters who heckled, were openly misogynistic to Maria Gaidar and someone threw a bottle. One thug tried to monster Navalny outside the venue. Navalny pulled out a handgun and fired into the air. The police arrested Navalny but Russia hadn't sunk into full authoritarianism at this stage; the gun was in fact an air pistol, and there were enough witnesses to the thug's previous unpleasantness for the charges to be dropped, six months on. Navalny got away with his foolishness.

But the Committee and the DA! debates were an entertaining sideshow. The big picture for Navalny's party of choice was bleak and getting bleaker by the day. Yabloko's numbers kept on going down and down and down. In 1995, in the elections to the Russian parliament or Duma, Yabloko got almost seven per cent of the vote, did worse in the subsequent elections and, in 2007, got less than two per cent and no seats at all.

As ever in politics, policy and personality got entwined. Yavlinsky was a solid liberal but also his detractors accused him of running Yabloko as some kind of cult. And the cockiest of those critics was Navalny. After the terrible results in 2007, Navalny went on the attack: 'I argue that Yabloko has collapsed because it has turned itself to a sect. We demand that everyone must be a democrat, but we don't want to be democrats ourselves . . . And the worse the results, the stronger the leadership's position.' He called for the 'immediate resignation of the party chairman and all his deputies, re-election of at least 70 per cent of the bureau'. Navalny conceded that the elections were 'dishonest and unfair. But we would get even less in fair elections. Because fair elections should not be just a live broadcast for Grigory Alekseevich [Yavlinsky].'

Navalny was arguing that the odds were stacked against Yabloko but that Yavlinsky had made a bad situation worse by hogging the limelight, blocking out other, more popular stars in the liberal firmament like the chess grandmaster Garry Kasparov, Putin's first prime minister, Mikhail Kasyanov, and the more Communist Party-leaning Nikolai Ryzhkov.

This went down like a cup of cold sick. Navalny was kicked out of Yabloko, officially for his nationalist views and marching with the far right. His friend, Ilya Yashin, said that the real reason was his challenge to Yavlinsky. It turned out that both were probably true. Frustrated at Yabloko's failure, Navalny turned to the far right and in doing so made the greatest mistake of his life, so far.

CHAPTER THREE

Bit of a Fascist?

Russian democracy under Yeltsin had been bloody, violent, extraordinary but always fascinating. Putin made politics boring, overnight. Enthusiasts for strongmen never quite get this, just how dull it is to read and recite the leader's dreary nonsense all the live long day. And the next day. And the day after that . . . Public life under Hitler, Stalin, Mao, Kims One, Two and Three in North Korea, Russia under Putin, China under Xi is an endless series of bowings and scrapings. Democracy is so much more fun.

True, Putin reduced the bloodshed but only by channelling it at the people who dared oppose him. But what had been extraordinary became numbingly banal as parliament and the media were defanged. This process started within less than a year of him taking over effective power, triggered by the sinking of the Kursk submarine in August 2000. His failure to act swiftly to help the trapped submariners was one thing; his rejection of Western help another; but perhaps the most shocking was his unfeeling response when challenged about his lack of action. The most human response he could come up with was: 'It sank.' When he met relatives of the dead submariners they lambasted him.

One widow screamed at him but was silenced when an official came up to her and jabbed a syringe in her side. Putin's response was not to change but to switch off Russia's independent, free-wheeling media. Democratic politics started to die and the activists still out there fighting found themselves in a virtually airless vacuum, barely able to breathe. That was the context in which people started to look at the nationalist right as a possible force to combat Putinism. It looked tempting.

No mousetrap without cheese.

The person who encouraged Navalny down this route is not a fascist at all but Yevgenia Albats, a brilliant investigative journalist, a scourge of the KGB/FSB and an observant Jew. In a fascinating piece in *The New Yorker* in 2021, the great Masha Gessen tried to understand the evolution of Navalny's nationalism and her first port of call was Albats. In 2004, fresh back from Harvard, Albats, then in her late forties, hosted a group of around twenty young Russian movers and shakers in her Moscow flat for a Tuesday night seminar. Of them all, Navalny was, Gessen writes: 'the oldest among those who gathered at her house but also the least articulate and least educated: most of the others had gone to prestigious colleges, while Navalny was a military brat with an undergraduate law degree from a decidedly second-tier school.'

But Albats took a shine to the grunt of her literati. For as long as she has known him, Albats told Gessen: 'Navalny has been teaching himself how to be a politician: he taught himself public speaking; while he was under house arrest a few years back, he taught himself English.'

And, frustrated with liberalism's failure to gain traction in Putin's new order, he taught himself nationalism. Gessen notes that this wasn't just a preoccupation of Navalny. Garry Kasparov, the grandmaster, for example, when he exited chess to get into politics in 2005, launched his new career with figures from the National-Bolshevik Party. Kasparov told Gessen back then that only a united front could overthrow the Putin regime – and that meant, effectively, holding your nose and hanging out with the nationalists.

It is also true to say that throughout his twenty-four years in power and counting, Putin had brutally suppressed politicians from the moderate left, the centre and the moderate right, but allowed the Communists to do their shop-soiled shtick to the far left and gave space for a degree of open dissent to the far right. So it was that Navalny, experimenting with hanging out with nationalists and beyond, went along with Albats on the 'Russian Marches' for three years on the trot. They were an annual fun day out for Russian patriots, uber-nationalists, monarchists, white supremacists and neo-Nazis, Slavic versions of the Ku Klux Klan. Albats told Gessen that she and Navalny went together: 'I wore a giant Star of David that I made sure could be seen from a distance. He took a lot of shit for walking with a kike.'

Marching with a self-declaring Jew alongside a bunch of Nazis is one thing. If that was Navalny's only digression, so be it. But it wasn't. In 2007, while still in Yabloko, he formed a group called NAROD – Russian for 'people' but it was an acronym for the Russian National Liberation Movement. He launched NAROD with two short videos, his baptism on YouTube.

The first video is forty-two seconds long. Its title is 'PEOPLE [NAROD] for the legalisation of weapons'. Navalny stands behind a desk and there is a video screen to the left; on the desk is a fly-swatter, a kid's pink slipper and a handgun. He introduces himself as a 'nationalist'. The set-up is naff and cheap, a low budget ad you might see on the telly in Alabama with someone selling you the latest gizmo in bug-killing. The patter is no better: 'Hello, today let's talk about pest control. None of us can prevent a cockroach creeping into our home or a fly coming in through a window.' On the video screen next to him, a cockroach and a fly pop up. 'Everybody knows that a fly-swatter works against a fly and a slipper finishes off a cockroach. But what happens when the cockroach gets too big? Or the fly too aggressive?' On the video, you see five bearded fighters – nothing is stated but they would appear to be Chechen – captioned 'Borderless Homo Sapiens'. Then to the soundtrack of a man-beast roaring 'something something', an attacker in a flowing black robe comes for Navalny. The 'something something' has been deliberately distorted, a bit like the guitar in *Tubular Bells*, but if you listen to it a couple of times it sounds very much like 'Allahu Akbar'.

Navalny shoots the intruder: 'In this case I recommend a pistol.' The parting message appears on the screen: 'Firearms should be permitted.' The video clearly lumps flies, cockroaches, bearded Muslims and murderous jihadis together. It is racist.

The second video is one minute long. Its title is 'Become a Nationalist!' Navalny plays a dentist in his surgery, a male client sitting in the chair, occasionally waving the dentist's traditional instruments of torture in his hand. 'Our society is corroding,' says Navalny the dentist. The screen cuts to skinheads beating someone up; then a rictus of bad teeth; then Nazis wearing swastikas; then back to Navalny; then more bad teeth; then to East Asians – Chinese, Koreans, Mongolians, it's not clear – then back to Navalny.

The words are revolting: 'The clinical picture is plain enough to a non-specialist. There is no need to inflict pain on anyone. Anything that causes harm should be carefully extracted. Only someone with half a mind thinks that nationalism leads to violence. A tooth without a root is dead. A nationalist is someone who does not want to extract the root from our sense of "Russia". We have the right to be Russian in Russia and we will protect this right.' The video ends with a tagline: 'Think about our future. Become a nationalist.'

Both videos are moronic, poorly made, yucky. He was thirty-one at the time and comes across as a bit of a fascist. He never repeated anything like these videos but, also, he never apologised for them. Down the track, I suspect that more than anything else, these videos cost him the Nobel Peace Prize and that, in turn, may have cost him his life. Putin can be fabulously reckless but, more often than not, he moves cautiously, sensing the mood before he strikes. Killing a Nobel Prize winner would have been a big step, even for him.

What the fuck was Navalny doing?

The evidence points to the videos being made when Navalny's fury at the ineffectiveness of the liberals to land a punch on Putin was at its most extreme and irrational and that he later regretted them but, Navalny being Navalny, he couldn't bring himself to take them down. Over the next three years he pursued his grand strategy of trying to get the nationalist right to wake up to the threat from Putin's fascism. When he realised that strategy wasn't working it was, for him, too late, and a tad embarrassing, to delete the videos, so they stayed up. He didn't get it, that the liberal world hates this kind of stuff and the stink of it followed him down the years even though he had turned himself into something quite different. This defence rests quite a lot on how both Albats and Gessen understood him, that he was forever experimenting and thinking of new ways of defeating the Kremlin. When one avenue of fire failed, he would pursue another, and then another. The goal was to defeat Putin; he didn't realise that with the NAROD videos he ended up defeating himself.

But perhaps he did. Leonid Volkov was the Jewish Tonto to Navalny's Lone Ranger, doggedly at his side in so many scrapes. Volkov told Masha Gessen for her article about Navalny's nationalism that his hero regretted making the 2007 dentist video in which he advocated deporting Asian migrants. The reason he did not delete it from YouTube was 'because it's a historical fact'.

So the videos were a mistake, one that he was too arrogant to admit. Once again, if you spend your time mocking the serial killer in the Kremlin, it's fair to say that an arrogant insouciance comes with the day job. What about Navalny's wider strategy of seeking the help of the nationalist right, the far right and beyond to dethrone the tsar in blood?

The Polish historian and sometime political prisoner Adam Michnik sat down with Navalny and thrashed a lot of this out with him, turning their conversations into a book, *Plotting the New Russia*, first published in Russian in 2015. Navalny conceded that many people regarded him as a nationalist: 'These are mainly people who find it comforting to live in a world of ideological clichés. There are some topics that are considered virtually taboo in liberal circles – issues surrounding migration, for instance.'

Hardly anyone on the right – Donald Trump, say – knows

much about the make-up of Russian society, so they don't understand that there is a huge number of migrants in Moscow, officially two million out of a population of thirteen million, although the number is almost certainly higher, perhaps double that. Moscow, like London, New York, Paris and so on is a world city in the twenty-first century. The power of money sucks in poor workers from the far edges of the old empire to do the jobs that ethnic Russians don't fancy, just like everywhere else. A lot of the cleaning staff at the hotel we stayed at in Moscow in 2018 while making our BBC *Panorama* 'Taking on Putin' were Buryats from the Soviet republic north of Mongolia. These are a Buddhist people who live on the shores of Lake Baikal and the surrounding steppes. Four years later, just after the Russian army left the Kyiv area, Ukrainian friends took me to the aftermath of a tank battle in Bucha. Just outside a fried tank was the burnt corpse of a soldier. The flames had left his face untouched. He was a Buryat. Add Kabardins, Kalmyks, Karachays, Kazakhs, Khakas, Khanty, Komi, Koreans, Koryaks, Kumandins and Kurds and you get a flavour of just how multi-cultural Moscow is. Oh, and by the way, that's just the letter K. Away from the fancy hotels, waterholes and the palaces of the wa-Benzi – the people who drive a Mercedes – Moscow feels much more like the set of *Blade Runner* than, say, London.

The ethnic minorities the far-right Russians hate and fear the most are the Chechens and Daghestanis from the far south of the old Russian Empire in the Caucasus who are, of course, Muslim. It was the Chechens who first told the world that Vladimir Putin was a monster. Under the false flag of revenging the September 1999 Moscow apartment bombs – not Chechen terrorists but the FSB were responsible – Putin started the second Chechen war. The Russian army flattened Grozny, used fuel air bombs against civilians and bombed white flag refugee convoys. I saw evidence of those last two war crimes with my own eyes. And the Russians tortured on an industrial scale. But because the Chechens were (light) brown and followed the wrong religion, they were ignored by London and Washington DC. I know this from personal experience because, when I returned from Chechnya in 2000 having seen the war crimes and said there is a big problem with Putin, no one would listen.

Just like everywhere else, poor white Russians look down on their immigrant neighbours and hoover up vicious anti-immigrant populism. As with so much else, Putinism echoes the Soviet mindset. The Soviet Union barked egalitarian rhetoric while being, in practice, ferociously racist; Putin's regime is just the same. No one around him is from an ethnic minority. Nearly all his old guard are pale, male and KGB.

Navalny's outlook changed over time, becoming markedly more liberal towards the end of his life than he had been during his grisly 'cockroach' phase. Furious at the liberal worthies in Yabloko for not sticking it to the Kremlin, he over-compensated and ended up in a dark place. Navalny confessed that he had been branded a nationalist by the liberals and a liberal by the nationalists: 'So far, I've got to admit it, I've done nothing but damage my own image.'

The joke at his own expense is well made.

Daniel Roher, the director of the *Navalny* documentary about his poisoning by Novichok in 2020, is Jewish and pushed his subject on the issue of him taking part in the Russian Marches. Navalny replied: 'Within all my career, I've been asked the same fifteen questions all the time.

"Are you afraid?"

"Are you working for Kremlin?"

"What is your family doing?"

"You have a responsibility for your family?"

'If it is a foreign journalist, they are asking about nationalism and Russian Marches. Every one of them, Jesus Christ! Just watch the previous interviews.'

'Hold on,' said Roher, 'were there not a couple of Sieg Heil-ers at that thing?'

'Sorry?'

'Were there not a couple of Nazi guys at that march? Certainly Sieg Heil-ers are a different category that you would not want to associate with or march beside?'

'Well,' replied Navalny, 'in the normal world, in the normal political system, of course, I would never be in the same political party with them. But we are creating coalition, broader coalition to fight a totalitarian regime, just to achieve the situation where everyone can participate in election.'

'A lot of politicians would even be uncomfortable to be associating or being in the same photograph as one of these guys. You're comfortable with that?'

'I'm OK with that and I consider it's my political superpower – I can talk to everyone. Anyway, well, they are citizens of Russian Federation and if I want to fight Putin, if I want to be a leader of a country I cannot just ignore a huge part of it. There are a lot of people who call themselves nationalists. OK, let's discuss it. We're living in a country where they are poisoning a politician and killing people. And arresting people for nothing. Of course, I am totally fine to sit with a guy whose rally looks kind of not very good for me.'

In the documentary, Navalny kind of slumps at the very end of his defence of himself, so the last phrase feels like a bit of an apology for what has gone before.

Navalny was consistent, telling his friend and sponsor Roman Borisovich that he went on the Russian Marches to make himself seen by the less radical right, so that he could bring them over to his anti-corruption agenda. Borisovich argued with Navalny about the wisdom of this strategy but, he told me, 'Navalny's view was that these people would be naturally supportive of his slogan against Putin's United Russia gang, "DON'T STEAL AND DON'T LIE!" Navalny assumed that these elements would be militant against people who were stealing from them just like they were against immigrants. He tried to channel their militancy into support for his battle against corruption. My argument was that his anti-corruption agenda was more of a liberal even leftist thing and he should look for this kind of support on the extreme left, not the extreme right. They had an even bigger grudge against the personal enrichment of the elites and were no less militant about it. Navalny thought about this and said: "You are right. Indeed, Russia is a left-wing country by definition. I could get the same popular support from the commies."'

After his dalliance with the far right ended, he became much closer to Sergei Udaltsov, the leader of the Left Front, with whom he led anti-Putin protests in 2012. Once, Borisovich recalled, Navalny told him of a conversation with Udaltsov when the leftist was calling for a march on the Kremlin.

'So who's gonna join from our side?' Navalny asked. 'Yavlinsky and the liberals? They will shit their pants. We need the right-wingers too.'

That, in a somewhat inelegant nutshell, was Navalny's motivation for hanging out with the people who march in step.

There's an abundance of evidence that Navalny wasn't the least bit anti-Semitic. But was he racist to non-whites? In the autumn of 2010, Navalny spent a term at Yale, as part of its World Fellows Program, where sixteen rising stars in politics from around the world get to chew the fat with like-minded souls and misunderstand the rules of American football. One of his closest think-mates was Marvin Rees, who went on to become the first black mayor of Bristol and, indeed, the first black mayor of any big city in Europe. Rees, who describes himself as the mixed-race son of a Jamaican father and a white single mother, and Navalny became firm friends. For this book I interviewed Rees over Zoom.

What did Rees think about the charge that Alexei is a racist?

'When I first got there [Yale is in New Haven, Connecticut, down the beach from where the Americans threw tea into the sea in 1773], I didn't have a car. Alexei took me shopping. He sat outside waiting while I got my supplies in the supermarket and then he took me back to the complex. In terms of the charge of being racist, I take someone as I find them. I didn't meet someone who approached me with any sort of hate or hostility. No two people agree totally on our world views. But I met someone who treated me with respect. He treated me as a friend, helped me when I needed it. Later on, after the Yale programme had finished, I met Alexei a couple of times at reunions, and bumped into Alexei and Yulia at an airport. We just met and talked as friends, with me being a black man and him being a white man. It wasn't an issue. That's how I experienced Alexei.'

Navalny being Navalny, Rees had to put up with Alexei's impression of Terminator.

'One of the elements of the Yale programme was to spend time with a really well-known psychologist who I actually thought was fantastic. I loved spending time with him, talking about ourselves, our motivation, why we did things, how groups work, people's emotions and all the rest of it. Alexei described it in his own Terminator voice: "What's all this mumbo jumbo?"'

When they were at Yale in late 2010, Navalny's investigation into Transneft popped up on his blog. The gist of it was that Team Navalny had got hold of documents that suggested that two years before, in 2007, an audit had shown that funds had gone missing during the construction of the East Siberia–Pacific pipeline. How much? Well, at least $4 billion or £2.5 billion in old money.

No other Yale fellow was causing trouble for their home governments like Navalny. Rees told me: 'Some of the other [Yale World] fellows were saying that "This is big, this is a lot of money. This puts you in danger, you might want to think about not going back." A number of them were very politically experienced and predicted that his opponents would start saying that he "was a member of the CIA, that he'd been in the USA collaborating". And he said, "I have to go back. Because if I don't go back now and push back against all those bullies out there, that would undermine the exposure of the crooks and thieves that I've been bringing into the public domain." And I think people were really struck by his resolve.'

How Russia deals with dissidents like Navalny's friends shocked Rees. 'One evening, Alexei and I were late in the office, just the two of us. I was at my computer terminal, he was at his. We were finishing an exercise on negotiation and a link was sent through to him. And he said, "Oh, Marvin, come look at this." It was a video of a journalist friend of his being beaten, one of the most savage beatings I've ever seen. That was when I first properly understood how serious the situation was that Alexei was in.'

Navalny's friend, Oleg Kashin, was a reporter on *Kommersant* who had upset the wrong kind of people. On 6 November 2010, two men hit Kashin fifty-six times in the head and legs with a steel pipe. When he was down on the ground, they used the pipe to smash his fingers repeatedly so that one had to be amputated. Which wrong people? One lot were the Kremlin's version of the Hitler Youth, Nashi, which means 'Ours'. That August, Molodaya Gvardiya, the boss of the youth wing of Prime Minister Vladimir Putin's United Russia party, called Kashin a 'journalist-traitor' and published his photograph with the caption: 'To be punished'. *Kommersant*'s editor, Mikhail Mikhailin, said the fact that several of the journalist's fingers had been crushed gave a clear indication of why he had been targeted: 'It is completely obvious that the people who did this did not like what he was saying and what he was writing.'

What Navalny was sent and showed Rees was uncut CCTV footage of the attack on Kashin. I could tell from Rees's voice that, years later when he recalled it to me, he was truly shocked by the savagery Russians critical of the powers that be were subjected to. Rees acknowledged that Navalny had held some views that he was not at all comfortable with, but that on a personal basis, there was no hostility towards a black Briton. On the contrary, they became firm friends, so much so that when their families came out to join the lads, they teamed up: 'We ended up taking our kids apple-picking together. We had two cars, drove out to the fields for the day, picked apples, rode back in the trailer driven by a tractor, my kids, his kids.'

Rees remembered warm, early autumn evenings when four fellows would hang out together: Navalny, Rees, Lumumba Di-Aping from South Sudan and Ricardo Terán from Nicaragua: 'We would sit on the back porch, Lumumba and his family, Alexei and his family, me and mine. Ricardo would bring out some Nicaraguan beer. We would sit there with some food, nibbles, on a warm Connecticut summer evening, just talking. Our kids would run off a little bit. At the time, his daughter, Dasha, was really into Lady Gaga.'

One more thing from Rees: 'In 2016, I was running to be the mayor of Bristol. If I won I was going to be the first black mayor of a big city in Europe. And then my comms director says, "Hey, someone just tweeted: 'Good luck in the election.' And he's got over a million followers."'

The tweet came from his fellow apple-scrumper: Alexei Navalny.

So was he a bit of a fascist? Yes, for a time. But I suspect that his spell in America changed him. At Yale, he could have hung out with all sorts, including white conservative neo-fascists in one of their yucky alpha beta frat houses. Instead, his gang were an African called Lumumba, a Nicar-aguan and a black guy from Brizzle. His three months at Yale would have opened his eyes to the land of liberty, its absurdities, its crassness, its cult of money, but also to the fact that power is, more or less, democratic, that the authori-ties, more or less, respect the rule of law, that liberal democracy, more or less, works, that an open society open to all talents is so much brighter than the dark Soviet basement he had been born into and the place Vladimir Putin wanted Russia to return to.

After Yale, the fascist in Navalny slunk off into a dark corner.

Who ripped off Transneft? The answer to that question might tell you something about how Russian corruption could have injected its poison into the lifeblood of British democracy. VNIIST was one of the companies accused by Navalny of stealing from the largest oil pipeline company in the world while working on Transneft's massive Eastern Siberia–Pacific Ocean (ESPO) project. 'They stole. They overstated prices. They connived with contractors to cheat.'

Navalny published the secret 2008 internal report prepared by Transneft which alleged there was 'an artificially engineered' scheme to benefit contractors on the ESPO pipeline project, giving them 'unreasonably high payments' from the state-owned company. One of the rip-off contractors, the report alleged, was VNIIST who stole £80 million from Transneft, which, because it is publicly owned, effectively meant the Russian public. The report stated: Transneft had 'no objective need to conclude a contract with VNIIST' and its part in ESPO was 'unjustified and economically unprofitable'.

No charges were laid. When Navalny cried cover-up, Putin said: 'If there had been anything criminal there, I assure you people would have been behind bars long ago.' No one knew who the ultimate owners of VNIIST were until, in 2021, the Pandora Papers were published. A massive leak of dodgy shell company information from around the world, they showed that a co-owner of VNIIST was Viktor Fedotov.

The fun fact about Fedotov is that after ESPO, he moved to Britain, bought a stately pile in Hampshire and was the secret face behind Aquind, a company aimed at building an electricity inter-connector between France and Portsmouth. The face of Aquind was a Ukraine-born entrepreneur, Alexander Temerko, who was close to the Russian Ministry of Defence but who now enjoys British citizenship. Temerko set out his stall as a pro-Remain, pro-EU Tory and an anti-Kremlin oligarch. In July 2019, in investigation by Reuters stood that on its head, showing that Temerko had applauded Brexit, endorsed Boris Johnson's bid to lead Britain out of the EU, and praised Kremlin hawk Nikolai Patrushev. Fedotov had tried hard to keep his role in Aquind concealed. Fedotov's entities have donated £700,000 to thirty-four Tory MPs and their local parties since the Aquind project began, beneficiaries including the current prime minister Rishi Sunak and the current chancellor, Jeremy Hunt.

Lord Callanan, currently a Tory minister, is a former director of Aquind; former minister Lord James Wharton took up a paid role as an Aquind adviser when he lost his House of Commons seat in 2017. A Conservative spokesman said donations are properly and transparently declared and the party 'perform compliance checks in line with the . . . legislation and requirements enacted by the last Labour government'. The spokesman said, 'Fund raising is a legitimate part of the democratic process. Government policy is in no way influenced by the donations the Party receives' and that the party is 'motivated by the priorities of the British public, acting in the national interest'. Lawyers for Aquind said their donations were 'entirely lawful, properly declared and have not been made in return for any special treatment'. They said there was 'no evidence that funds were embezzled' from Transneft. Fedotov 'denies any allegation of wrongdoing' and says that he 'has never had any interest in British politics and has operated in an open and transparent manner throughout the course of his career'.

Back in 2010, Navalny had blogged about the people who benefited from the scam: 'We need information about their real estate and assets abroad, primarily in the UK. We all understand that all the houses and castles are due to the money-laundering of illegally obtained funds. The money was stolen in Russia and invested in the UK. That is a crime. The guys from Scotland Yard and Baker Street need to start investigating!'

No one is suggesting that the thirty-six Tory MPs, including our current prime minister and Chancellor of the Exchequer, who took money from Fedotov's entities knew that the money came from a potentially tainted source. However, that source of the cash was opaque, concealed from open view, and that was Navalny's point. The guys from Scotland Yard and Baker Street did not investigate and so the thirty-six Tory MPs kept the money. Once again, all concerned deny any wrongdoing. But why did Fedotov spend his money? To buy influence? The Conservatives pocketed the cash and the whistleblower, Navalny, ended up dead.

CHAPTER FOUR

Jailhouse Rocker

Democratic Russia had, just like the USA, a rule to prevent presidents becoming kings, that a president could only serve for two four-year terms and after that it was 'hasta la vista, baby'. Vladimir Putin ran out of road in 2008, anointing his deputy prime minister Dmitry Medvedev to be his successor. When he announced the passing on of hands, Putin said: 'I am confident that he will be a good president and an effective manager. But besides other things, there is this personal chemistry: I trust him. I just trust him.'

Putin didn't add that at five feet, seven inches he towered over Medvedev who barely scrapes home at five feet, four inches. With the benefit of hindsight, the two outstanding qualities of Medvedev for Putin's benison are that he is the shorter man and that he would never dream of saying boo to the boss. Medvedev was duly elected as president in March 2008. His first appointment was to make Putin his prime minister. Power drained from the high red walls of the Kremlin and flowed to Russia's White House, where the office of the prime minister is stationed. For a time, Medvedev steered or appeared to steer a path to a different future. That was a charade. In fact, he owed fealty to Putin.

What you got was liberal lipstick but fascist substance. For far too long, the West went along with Medvedev's shtick as a reformer with an interest in new tech, blah blah, blah blah.

Team Obama fell for the lipstick, big time. In spring 2009 in Geneva, US Secretary of State Hillary Clinton presented Russian Foreign Minister Sergey Lavrov with a red button with the English word 'reset' and the Roman alphabet transliteration of the Russian word перегрузка / 'peregruzka'. But someone in Foggy Bottom – the all-too-accurate location of the US State Department – had made a big boo-boo. Перегрузка / 'peregruzka' means 'overload'. The word the State Department was actually looking for was the subtly different перезагрузка / 'perezagruzka'. How Lavrov must have laughed.

In September 2011, Medvedev wiped the lipstick off, proposing that he would stand down to make way for a new presidential candidate in the following year's election and the winner would be . . . Vladimir Putin. This single political act angered liberal, sophisticated Russia like nothing else in the twelve years of Putin's effective tsardom. And there was an opportunity to register their fury, the elections to the Duma on 4 December where Medvedev, now candidate prime minister, would be running as the figurehead of the United Russia party.

Evidence that Navalny was becoming a target of bad people in high places came in October 2011 when an anonymous blogger leaked one thousand pages of his private emails. The leaker claimed that the emails exposed Navalny as a corrupt ultranationalist financed by US authorities but they did no such thing. The *Moscow Times* reported that their review of the leak found 'they contained little in the way of incriminating evidence. The incident is reminiscent of the 1990s, when drudging up dirty laundry was a staple of political life. Once used in Kremlin turf wars, the practice has been recently applied to opposition activists and, as such, the leaked letters may confirm Navalny's clout with the opposition rather than ruin it.'

The leak was evidence that the powers that be were getting nervous about Navalny and were finding it hard to lay a glove on him. The *Moscow Times* went on to summarise recent smear campaigns against opposition figures: how Ilya Yashin had been filmed allegedly bribing a traffic cop; while Eduard Limonov, the founder of the National Bolshevik Party, Viktor Shenderovich, a liberal columnist and aesthete, best known for writing the scripts for the 1990s *Puppets* TV show – a Russian version of *Spitting Image*, canned under Putin – who had signed the 2010 anti-Putin manifesto, 'Putin Must Go', and far-right activist Alexander Belov popped up in separate kompromat videos having sex with the same woman. If it happened, why would the woman do what she is alleged to have done? Well, the only thing that unites the two far-right figures and the famous liberal writer was they were all thorns in the flesh of Vladimir Putin. The former secret policeman has, of course, got previous for being a moral degenerate using sex kompromat against people. Back in 1998, at the fag-end of the Yeltsin government, the then president's family were being investigated for corruption by Yuri Skuratov, Russia's Prosecutor General, when a video appeared of a man looking very much like the country's top law enforcement officer in bed with two prostitutes. One powerful Russian oligarch who, according to his own book, *Hunt the Banker*, was investigating Skuratov, was Alexander Lebedev, the former KGB spy in London and father of Evgeny, now Baron Siberia, because Skuratov was investigating his National Reserve Bank. Skuratov denied being the man in the video but the then head of the FSB, one Vladimir Putin, went on telly to push for him to go. The Prosecutor General resigned, his investigations bit the dust and Putin got the keys to the Kremlin. All concerned deny any wrongdoing.

But Navalny was proving a tougher nut to crack. His love for Yulia was deep and genuine and so, unlike other opposition figures, he proved impossible to destroy through sex kompromat. Other mechanisms to close him down would have to come into play.

The December 2011 Duma elections were the first where the mobile phones of ordinary people stood in for the failure of the official Russian election commission to do their job properly. Across Russia's eleven time zones, phone cameras captured ballots being stuffed, coachloads of voters being shunted from one polling station to another – so-called carousel frauds – and cheating on an epic scale.

Navalny's blog on the day following the results, 5 December, headlined 'Political Botox Not Gonna Help Them', is a minor classic of the genre, funny, cool, sardonic: 'On Friday we had a dispute regarding United Russia's election results in our office. Everybody had made a prediction, everything was written down on paper. These forecasts were for the "official results", i.e. the results adjusted after fraud. The winner would dine out in restaurants for a week, paid for by the others. They won't be feeding me.'

In the Team Navalny election fraud sweepstakes, Navalny, to his shame, had forecast '54 per cent for the PCT (Party of Crooks and Thieves)' – his brilliantly successful nickname for Putin's United Russia Party. Only one member of the team predicted that United Russia would get less than

50 per cent. Navalny blogged: 'If I had known on Saturday, that the "official result" of the PCT was gonna be less than fifty, I would have worn a happy smile round the clock. So, we woke up. 49.54 per cent.'

But what mattered was that so many mobile phones had captured hard evidence of vote-rigging, in Navalny's words, 'videos of brazen swindling at election sites'. On the following day, Vladimir Churov, the grotesquely fraudulent Chairman of the Central Electoral Commission, said: 'These videos show signs of editing and have been published on the American YouTube server.'

United Russia did get a pasting outside the metropolitan areas to Navalny's joy: 'We are proud of the Far East, Siberia, Ural and Central parts of Russia, St Petersburg and the North-West region, where the crooks and thieves are totally screwed. We didn't give them the chance to steal victory. When the Vladivostok results start coming in, I wanted to run, buy a ticket, fly there and start kissing people on the streets.'

Lots of the results were funny peculiar, fantastically so in some cases. In Chechnya, an autonomous national republic, part of Russia but ruled by Vladimir Putin's psychotic quisling, Ramzan Kadyrov, United Russia scored 99.48 per cent in the Chechen Republic. Navalny commented: 'United Russia is a party which represents Chechnya, the top thief of the national republics, oppressed rural areas and Moscow municipal pilferers. They saved United Russia from total failure. Putin is the president of the Dagestan, Chechnya, Ingushetia national republics but surely not of Russia.'

He was cast down by how massively the vote had been rigged in Moscow: 'The victory was stolen here, and we failed to protect it. This is our major disappointment. All exit polls showed 27 per cent maximum, but the official results appeared twice as high . . . Moscow is not 100 per cent homogenous, of course, but it's unbelievable that the PCT got 27 per cent in one district, yet 70 per cent on the opposite side of the road. A huge amount of evidence proving falsification has been collected. Dozens of videos. We have created a new political space in this country: Everybody is against United Russia. It is Russia against the Party of Crooks and Thieves.'

President Medvedev announced an investigation into alleged irregularities. Yuri Chaika, the fabulously corrupt Prosecutor General of Russia, said that the data on falsifications would be analysed, but also that violations were local and didn't affect the overall result, and that therefore there was no reason to cancel the results of the elections. But the cat was out of the ballot box.

Navalny called for demonstrations to begin that very evening at Clean Ponds, a famous place of calm and beauty in a Moscow which doesn't have so much of either. In the eighteenth century, people had dumped their rubbish in the ponds, so that the area was known as 'Dirty Ponds'. Then a nobleman came along and tidied them up, hence the new name. One lives in hope that the same trick will be pulled off for the whole city. He blogged his call to arms, noting that cities in the sticks had done their bit, but the numbers in the capital were much better for United Russia: 'I'm ashamed, that guys from Ekaterinburg and Novosibirsk cities are telling us: "You fucking Muscovites! You called us and urged us to fight against fraud. We fought and finally got fair election results. But you achieved nothing!" I don't want Moscow to be the weak link. I don't want Moscow to hold this dubious position. We don't have to be silent while these bastards just throw our votes in the bin, gifting them to the Crooks and Thieves.'

He was worried that only a few hundred people would turn up. His pal, Ilya Yashin, later explained: 'I had a funny correspondence with Navalny an hour before the rally. I wrote him a text: "An hour ago, the Communists got 100 people on Pushkin Square." Navalny replied: "I'm afraid that not much more will come along to our thing."'

Navalny's fears were misplaced. There were thousands and thousands of people, not the usual suspects but tons of new-comers. Funnily enough, there were no representatives of the parties that had taken part in the election, especially the Communists who always came second. Navalny noted sarcastically, 'They couldn't care less that their votes had been stolen.'

On brand, his first gag was aimed at himself: 'Hi, every-body. While jumping over the fence to get to this rally, I forgot everything I was going to say.' He was only joking. Navalny had a knack of talking to a crowd, of getting them to roar back.

'Hear our voices. Here we stand!' he roared.

'Yes!' replied the crowd.

'Here we stand! They hear this sound and they're scared.'

He had a pop at the tightly controlled official media on the TV or, in Navalnyese, 'the zombie box'. He mocked their insults: 'They can call us micro-bloggers or internet hamsters. I am a net hamster! And I am going to cut the throats of these beasts! Together we'll do this. Because here we stand! One for all and all for one!'

After the rally, people headed to the Central Election Commission: 'It couldn't be called "a march",' wrote Nav-alny, 'just a chaotic procession along the side streets. We didn't know where or why we were marching in the rain. We knew the police would disperse us. Moreover, they could give any one of us a bash with a truncheon, just out of principle.'

That night, roughly six thousand people had heeded his

call, many people wearing white ribbons. The police moved in and three hundred were arrested including Navalny himself. The cops whisked him to a distant lock-up to prevent his supporters from mobbing the jailhouse rocker. Then he and others popped up in court and were sentenced to a maximum of fifteen days 'for defying a government official'.

Alexei Venediktov, the head of the Echo Moscow radio station, the last independent broadcaster in the city, called his arrest 'a political mistake: jailing Navalny transforms him from an online leader into an offline one.' In January, Viktor Shenderovich put it more pithily, also to the listeners of Echo Moscow: 'Navalny went into jail a blogger and came out a presidential candidate.'

On 7 December, Judge Krivoruchko – his surname translated means 'Crookshanks' – confirmed the fifteen-day sentence. The judge had previous, ruling twice in the infamous Sergei Magnitsky case, refusing him bail. Magnitsky was tortured by denial of medical treatment and then killed in custody on the orders of corrupt tax officers who had stolen millions from Hermitage Capital, Bill Browder's venture capital company.

Three days later, Navalny blogged from inside jail to his followers: 'We are not cattle or slaves.'

Navalny was locked up in the same jail as fellow protesters Ilya Yashin, who was soon to become a good friend, and Sergei Udaltsov, the unofficial leader of a radical Russian Communist youth group. While they were inside, their comrades organised a second big protest in Bolotnaya Square for the evening of 10 December. Navalny blogged about what it was like to hear accounts of the movement growing from inside his prison's walls: 'We were arrested for fifteen days in one country and released in another.'

Prison didn't scare Navalny one little bit. The moment he was back on the streets, on 21 December, he posted that he had to hurry off to be disinfected: 'My wife's joking about powdering me with bleach.'

Out of jail, he started to organise another protest against the rigged elections, and this one, on Christmas Eve, 2011 was the big one, far bigger than the first, attracting as many as 120,000 Muscovites, according to the organisers of the protest, or 29,000, according to the police. Given the temperature was minus 5 degrees C, even the police numbers were big. What became known as the Snow Revolution started to gather pace. And the venue, Sakharov Prospect, had poignancy too, a broad avenue named after the grand old man of dissent, the father of the Soviet H-bomb who turned on the Communists' denial of human rights.

Venediktov's prediction had come true. Other opposition leaders spoke too but Navalny, hatless despite the cold, in grey knotted scarf, black coat and jeans, was the rising star. When Navalny stepped up, the *Guardian* reported, 'a frisson of excitement passed through the crowd'.

By this time, Navalny was a hero because the regime had locked him up for fifteen days and his blog had properly established him as a thing. For the past two years, he had made a series out of his 'How They Saw [Slice Things Up] At . . .', prying open cans of worms at the state-owned bank, VTB, the state-owned oil company, Rosneft and elsewhere. His investigation into hey-nonny-nonny at VTB, where an arm of the bank had leased a ton of Chinese drilling rigs, dumping a number in the Siberian wastes, was a spectacular success. Andrei Kostin, the head of VTB, fired the head of VTB Leasing and announced a clean-up operation, all of this triggered by Navalny's 'How They Saw At VTB' work.

In a stroke of genius, Team Navalny had also created RosPil – 'Pila' meaning 'saw', suggesting a slice of the action. RosPil's shtick was to invite everyone on the internet in Russia to do the team's anti-corruption sleuthing for them, surfing on the back of a new initiative by President Medvedev's government to make tendering for state contracts public. To rub home the point, its logo spoofed the Russian coat of arms by having the traditional double-headed eagle holding two handsaws. In September 2011, he brought all his sleaze-busting ducklings into one duck house, the Anti-Corruption Foundation.

So, that Christmas Eve, everyone in the crowd knew that he was ferociously brave, that he was unbribable and that he was going for Putin. What many didn't know was that as well as having a lawyer's forensic mind for sniffing out anomalies in the small print, he could be a bloody good rabble-rouser. Not that the people he was stirring up were any kind of rabble.

'I've been reading this little book,' Navalny roared. 'It's called the Russian constitution. And it says that the only source of power in Russia is the people. So I don't want to hear those who say we're appealing to the authorities. Who's the power here?'

'We are!' the crowd yelled back.

'Who's the power?' Navalny repeated.

'We are!' the crowd roared again.

'I see enough people here to take the Kremlin or White House right now!'

This kind of language is heavy, heavy as lead. Navalny turned the rhetoric down a notch: 'But we are a peaceful force – we won't do that, for now. But if these crooks and thieves continue to try to cheat us, to try to lie and steal from us, we will take what's ours.'

He had a warning for President Medvedev and Prime Minister Putin who were about to play swapsies: 'Those two guys in their offices have no guts; two crooks and thieves huddling up to one another to seek a bit of warmth and support. They're snuggling up to one another with their cheeks fresh after a recent facelift, trying to keep warm. Alas, Botox doesn't warm you. It's you who make me feel hot! So tell these guys we are not alone. We are united in solidarity. All for one and one for all! We'll win! In the coming year the power will belong to the people! We don't want to wait any more.'

The Christmas Eve, 2011, demo was the biggest against the government since the fall of the Soviet Union in 1991. Afterwards, Navalny blogged: 'I have never seen so many people in my life.' Medvedev was not the target of the crowd's contempt but the puppet master in the White House.

A few days after the first rally on 5 December, Putin had hosted his annual 'telethon', a wretchedly dreary event where he answers pseudo-questions from dozens of placemen, Uriah Heeps and the creeping things that creepeth upon the face of the earth. Putin had claimed that 5 December was all stage-managed by the United States, adding that he thought that the white ribbons people sported were condoms, something to do with the campaign against the spread of Aids. Reacting to Putin's taunt, protesters gaily sported contraceptives, some inflated like balloons, others dangling limply from coats. One poster compared Putin to Muammar Gaddafi, who had been stabbed in the bottom by the no longer adoring Libyan masses two months before; a second to Kim Jong Il, the uber-creepy North Korean god king who had died on 17 December, just a week before the Christmas Eve demo. One protester summed up the logic driving her defiance to the *Guardian* rather beautifully: 'I'm for honest elections, for a lawful state. I want politics to be polyphony, not monotony. It's the cynicism and the silliness of the ruling power that I can't stand any more.'

As New Year's Eve approached, there was more wonderful news for Team Navalny. *Vedomosti*, a Russian version of the *Financial Times*, polled their readers as to who was the country's 'Politician of the Year' and the winner was: Navalny.

Crossing out Kremlin-inspired unthink was one of the many personal touches Navalny brought to his blog: 'While I have no doubt that the editorial board was bribed by the US Department of State and global players behind the scenes – the readers ~~(despite being brainwashed by massive Western propaganda)~~ voted freely.'

While Putin was the Man in the High Castle, as remote as a pharaoh, Navalny was now communicating directly with tens of thousands of ordinary Russians – not hyper-liberals, not uber-nationalists, not neo-Nazis – and he was on a roll. But he wasn't on the presidential ballot. The pharaoh still had that, the heart of Russian democracy, under lock and key.

'*Feliz Navidad!*' Navalny blogged from Mexico, where he had taken Yulia and the kids for a holiday. You get a flavour of just how extraordinary Navalny's life was then: a promising rally; fifteen days in the slammer; then the hottest attraction at the biggest anti-government rally for twenty years; then the beach and tequilas at sundown.

Navalny, of course, wasn't just soaking up the sun but working hard: 'I was drawn away from the Mayan legacy by tons of emails'. Then he went on to predict the future, that the next step in repression would be:

'1) they will try to restrict the spread of information on the internet by means of various anti-extremist laws etc.

'2) by allocating suitcases of money to create a new pro-Kremlin internet with their own public opinion makers and well-known media people.'

The Kremlin's patsy media were keeping up the attack. *Argumenty i Fakty* was, in Soviet times, a great magazine but it got muzzled under Putin and became just another yapping Kremlin attack dog. When it posted a photo of oligarch Boris Berezovsky laughing with Navalny, he was moved to mock. Back in the day, Berezovsky had picked out Putin for preferment, seeing in him a useful tool who could be manipulated. Putin became the head of the FSB, then Yeltsin's approved successor at Berezovsky's urging, but once Putin was in power, the old, quasi-submissive retainer turned nasty, very. Soon Berezovsky was forced to flee the country for the not that safe sanctuary of Britain. So it was revealing that Berezovsky and Navalny were seen to be palling around. But the picture was fake. The original was of Berezovsky and fellow oligarch Mikhail Prokhorov. The magazine had cut him out and photoshopped in Navalny. To entertain his readers, Navalny did the same trick, offering up photos of Stalin enjoying a joke with Navalny, then Putin with Navalny, then a space alien with Navalny. Yet again, the Kremlin lie factory was shown to be dishonest and stupid, both at the same time.

In Russia, Putin knifes the spirit of the law while enforcing administrative law against his enemies. If you try to stand against him, and you are a candidate of quality, then you will face a series of hurdles that make it impossible. At no time will the word be: 'you cannot stand, full stop'. There is always some quasi-legalistic excuse. In late January, Navalny correctly predicted that his old liberal opponent, Grigory Yavlinsky, would not be qualifying for the presidential elections in March, even though supporters of Yabloko had supplied more than the necessary two million signatures to pass the threshold. Navalny blogged: 'Yabloko received 2.25 million signatures of voters. Is this not enough to run for presidential election? This is the usurpation and illegal seizure of power.' Underneath a laughing photo of Putin, he wrote: 'This crook sits and decides which candidates he will fight in "fair elections", just to be 100 per cent sure.'

An election where one of the candidates has total control over who the other candidates are is not an election but a coronation. With Yavlinsky out of the way and Navalny not well known enough to run, Putin's hand-picked opponents were Gennady Zyuganov, an elderly Commie, trusted to rock the boat of his geriatric supporters and that alone, Mikhail Prokhorov, a giraffe-like oligarch, Vladimir Zhirinovsky, the fool's bladder on a fascist stick, and Sergey Mironov, a nonentity with the flavour of the actor who gets killed in the first five minutes of a movie.

Undaunted, at the start of February 2012, Navalny targeted his volunteers at election centres that had got form for voting anomalies, such as suspiciously high turnout compared to neighbouring places. Come the big vote on 4 March 2012, Putin, with no serious rivals, with near total control of the mainstream media, the courts, the police and the money of the oligarchs who owed him fealty, won a landslide. Navalny and his gang hit the streets the next day to register their contempt for yet another rigged election. The crowd wasn't massive and as people went home, Navalny was arrested and shoved into a Black Maria.

'Our police wagon is Number 2012. Attention!' he warned his followers: 'DO NOT SET IT ON FIRE. Just puncture the tyres.'

How Putin must have hated him. Navalny was the tsar of

charisma, courage and connecting with people; Putin the tsar of the knout, the cosh and the hypodermic syringe. The battle could only end with one tsar standing and Putin was now back in the Kremlin, with all its machinery now once again under his direct control.

On 6 May 2012, the day before Putin's inauguration, something nasty this way coming was signalled when what was left of Russia's independent-ish media were subject to 'Denial of Service' attacks. Echo Moscow radio station, *Kommersant* daily, and TV Rain channel were all hit. Even so, 20,000 protesters got to Bolotnaya Square to make the point that there should have been no such thing as a third presidential inauguration.

Ilya Ponomarev, an opposition MP, said: 'The police started it. Bolotnaya Square filled up and the police sealed it off. When they started to push demonstrators, people reacted.' The OMON riot police played it heavy from the get-go, clubbing people here, there and everywhere, leaving eighty with nasty injuries. Putin's PR man, Peskov, said he believed the police were being too soft on the protesters: of course he did. Around 400 protesters were arrested, among them Navalny, Nemtsov, the left-wing activist, Udaltsov, and another leftist, Leonid Razvozzhayev. The big names were freed relatively quickly but thirty-seven less well-known activists were locked up and faced a run of court appearances leading to serious prison time.

The master of the Kremlin would have noted that Navalny had managed to get five times as many protesters on the streets the previous Christmas Eve as he did on 6 May. Now the crowd was thinner; the tide was turning against Navalny; now was the time to break the butterfly upon the wheel.

A YouTuber captures the scene, close up on Navalny, as

he walks through admirers and hostile cops towards the open-air stage protected from the weather by a marquee. He gains access and is at the back, poised to speak next, when riot police, wearing full body armour with plastic face shields down, take over the stage and arrest the current speaker to a chorus of booing from the crowd. The phone-camera pans to see a big fat cop and a riot cop run with an arrested man down the street, away from the crowd, escorted by a dozen riot cops. Backstage, you can see from the look on Navalny's face that things are not going to plan.

'Where is Tsarkov?' Navalny asks. Peter Tsarkov, who sports a truly fabulous comb-over, is one of the organisers of the protest.

Then the sound of the PA is cut off by the police.

'Why don't we have sound? Give me the mic?'

'It needs to be charged,' an aide replies.

'Is it working?'

There is no time. While Team Navalny wrestle with the practical problem of solving the sound issue, two big cops sporting the silly, oversize hats Russian cops wear move to arrest him.

'We are taking you,' says one of the cops.

'Taking me where? I haven't done anything.'

He darts around them and mounts the steps to the sound stage, but two riot police and the two arresting cops, one of whom is very big and aggressive, grab him from behind, the very big cop putting an armlock around his neck. Navalny knows that if he gets to the top of the steps, the crowd will see what is happening while the four cops put a lot of force into stopping exactly that. He is a strong man but it is four against one and he loses the physical battle. He has one shot left.

'Stay where you are!' he roars at the top of his voice. 'Don't go home! Stay here!'

But the four cops, taking a limb each, manhandle him away from the stage without the crowd seeing that their star act has been kidnapped. The YouTuber's shot goes crazy as he runs parallel to the cops, squeezes through some metal barriers, and then he is back on. The very big cop is good, technically, at the rough stuff. When they are at the side of the square, they switch positions, the big cop forcing Navalny's arm behind his back and making him run, away from the crowd.

'You are breaking my arm,' he cries out in pain.

The cop ignores him, gains precious more metres away from the crowd, and then lets up: 'OK, now. Can you walk on your own?'

'Yes, I will walk on my own.'

'Don't fidget. Walk properly or I will break your fucking arm.'

'I will have you arrested.'

The cop reacts badly to that, jerking his arm back cruelly.

'You are breaking my arm,' Navalny screams, then, pleading, adds: 'Let go of my arm a little, please.'

The YouTuber's last shot is the back of a riot cop's helmet ballooning towards the viewer as, moving closer and closer towards the camera, the police officer blocks out the picture of Navalny disappearing into the bowels of a police station.

CHAPTER FIVE

One Russia, Two Tsars

Secret policemen know all the dark arts of that disgusting profession: bribery, sex shaming, intimidation, torture, murder. As a former KGB colonel and, later, head of its successor agency, the FSB, Vladimir Putin would have his goons tap the phones of any political rival with promise, would have his goons bribe, corrupt or shame people to inform on what the target was up to.

The Russian dark state listened in. That was a given. They would have you followed. But there would always be a grimmer possibility, that if you seriously troubled the Kremlin, you might suffer physically. In fact, you could die. For a very long time, Navalny was or seemed to be almost contemptuous of this possibility. In 2010 he gave a revealing interview to Gregory Asmolov who titled his piece: 'Blogger Navalny Tries to Prove That Fighting Regime is Fun'.

Asked about the real-world dangers his anti-Putin campaigns might trigger, Navalny replied: 'I've never received threats related to my professional activities. Although, from time to time, there are some strange calls or strange cars out there that follow me. It doesn't happen often and I never got immediate threats. I think that the whole threat issue is exaggerated. Of course, they can without any problems knock down a specific person in three seconds, including me, but someone will resist longer while someone resists less, someone will break sooner and someone later, but there's no need to exaggerate their ability to put pressure on everyone.'

That's bonkers.

The pressure was ever-present. Take, for example, what happened to Ivan Rybkin, the former leader of the Duma who was nominated by Boris Berezovsky's Liberal Party for the Russian presidential elections in 2004. At the start of his campaign, he directly accused Putin of masterminding the September 1999 apartment bombs and blaming them on the Chechens; that the president of Russia had, to get elected four years before, blown up Russia. Then he vanished for four days, popping up in Kyiv. Later, he explained that he had gone to the Ukrainian capital for a secret meeting with a Chechen leader. While waiting for the meeting that never happened, he took refreshments, then felt 'very drowsy' and passed out. When he came to, four days had gone by. Upon waking, he said he was shown a videotape in which he was performing 'revolting acts' conducted by 'horrible perverts'. Rybkin was told that the tape would be made public if he continued with his presidential campaign. In early March, he officially withdrew from the 'farce' of the race for the Kremlin. Rybkin blamed the FSB for his treatment but, since then, has held his tongue. The 'revolting acts' tape has never been made public.

Rybkin was temporarily removed from the scene until the electoral danger he posed to Putin passed. But what about those who stayed around, who wouldn't buckle under? The long list of people who were critical of Vladimir Putin and his regime and ended up dead is very long indeed, but at the end of this book there's a short list of those killed; what they were investigating or talking about when they were killed; and how they were killed.

For the avoidance of doubt, I do not believe that the evidence is anything like strong enough to call Vladimir Putin a paedophile. True, in the summer of 2006 he got out of his Kremlin motorcade, walked a few hundred yards, came across a slight, blond young Russian boy, knelt before him, lifted up his T-shirt and kissed him on the stomach, patted him on the head and then hurried off to his high castle. You can see it on YouTube here: https://www.youtube.com/watch?v=5uWEaKLzwUg

It is beyond creepy but that one instance is not enough to jump to the conclusion that Putin is a paedophile. Alexander Litvinenko was the former KGB colonel who clashed bitterly with Putin over corruption inside the renamed FSB, so much so that he had to flee the country for London. After he saw this video, he wrote a blog, alleging that the reason that Putin got a poor posting when he started out in the KGB was because the high-ups discovered he was a paedophile and felt they could not trust him to serve in the West, so he had to work first in Leningrad, now St Petersburg, then Dresden in East Germany where they could keep an eye on him. Litvinenko cited sources, old KGB officers, for this allegation, but he never came up with any written or other corroborating evidence. Artyom Borovik and Antonio Russo are believed to have been working on the 'Putin may be a paedo' story before they were killed in 2000.

Once again, Putin's fog machine is working full blast here. Of course, there are many other reasons why these three men could have been killed. But both Paul Joyal, a former

US intelligence analyst, and I are confident that Litvinenko was poisoned with Polonium 210 because he blogged that Putin was a paedophile. Not long after Litvinenko was murdered, Joyal sat down for a long interview with NBC *Dateline*. The NBC team did not broadcast his statement that 'the tipping point was Alexander's allegation that Putin was a paedophile in the Kremlin'. Joyal said that Litvinenko was wrong. He believed that Putin was not a paedophile, but he was bisexual. This, too, was not broadcast. Joyal suspects that the Russians got hold of a transcript of his extended interview. In Russia in the nineties, Joyal had met a couple who had told him that when they met Putin, he faked interest in the woman but was actually going after the man. Joyal's story chimes with Putin's strange affection for being photographed going topless on horseback and, during one of his long Q&A sessions with the Russian public, openly flirting with a handsome young man from the Caucasus. When I challenged Putin about the shooting down of MH17 in 2014, I was struck by how effeminate he was to me. By the way, there is nothing wrong in being bisexual or effeminate. But in Putin's Russia, you can go to prison for advocating homosexuality. It would be ironic if Putin is like some British Conservative MP in the 1960s, condemning the repealing of the law against homosexual acts in public but doing something completely different in private.

Four days after the NBC broadcast, Joyal was at home near Washington DC when two men attacked him, shooting him with a nine-millimetre round which went through his colon and bladder. They tried another shot to the head but the gun jammed. Then his big dog went for the attackers and they fled. The men who tried to kill Joyal have never been caught.

The point of this digression on Putin's alleged paedophilia – unproven – and suppressed homo-eroticism – to my satisfaction, proven – is that, to use the language of a milquetoast, the president of Russia does not warm to criticism. In the early days of his rule, in 2002, when Putin was visiting the European Union headquarters in Brussels, a French journalist challenged him about Russia's 'extermination' policy in the rebel region of Chechnya. Putin replied: 'If you are prepared to become a radical Islamist and undergo circumcision, I invite you to Moscow. We have specialists who can deal with this problem. I suggest that you have an operation so radical that nothing grows out of you again.'

This is the true voice of the tsar in blood. When challenged about human rights abuses on a massive scale, he threatened to have the journalist castrated. It may well be the case that a few of the people on my list of murdered Putin critics were killed for other reasons, but he has created a system where those who commission such killings go unpunished and that is his fault. A twenty-first-century tsar, ruling in a police state, should never be given the benefit of the doubt. My list is not exhaustive by any means. It could be tripled by adding local reporters and civil rights activists who were killed by party bosses in their area, enjoying a culture of immunity handed down from the Kremlin.

But Navalny would have known, or known of, a good dozen politicians or journalists who were killed defying the Kremlin. When he said, 'There's no need to exaggerate their ability to put pressure on everyone,' he was talking poppycock. Navalny knew he was in constant danger so why understate the risks?

Cognitive dissonance is that bit of psychology when someone holds two contradictory beliefs at the same time; that, for example, Vladimir Putin is a murdering fascist; and that challenging Putin is not to gamble with your life. The problem is that if you accept the second premise and you're someone like Navalny, you would grind to a halt. Navalny used to joke that he was asked the question, 'Why are you still alive?' so often that it was boring but he gave one of his more revealing answers to the US TV documentary *60 Minutes* in 2017 when he said: 'I don't know. Maybe they missed the good timing for it, when I was less famous . . . actually I am trying not to think about it a lot because if you start to think what kind of risks I have, you cannot do anything.'

Roman Borisovich is the former Russian insurance boss who got to know and, in a kind of way, love Navalny from 2011 onwards. Borisovich is a great barrel of a man, not at all fearful, full of subversive fun. When Navalny started asking around for Russian sponsors for his Anti-Corruption Foundation, he knew that many, many Russians would duck the test for fear of the consequences. Their businesses would be stolen by the practice of 'raiding', where rivals set up secret board meetings in the middle of nowhere, create new company seals, get their thievery rubber-stamped by a bent judge and suddenly a thriving company and all the money it generates has been hollowed out from under their noses. Or worse, something like what happened to Yavlinsky's son back in the nineties or Rybkin in 2004. Or much worse, like waking up a dead man walking.

Still, in February 2012, Navalny found sixteen Russian sponsors, eleven people from business, five from the arts and science. Why not look for more money from people safely abroad? Borisovich told me: 'Being a Russian taxpayer was the killer condition. After half a year of searching, only eleven businessmen and five public figures agreed to have their sponsorship disclosed. Navalny was, as usual, a seer. After he launched the Anti-Corruption Foundation, he was accused of being a foreign puppet sponsored by the CIA, MI5 and the usual suspects. The Duma started a formal investigation of his funding sources. Navalny came out publicly disclosing his sponsors. In his brilliant matter-of-fact manner he said: "Relax, there is nothing to investigate, you only had to ask. Here are my very public sponsors, the crème de la crème of Russian business and well-known Russian scientists, writers and journalists." The Brave Sixteen he called us.'

Borisovich was number two on the list; at number nine was Alexander Lebedev, a former KGB spy in London from 1988 to 1992 and the father of Evgeny Lebedev, whom Boris Johnson made Baron Siberia. On the face of this evidence, it would appear that Alexander Lebedev was an anti-Kremlin oligarch, not afraid of standing up to Putin. But the closer you get to the Kremlin, the murkier everything gets. In Russia, nothing is as it seems. In 2022, old man Lebedev was sanctioned by the Canadian government following Russia's full-scale invasion of Ukraine, suggesting that there are people inside Canadian intelligence who may suspect that there is no such thing as an anti-Kremlin oligarch. All concerned deny any wrongdoing.

One of Borisovich's first questions to Navalny when they met in the flesh in 2011, was: 'Are you not afraid?'

Navalny replied: 'What will they do? Kill me?'

Borisovich told me: 'His voice, these words rang in my ears every time his life was in danger, when some chemical liquid was thrown into his eyes, when he was poisoned with Novichok, when he was very poorly in jail. But when I learned of his death, it stopped. I no longer hear this voice say, "What will they do? Kill me?" Because they have.'

Back in 2011, when Dmitry Medvedev was minding the Kremlin shop and Putin his nominal prime minister, Borisovich and Navalny both dismissed the idea of Navalny being killed as ludicrous: 'I replied, "No, you are way too public at this stage, they would not dare. But they can put you in jail?"'

Navalny: 'What for?'

'Whatever, they can fabricate something?'

Navalny: 'Don't forget, I am a lawyer. I know the Code. I won't give them a reason.'

Borisovich continued: 'He had enormous charisma. He was the most charismatic Russian I ever met. Most of them have the charisma of a concrete slab. The second thing that comes to mind was his necessity, his need to lead. He was a leader, and in any sort of small or large group of people, whether talking to a crowd, or whatever, he enjoyed it so much. He had this gift of leading people.'

All sixteen sponsors became instant celebrities overnight. The night before, hardly anyone knew their names; in the morning, *Izvestia*, *Vedomosti* and all major news outlets published the list of Anti-Corruption Foundation sponsors; in the evening they were all over the media. Borisovich went on the prime-time news show of TV Rain – the last truly independent news channel then working in Russia – where they asked him the same question he had asked Navalny in their first meeting: 'Are you not afraid?'

In retrospect, Borisovich considers his answer incredibly naïve: 'Afraid? – I said – Of what? Of repercussions for supporting an anti-corruption foundation? In the country where corruption is the main impediment of progress, every citizen should be doing the same. It is not bravery, it is merely my civic duty, nothing more.' Little did he know that three months later, his civic position would force him to flee the country.

That question 'Are you not afraid?' is irritating, very. I can say that with confidence because I get asked it or versions thereof rather more often than I'd like, which is never. Obviously, the risks to me were, are and will be pathetically small compared to the dangers Navalny and Borisovich faced, but the question requires you to consider the quality of your armour, dented though it may be.

Challenging Putin is like gripping an electric fence by the hand. You may not die, you might not even get electrocuted, but the likelihood of getting off unscathed is low. When I doorstepped him in 2014, a few hours later I got punched in the gut: a very light chastisement indeed. But then I was working for the BBC, am British, and his goons knew from my visa that I would be leaving Russia soon. Writing *Killer in the Kremlin* and now this book feels like gripping the electric fence again, but the idea of Putin getting away with the things he does, unchallenged, revolts me. Anger rides fear.

Navalny, I suspect, was consumed by that anger too. And he was intensely hyper-focused, so determined to stand up to Putin that he deliberately suppressed sensible fear, in the same way that he didn't stop to consider the downsides of doing his ghastly NAROD videos. And, as he says in the quote at the very beginning of this book, not to challenge Putin was 'boring'. But Borisovich's judgement that he was a natural-born leader is right too. With Navalny, not just anger but also ambition rode fear.

As time passed, and the truly exceptional nature of Navalny's challenge to Putin's regime stood out, it became obvious that there were only two people in Russia who enjoyed true political free will: Vladimir Putin and Alexei Navalny. The first was the Tsar of Corruption; the second the Tsar of Anti-Corruption. One Russia: Two Tsars was never going to end sweetly but, for a time, such was the power and majesty of the contempt for the thievery and crookedness of the first Tsar's regime that things looked good for the Second Tsar.

Navalny didn't start out as an anti-corruption warrior but as someone who fancied making a little bit of extra money from owning stocks and shares. In 2009 he had sat down with *Kommersant*, one of Russia's leading financial papers, and explained what got him into this in the first place: 'I made almost all of these investments for the purpose of growing capital; there was no goal of buying shares in order to sue. Today I have stakes in Rosneft, Gazprom Neft, Surgutneftegas, LUKOIL, Sberbank, VTB, Gazprom, Transneft, E.ON Ruhrgas, ENI and more than ten companies in the electric power industry.'

Then he started causing trouble. Why was that? asked *Kommersant*.

'Because of the dividends. After buying the shares, I began to regularly read company reports, monitor what was written about them in the press, and I was horrified. At that time there was no sign of a crisis: oil prices were breaking all records, the companies whose shares I purchased were "in clover", but the company reports said: "no dividends". As a shareholder, this did not suit me, and I decided to find out where the companies' profits were going and why they weren't sharing them with me . . . At some point, it became a matter of principle.'

Golfers dream of a hole-in-one; investigative journalists and activists orgasm on anomaly. In December 2008, he found a big anomaly in the books, not of some nasty little worm in the primeval soup of Russia's gangsta-capitalism, but the Tyrannosaurus rex itself. Navalny's first great anti-corruption trophy was having a pop at Gazprom, in its pomp the largest publicly listed natural gas company in the world, with sales in 2019 of more than $120 billion, based in St Petersburg in the tallest building in Europe. Gazprom is majority-owned by the Russian state so the only way its bosses could seriously enrich themselves was, Navalny's hypothesis alleged, by defrauding the company by creating unnecessary transactions through murky go-between companies which were, in fact, controlled by those self-same bosses. All concerned deny any wrongdoing.

Navalny hopped on a prior complaint and stuck with it, like a dog gnawing a bone. He had bought shares in Gazprom and said that fraud had reduced the value of his shareholding, so that he was a victim. The details are hard to follow and involve a lot of companies with irritatingly long Russian compound names, but stick with it. He explained it all in a blog on 28 December 2008, called 'How They Saw At Gazprom' – 'Saw' being Russian slang for nicking money on the sly, as in sawing off a branch or a slice of the action.

This piece of alleged embezzlement was a work of art.

His blog started: 'Today, my dear friends, I will tell you about one of the fun money-drinking schemes adopted by Gazprom OJSC. Our "national treasure".'

Navalny's style is fun but let me try to set out the scam in simple language. The anomaly was that Gazprom subsidiary Mezhregiongaz had bought gas from a supplier, Novatek, in a funny peculiar roundabout way. The simple, cheap way was for Mezhregiongaz to buy the gas direct from Novatek. It did not. Instead, a go-between, Trastinvestgaz bought the gas, then sold the very same gas, moving along the very same pipeline, to Gazprom for nearly double the price. When Gazprom officials were pressed to explain why they hadn't bought the gas at the outset for the lower price, they initially insisted Gazprom didn't have the cash to complete the transaction. As explanations go, that is a bit rubbish frankly. Navalny continued that Trastinvestgaz had bought the gas using a loan from Gazprom.

Navalny used his ten shares in Gazprom to claim that he had lost money because of the shenanigans. The investigating authorities after a lot of slipping and sliding registered Navalny as a potential fraud victim.

The death threat was not long in coming.

'Last thing,' Navalny blogged: 'The investigator in the case, such a cheerful lieutenant colonel, told me at the first meeting: "Alexei Anatolyevich [Navalny's first name and patronym, the normal form of address in Russia], I will now make a decision recognizing you as a victim, but I consider it my duty to warn you. One of the bosses at Novatek, who was across the scheme and signed everything, tragically died under strange circumstances after the investigation began. Looks like he crashed on a snowmobile. There has been no investigation, but some consider the death suspicious."

'I don't know the details, I didn't find out one way or another. But just in case, I officially declare:

o I don't ride snowmobiles.
o I don't plan to ski this year or next.
o I'm not into rock climbing or hang gliding.
o I drive the car carefully.
o I don't wash windows, especially when they are open.
o I don't like eating Fugu fish or something like that for breakfast.

o I don't run across the road when the lights are red.
o I swim well.
o I don't have the habit of walking where bricks,
   slates or pianos are falling from above.

'This is not to say that I am very afraid of "countermeasures". Just in case.'

Fugu fish, by the way, contain the poison tetrodotoxin in their skin, eyes, ovaries and liver. The poison paralyses the muscles while the prey stays fully conscious; the victim is unable to breathe, and eventually dies from asphyxiation. Nasty.

Navalny, then, was fully aware that what he was doing could end up with him being killed. But if he were to fear death, then he would have to fall silent. And that would be boring.

What happened to Borisovich after his sponsorship of the Anti-Corruption Foundation was made public tells you something about how democracy got crushed in Russia. To begin with, everything seemed to be going well. Borisovich, by this point the vice president of Russia's insurance giant, Rosgosstrakh, explained: 'I loved the empathy and support we were getting from the people we knew and most importantly from strangers. I vividly remember a shy young lady approaching me in a crowded office elevator: "Roman Vitalyevich, you don't know me, but I just want to tell you I am so proud of you! I love the fact that one of Navalny's sponsors works in our company. I am proud to work for Rosgosstrakh with you!" Strangers asked to shake my hand, or have a selfie with me, or simply waved hello. These were the best compliments I ever got. But on the dark side, FSB and the other *siloviki* [literally 'men of force' or 'strongmen'

but better conveyed by 'secret police' or 'the connected']
were after our careers, businesses and lifestyles. The eleven
businessmen sponsors started having all sorts of problems:
some were fired, others had important contracts revoked,
state-owned bank loans called in, business arrangements
cancelled. Every single one of us got screwed.'

Borisovich continued: 'My experience was easier than
others. My boss covered my back and I had my British passport as a Hail Mary. First thing I noticed was being put on
the special passport control list – that's when you cross the
Russian border and the passport officer has to scan every
page of your passport to send the scans to the FSB. I travelled abroad almost every week that summer, so I quickly
noticed the changes when I went through passport control.
What used to take a few seconds, all of a sudden started to
take more than ten minutes. The reaction of the border
control officers was priceless. The experienced ones would
tell you to ask people behind you in the queue to go to other
counters because you would be held up for a while, and the
rookies would gaze in stupor at their screens and start calling their superior officers for help. I was also being followed.
This did not bother me much. I merely told my counterparts that I had a tail, leaving it up to them to confirm or
cancel our meetings. Nobody was bothered by my surveillance and most people thought I must be imagining things.

'The router in my apartment was also bugged, but so
unprofessionally that some applications like Gmail refused
to function, citing cybersecurity issues. All of a sudden, after
I was named as one of Navalny's sponsors, a neighbour
wanted to become friends, inviting himself over to our
apartment and asking to use our Wi-Fi while he was there.
I simply stopped using home Wi-Fi for anything other than

TV. I used my UK phones for email, leaving all sensitive stuff to be done when I was outside of Russia. I also think someone bugged the apartment.

'At the end of August 2012, when my family was returning to Moscow after the summer in France, my wife was subjected to the same extraordinary passport control procedures that they had been using against me for some time. Then I had to confess, I told her about the special passport watch list, about me being followed, the electronic surveillance and the bugs. Masha was shocked. Three weeks later we left Russia for good. As I was saying my goodbyes in the office I had a major discovery. Not the FSB but the SVR, the foreign intelligence agency, had come to see my boss, the CEO and majority owner of Rosgosstrakh, Danil Khachaturov. The SVR asked for me to be fired. Danil had asked everyone in the office to keep this secret from me, only telling me the day before I left Russia. He told me that: "Some idiot general came over with his deputies and told me that we cannot have a person like you second in command of the national insurance flagship. I told this moron that you are a very highly regarded manager, that I had nothing but praise for you among the senior management and employees of the company. If I fire you now I would be forced to explain that I was ordered to do so by the security services. So unless he gives me the order to fire you, him and his stooges can leave my office, I have an insurance company to run. The meeting was over in five minutes." God bless Danil, but it was 2012 back then, when things were not as terrible as they are today. I am sure his departure and the re-nationalisation of Rosgo was partially due to him defending me back then.'

Borisovich made sure his wife and kids were safely out of

Russia before leaving himself. He had called Navalny in early September 2012, to tell him he was leaving the country: 'He did not take it well but did not accuse me of anything. But I could feel in his voice that he did not like what he was hearing. I had to remind him of the arrangement we made in our very first meeting, when I said that I did not want to get into Russian politics. I told him that as my sponsorship and advisory function had been made public, it had involuntarily dragged me into politics and all the repercussions of being involved in the political opposition in Russia at the time.

'"So, you have made your decision. It is regrettable," he said in a cold voice. I did not want to end it like this and ask for a meeting before I leave.'

They met in late September in a small Asian restaurant just by the Anti-Corruption Foundation's office: 'We sat near the entrance by the glass wall observing the midday traffic. He ordered a rice dish, I had noodles. To my big surprise, in the meeting, Navalny was exactly the opposite of how he had sounded on the phone. He was very upbeat and optimistic, joking about my return to "foggy Albion" as if he was totally OK with it. We discussed how I could be helpful to his cause from London. Navalny said that I should try to look into the offshore ownership problem, but when I promised to try to do something about it, in his eyes, I saw how people must have looked at Don Quixote gearing up to fight his windmills.

'I could not hide the fact that I was surprised by the sea change in Navalny's reaction to me leaving Russia. I asked him directly, as usual: "What has changed between our phone call and this lunch?"

'As usual, Navalny was not shy of admitting his mistake:

"Sorry, man, I had a bad day. Lot of negative news that day. And then your phone call. I lost my temper." I told him that he had not, that he was very calm and courteous. "Well, you felt the negativity, it was how I was feeling then, so I apologise." "What has changed?" I asked, and this is when he shared his prophecy: "Look, they keep trying to implicate me as a foreign puppet. They have tried so many times and will not stop. You are the weakest link: you spent your life outside of Russia, you worked and lived abroad, you have properties, bank accounts and whatnot in the West, you are here temporarily, you said it yourself. So, what prevents them from parading you as a foreign spy? With a little simple hacking, they can obtain some documents, and there you go, NTV Investigations or even Rossiya 1, Kiselyov [Dmitry Kiselyov is one of the star propagandists of Russia's state TV channel, Russia One, Squealer to Putin's Napoleon in George Orwell's *Animal Farm*] will have it all over the telly: here is his British passport, these are his foreign bank accounts, this is the house he owns in London and his children's birth certificates, or some other documents they find. Hurrah, we have uncovered a British spy in Navalny's organisation! Roman is the puppet master, the ultimate link between the Anti-Corruption Foundation and MI6. We always thought that Navalny is a foreign agent, here is the proof. They might even reward some SVR general for uncovering the MI6 plot in the heart of Russia. Put this on the telly and 90 per cent of the Russian population will believe their story!"

'I very much liked Navalny's change of heart, but in my own mind I dismissed what he was saying. It didn't make sense to me. Why on earth would a British spy want to make the lives of ordinary Russians better?

'It was eerily quiet in the restaurant, then, in the middle of our meal, a chap rose from a table at the far corner of the restaurant and approached us. He sat down at a table next to ours, ordered a coffee and took out a pack of cigarettes, lit one and placed the pack on the edge of the table facing us. He started reading his phone while waiting for his order.

"Ah, he's with me," Navalny joked loudly. The chap was his tail who had followed him from his office to the restaurant and entered sometime after Navalny had come in. I did not notice the man when he had walked in and disappeared from my sight to the corner.

"Don't worry," Navalny told me in the same loud voice, "he won't sit here long. He has come closer to take a few photos of you, as he does not recognise you. You are not one of my daily contacts whose faces they know by now. So, he needs to report a new contact, and for that, he needs to photograph you." The dude heard him perfectly well but did not show any reaction. He finished his coffee, stood up and went back to the corner table. The pack of cigarettes remained sitting on his table; I pointed it out to Navalny with my eyes. Navalny called the waiter and told him to return the cigarettes to the absent-minded spy in the corner. "Probably a small recorder or microphone," said Navalny when the pack was taken away. The dude did not bother us again.

'Navalny said he regretted that I had to leave Russia, but it was, in his opinion, better and safer for me and my family and better for him. At the end of lunch, Navalny said his goodbyes and warned me that there would likely be a tail for me waiting outside, and there could even be a car to follow me. As he walked away with his tail following him, I could see a black Audi with dark windows had stopped nearby and put on hazard blinkers. One could not but notice it as it was creating a problem in the choc-a-bloc Moscow traffic and other drivers were angrily beeping. The traffic gave me an idea. I called my driver and asked him to come and collect me on the opposite side of the street from the Audi and give me a buzz just when he was arriving. I paid the bill, and soon my driver rang me. I briskly walked out of the restaurant, noticing a man following me on the sidewalk, went behind the black Audi and dashed across Novospassky, weaving through the cars amidst the crawling traffic. My car was just pulling up; I quickly got in and laughed at the black Audi frantically trying to make it across the traffic lanes to make a U-turn. We turned off Novospassky at the first opportunity and soon were far away from Taganka without any surveillance.'

Borisovich left Moscow at the end of September 2012, driving out of the country via the border with Estonia in his G-class Mercedes SUV on his own. The Russian border guards were waiting for him: 'They subjected me to the most scrupulous search imaginable: every single seam of kids' clothes was finger-tested, all music CDs were scanned for extremist material, and the car was even X-rayed. The security services were seriously looking for spy shit: they even crushed a pebble discovered in the pocket of my three-year-old son's jacket to see if anything was inside. When X-raying my G-wagon, the operator was showing me guns and electronics he was very proud to have found in other vehicles, checking my reaction. In retrospect, Navalny had been right all along. I think I left Russia in the nick of time.'

They let Borisovich go after a search lasting eight hours. He left Russia, never to return.

CHAPTER SIX

The Man Who Stole a Forest

One of the striking qualities about Vladimir Putin is his longing for legitimacy. Putin's thesis for his degree at Leningrad State University – he graduated in 1975 – was on 'The Most Favoured Nation Trading Principle in International Law'. When I met him in 2014 and challenged him about the Russian shoot-down of MH17, his answer was long and boring and overly legalistic. My working hypothesis is that Putin is a psychopathic serial killer who loves to dress up his bloodlust as legal necessity. Just like Joseph Stalin who always preferred his enemies to be convicted at a show trial before being sent to prison 'with no privileges', code for being shot.

Stalin had studied for the Orthodox priesthood, hoovered books, reading up to 500 pages a day, and had a library of 20,000 books. In his book *Stalin's Library*, Geoffrey Roberts reports that Stalin liked to make notes in the margins, often excoriating authors for grammatical or ideological errors. Stuff he liked got: 'yes-yes', 'agreed', 'good', 'spot on', 'that's right'. Stuff he hated got: 'ha ha', 'gibberish', 'nonsense', 'rubbish', 'scumbag', 'scoundrels' and 'piss off'. (I fear I am much more like Stalin than is comfortable.)

Putin's great mentor at the start of his life was Leo 'The Sportsman' Usvyatsov, a wrestler, rapist and gangster whose gravestone reads: 'I'm dead but the mafiya is immortal'. Long before Putin became a spy, he was beholden to a crook but one who got him into Leningrad University on an athletic scholarship to study law. I suspect that Putin's degree thesis was plagiarised. Years later, in 1996, Putin got a PhD by writing a doctoral thesis: 'Strategic Planning of the Reproduction of the Mineral Resource Base of a Region under Conditions of the Formation of Market Relations' which, there is no doubt whatsoever, was plagiarised. Clifford Gaddy for the Brookings Institute analysed Putin's paper and concluded that much of it copied whole chunks out of *Strategic Planning and Policy* by William King and David Cleland: 'I calculate that there are more than sixteen pages' worth of text taken verbatim from King and Cleland. Also, there are at least six diagrams and tables lifted directly or slightly modified from King and Cleland, with no attribution whatever.'

Putin is a thief, of words, of money, of votes, period. But also, just like Stalin, he is a thief who loves to blame others for what he himself has done. He is the Tsar of deflection. When faced with an opponent like Navalny, uxorious, honest and wary, it was only a matter of time before the crooked arm of the Russian state reached out to frame him. And frame him they did.

At the same time, Putin wanted to show to the democratic world that Navalny wasn't that popular, so he stage-managed a mayoral election in Moscow in 2013 in which Navalny was allowed to run. What happened was that two forces that drive Putin's weird, paranoid psychopathy, his longing for legitimacy and his love of placing his

enemies on the wrong side of the law, came into conflict
with each other, to comical effect. Navalny couldn't lose the
mayoral race if he was banged up; but if he was banged up,
Putin's legitimacy as a political actor with nothing to fear
from Navalny would look squiffy. The details are horribly
complicated but also farcical, a Russian version of Dario Fo's
Accidental Death of an Anarchist. Study this episode closely
and Vladimir Putin's contempt for and undermining of the
rule of law and the machinery of justice in Russia become
bleakly apparent.

Let's take the framing of Navalny first; then the mayoral
election hocus-pocus, although the two are intertwined.

Navalny had always got on well with a liberal politician
called Nikita Belykh, who had taken part in the first DA!
live political debate back in 2006. Two years later, at the
height of the Medvedev thaw, Belykh was made the governor of Kirov Oblast (or county), about 500 miles east of
Moscow, and he appointed Navalny to help clean up and
re-energise some of the local authority-controlled businesses
on his patch.

Navalny got stuck into Kirovles, a timber company
owned by the regional government where he suspected too
many forests got chopped up off the books. Leastways, it
was losing money for no good reason. Its boss was Vyacheslav Opalev. Navalny made a plan to make Kirovles more
open and profitable, bringing in a trading company, VLK,
run by a friend of Navalny's, Piotr Ofitserov. Kirovles would
cut down the trees and VLK, for a fair slice of the action,
would buy the timber off it and sell it on the open market.
VLK's true purpose was to stop Kirovles selling forests off
the books. For six months from April 2009, Kirovles sold
VLK timber worth around 16,000,000 roubles or £300,000.

That September, Governor Belykh sacked Opalev who then complained that he had been stitched up by Navalny and Ofitserov, saying they had pushed him into a deal that was bound to lose money. The Investigative Department of the Kirov Region looked into Opalev's complaint but in January 2011 decided that it was a bit rubbish because they could not identify that an offence had been committed.

Navalny seemed to be in the clear. Oh no he wasn't. In February 2011, federal cops, to wit the Central Office of the Investigative Committee based in Moscow, identified 'possible pressure' from regional actors. The COIC got new investigators to look into Opalev's complaint. In March 2011, the new set of cops also said there was no case. Navalny seemed to be in the clear, again. Oh no he wasn't. That May, investigators from the Central Investigative Committee itself accused Navalny and Ofitserov of deception in the Kirovles matter and/or breaching the trust of Opalev. Eleven months later, they admitted the whole thing was a dud, that there was no evidence of criminal wrongdoing. In late May 2012, Navalny blogged: 'All's OK.'

Oh no it wasn't.

Putin's old university classmate and faithful goon, Aleksandr Bastrykin, the head of the federal Investigative Committee, overturned the previous judgement that there was no case to answer, and had a swipe at his minions: 'You had a criminal file against this man, and you have quietly closed it. I am warning you, there will be no mercy, no forgiveness if such things happen again.'

This time, Navalny, the great enemy of embezzlers, was nicked for embezzlement, a much more serious charge than he had faced previously. To appreciate the irony, remember that the logo of Navalny's RosPil was that of Russia's double-headed eagle holding two handsaws – that 'saw' is Russian slang for embezzlement. As cases of deflection go, Vladimir Putin's proxies were engaged in a whopper. If convicted, and in Russia 99 per cent of trials end in conviction, Navalny faced ten years in prison and being banned from standing for political office.

A word about the lawman in the black hat. Aleksandr Bastrykin is one of the top law enforcers in Russia, roughly equivalent to the head of the FBI, but his performance harks back to the bad old days of the Feds, when J. Edgar Hoover made deals with the Mob and told his officers to target political figures who offended his dark sensibilities. Bastrykin is also a self-confessed kidnapper and a plagiarist.

The facts about Bastrykin the copycat are well evidenced, embarrassingly so. His 2004 book, *Signs of the Hand: Dactyloscopy*, about the science of fingerprinting, was a masterpiece of copying and pasting, principally from a book about forensics, *The Century of the Detective*, by German writer Jürgen Thorwald.

For example, Bastrykin wrote: 'Henry had only twenty-eight magistrates and several inspectors under his command. The back streets of Paris were a real paradise for numerous robbers and thieves. And only in 1810, when a wave of crimes was ready to flood Parpige, the hour of birth of the Sûreté Nationale struck. In the same year, the fate of its founder Eugène François Vidocq was decided.'

And Thorwald's original went like this: 'Henry had under his command only twenty-eight justices of the peace and several inspectors. The back streets of Paris were a real paradise for numerous robbers and thieves. And only in 1810, when a wave of crimes was ready to flood Parpige, the hour of birth of the Sûreté Nationale struck, and the fate of its founder Eugène François Vidocq was decided.' Apart from a few phrases, the passages are identical. But also Bastrykin copied across a great chunk of Anthony Summers' *The Secret Life of J. Edgar Hoover* to pad out his own rubbishy book.

The great Masha Gessen noted in *The New Yorker* that Bastrykin, when he gave a talk at the Sorbonne in November 2013, remained calm when he was heckled about the Russian Investigative Committee's use of torture, but lost his rag when he was personally accused of plagiarism. Dear Reader: I hope you have already worked out the theme here, that both Putin and his wannabe Sherlock Holmes steal other people's words.

In June 2012, Bastrykin made a nasty attempt to put the frighteners on *Novaya Gazeta*'s bloodhound, Sergei Sokolov. The paper has lost seven members of its staff to murderers. Its reporter had investigated the authorities' pathetically inadequate response to a horrific massacre in the town of Kushchevskaya in southern Russia in 2010 when a United Russia politician and gangster Sergei Tsapok and his goons murdered a farmer and eleven members of his family, including three children and a baby. Throats were slit, people were strangled, then the bodies were consumed by fire. The massacre was the culmination of a reign of terror where Tsapok's gang murdered and raped at will, protected by local police and above them, high-ups in Moscow, of which more later. One of the defendants got eight months for sitting on evidence of the massacre and a measly fine of 150,000 roubles. Sokolov's piece, two years on, was called: 'Ten thousand or so roubles for a life is the going rate'. Bastrykin encouraged the reporter to go with him on a fact-finding trip to southern Russia where he demanded an apology from him at a public meeting. Sokolov did apologise for the tone of some

103

of the article, but then went on to ask a number of pointed questions to which Bastrykin couldn't give a satisfactory answer. Infuriated, Bastrykin ordered Sokolov out of the public meeting. Worse, when they returned to Moscow, Sokolov was effectively kidnapped by Bastrykin's body-guards, taken to a forest where Russia's head of its kind of FBI took out a gun and threatened to kill the reporter, adding: 'Oh, and by the way, the investigation into your killing? I will be in charge.' Sokolov fled.

This was 2012 and some semblance of the rule of law, though not the substance, still mattered. When Sokolov's editor at *Novaya Gazeta*, Dmitry Muratov, wrote an open letter, complaining about what had happened, Bastrykin, Muratov and Sokolov all apologised to each other. In truth, neither Muratov nor Sokolov had done anything wrong, but their apologies provide some flavour of how *Novaya Gazeta*'s editor and staff made what they believed to be necessary or, rather, life-preserving compromises with the Kremlin.

What made Navalny stand out is not just the force but the crystal-clear clarity of his denunciation of gangsters in uni-form like Bastrykin. Others would give Russia's J. Edgar Hoover a wide berth. In June 2012, Navalny posted a blog called: 'Bastrykin in the Forest with a Gun', alluding to the kidnapping and death threat against Sokolov, but also to the official's fact-free vendetta against Navalny. He did not play the diplomatic milquetoast: 'Why has Bastrykin raised such a public stink? . . . He's just an ape, who's been given a gun by mistake.'

Not content with that remark, the next month, July 2012, Navalny's blog knocked the stuffing out of Bastrykin when he and his team discovered that the head of Russia's Investi-gative Committee secretly owned estates in the Czech

Republic and had a residency permit to boot. The next day he struck again in a blog headlined 'The Czech Spy'. Navalny's opening line is a corker: 'Well, the campaign to unmask the foreign agent Bastrykin is making faster progress than expected.' Navalny's readers will have noted that calling Bastrykin 'a foreign agent' and 'a spy' deliberately mimicked the language the Kremlin's patsy media used against him. The problem for Navalny is that mocking one of Putin's goons for being a thief was like pissing on marble. If convicted on the embezzlement charges, Navalny would be sent away for a very long time.

But then came the twist.

The certainty of Navalny being framed as 'The Man Who Stole a Forest' was about to be shaken by Putin's other compulsion, his longing for legitimacy. If Navalny was convicted as a thief, he couldn't run to be Moscow's mayor. If he couldn't run, he couldn't lose. If he couldn't lose, then it might look like Putin wasn't that universally popular a politician after all. So Navalny became Schrödinger's mayoral candidate, like the cat in the box, politically dead and undead, both at the same time.

CHAPTER SEVEN

Schrödinger's Mayor

Sergei Sobyanin is a semolina pudding Putin loyalist, has been mayor of Moscow since 2010 and has a distinguished academic record. Actually, I made that last bit up. He did write a thesis for his degree on 'The subject of the Russian Federation in the economic and social development of the state. The competence of government bodies and methods of its implementation', but whole chunks were, according to a Russian anti-plagiarism website, copied on pages 32 to 35, 90 to 91, 105, 149 to 153, 161 to 165, 168 to 183, 185 to 194, and so on. If you get the drift, you get the pattern.

When then President Medvedev sacked the previous mayor of Moscow, Yuri Luzhkov, in 2010, he had appointed Sobyanin for a five-year term, so he was safe until 2015. But the power of the people on the streets at Christmas 2012 had spooked the powers that be, and Medvedev started talking about appointees needing to be elected. On Valentine's Day 2013, Hizzoner Sobyanin gave an interview in which he said that a snap election was unwanted by Muscovites. There would be an election, but only in 2015, and that was jolly good by him: 'I don't yet feel such a desire from Muscovites. According to the polls that we have, 70–80 per cent of

Muscovites do not want any early elections. They believe that they need to work, and not engage in politics.'

Remember that in Vladimir Putin's system, the under-bosses don't have the final say. That's for the Godfather alone. The die was cast when Navalny told TV Rain in April 2013: 'I want to become president. I want to change life in the country. I want to change the system of government in the country,' adding that, given Russia's treasure in oil and gas, its 140 million citizens should live at least as well as people in neighbouring Estonia.

The little man in the Kremlin would have noted Navalny's ambition and not liked it one little bit. Putin doesn't do the internet but he is given a feed of news headlines from around the world and he would have known that his election in March was seen by many in the West as a bit of a joke. More to the point, no one had seen so many people on the streets of Moscow protesting against the government since the fall of the Soviet Union. That they had been shouting 'Putin is a thief' was not good. But the Kremlin made their calculations, and noted that Navalny, denied any kind of fair reporting by the patsy media, had taken something of a hit due to the constant drip-drip of negative reporting of the Kirovles case. Time to have a show election in the mayoral sandpit, to prove to Moscow and the wider world that Navalny was all mouth and no trousers.

On 4 June 2013, Navalny's thirty-seventh birthday, the underboss switched his story, now sensing a heavy ground-swell for a mayoral election, and declared there would be an election for Moscow's mayor. Navalny posted a lovely picture of him, Yulia and the kids on his blog and then went hard in, studs up, against Hizzoner Flip-Flop: 'I was watching yet another episode of their disgusting and deceitful clownery under the label of "the general public have asked the Moscow Mayor, Sergei Sobyanin, to call an early election, so Mr Sobyanin has heeded the voice of the people". Just a couple of months ago, Mayor Sobyanin proclaimed with his usual pompous manner that an early mayoral election would be "unreasonable" and that "Muscovites don't want it." But apparently, ALL OF A SUDDEN, people do want it now.'

Navalny went on to predict that the bad will get their just desserts and 'their ugly black castles (with depots for storing fur coats) will fall.'

It didn't work out like that.

Still, Navalny gave Putin's patsy mayor a run for his money. Team Navalny's slogan was feisty, on brand: 'Change Russia. Start with Moscow.'

But to do that, he had to run through a series of hoops created to make it nigh on impossible for someone like him to do so. To become an official candidate, he had to get either 70,000 Muscovites to sign up for him or to be pegged for the office by a registered party, and then collect 110 signatures from Moscow councillors from 110 different subdivisions, roughly three quarters of Moscow's 146 subdivisions. This is authoritarian bullshit, throttling democracy.

Only Mayor Sobyanin and the Commie candidate, Ivan Melnikov, got the 70,000 signatures. To secure the required 110 signatures of Moscow councillors, Navalny had to be sponsored by two parties: first, RPR-PARNAS, run by his friend Boris Nemtsov and, second, United Russia. To seek power he wasn't above going cap in hand to the enemy.

While running for mayor, the Kirovles trial kept on dragging him back to the sticks, to be placed on the rack of administrative justice for the Kremlin-hallucinogenic crime of forest-stealing. On 5 July, the Prosecutor Sergei Bogdanov closed his nonsensical case, calling for six years for Navalny and five years for his co-defendant, Pyotr Ofitserov. As so often, the court entertained the prosecution's dodgy and frequently self-condemnatory witnesses while refusing to hear key witnesses for the defence. The Kirovles prosecution was built not on timber but matchsticks. Navalny gave a truly noble speech from the dock which was picked up by the *New York Times* and is on YouTube. (Once again, I have fiddled with the translation in a few places because the literal word for word text sounds a bit tinny to my writer's ear.)

It's high summer and hot in the airless courtroom. Judge Sergei Blinov is exactly Navalny's age but looks like a boy dressed up in black gown, shirt and tie. Nervous, wary, Blinov does a pretty good impression of Private Frank Pike in the classic scene from *Dad's Army* when Philip Madoc's captured Nazi U-boat captain says he is keeping a list of names for when the Germans win and Captain Mainwaring shouts: 'Don't tell him, Pike!' Judge, prosecutor and goons are on edge; Navalny, in jeans and a white open-necked shirt, is the only force in the courtroom, watched on by a public gallery of around twenty or so Navalnyites, Yulia Navalnaya the most prominent. He takes a swig of water and sticks it to Russian fascism in judicial garb.

'Our remarkable trial is like a TV series – and sometimes it looks like a TV series resembling a trial – and is coming to an end. I am not even trying to insult the court by calling the trial a TV series because it really resembles a TV series.'

The goal of the trial-cum-TV series, says Navalny, is clear: 'so that the various state TV channels can mention me in the news in the context that this is the man who stole all the timber in the Kirov region; that this guy is a swindler.'

He apologises to his co-defendant, Ofitserov, and his family because they are accidental hostages. He tells the court: 'Stop torturing this man and his family. Everybody realises that Ofitserov is only here by accident. The demand to put him in prison for five years is absurd. Five years? How many million roubles are missing? A quarter of his tiny apartment in Ochakov has been put under lien. Isn't it enough to imprison a father of five, the only breadwinner? Do you want his five kids to go out on the streets?'

His voice dripping with contempt, he pours scorn on the trial created 'out of a world of fantasy and fairy tales', masking the reality that fifteen years of enormous oil and gas revenues has been stolen, leaving ordinary people with nothing apart from one thing: 'Vodka. This is why the only thing that is guaranteed to all of us, citizens of this country, is the degradation and the chance of drinking ourselves to death. And all these people who are building this feudal regime, having seized power, all the KGB generals who planted their children in the banks, all the United Russia deputies who sent their kids to Switzerland and opened bank accounts there, whole settlements in Marbella belong to Uni-Russians [his slang for people in Putin's United Russia party]. We shall destroy this feudal society that is robbing all of you sitting here.'

As so often in telling Navalny's story, the essence of his speech feels like a dialogue, its core message addressed to the other, smaller, greater tsar: 'If somebody [Putin] thinks that having heard the threat of the six-year imprisonment I would run away abroad or hide somewhere, they are mistaken. I cannot run away from myself. I have nothing else but this and I don't want to do anything else but to help my country. To work for our people.'

Is it worth it, all the grief, all the sitting around in court-rooms and police lock-ups, his mate heading to prison while five kids go hungry? Why bother fight the system? Navalny takes that one head on: 'None of us has the right to neutral-ity. No one has the right to avoid working to make our world better. We do not have this right. Because every time someone thinks, "Why don't I step aside?" he only helps this disgusting feudal regime which, spider-like, is sitting in the Kremlin. He helps the hundred families which are sucking the lifeblood out of Russia. He helps them degrade the people of Russia, to make them drink themselves to death, to rob the nation's common wealth.'

His conclusion is a rallying cry: 'I would like to call on everyone like me, the people who worked with me, people who want to work with me, don't be afraid of having a go. There's more of us. Hundreds of thousands, millions of us. But a strange thing happens because of inertia and apathy when these hundred families seize power.

'This cannot last. One hundred and forty million people, of one of the biggest and richest countries, are subjugated by a handful of bastards, nobodies. They are not even oligarchs who grew their capital due to their cunning or wisdom. They are a bunch of worthless former Komsomol [Young Communist] activists turned democrats turned patriots who grabbed everything. This is nonsense. And we will sort this nonsense out. Thank you very much.'

Not a word of this great speech was carried on state TV.

On 17 July, Navalny made it as a mayoral candidate, becoming registered as one of the six candidates for the Moscow election. The very next day, he was back in Kirov for sentencing. He got five years for embezzlement, his friend Ofitserov four years. Prosecutor Sergei Bogdanov demanded the prisoners be sent to jail forthwith.

Just before Navalny was led off in chains to the penal colony, he posted: 'OK. Don't miss me. And most importantly – do not be lazy.'

So that was the end of Navalny's hopes of running for mayor. Or was it?

He very publicly pulled out of the race and called for a boycott of the election. Immediately the sentence was announced, thousands hit the streets of Moscow, thronging the Manezhka, the open space next along to the Red Square, as close as you can get to the Kremlin without getting arrested automatically. The crowd called for Navalny to be freed.

By 2013, it is true that a whole series of Putin critics had been killed, but the Kremlin always went out of its way to turn on the fog machine, so that different stories, conflicting narratives, of why someone had been killed abounded. The state had been far more careful when it came to handing out jail sentences to political rivals, Navalny and friends routinely getting fifteen days' detention every now and then. Five years in the slammer was a jump to a different order of magnitude of repression.

The Kremlin smelt trouble and, lo, everything changed.

Prosecutor Bogdanov was, after all, just another underboss and now it was his turn to eat his own words. Two days later, the court sat again to hear the prosecutor call for Navalny to be freed on bail. Navalny was granted a speech and, on brand, he bit the hand that fed him, telling the three judges: 'I request that you verify the identity of Prosecutor Sergei Bogdanov. It's possible that it is his double because it was Prosecutor Bogdanov who demanded that I be detained in the courtroom.'

On the steps of the courthouse, Navalny noted the bizarre nonsense of being jailed and then un-jailed: 'Nothing like this has happened to anyone else.'

Navalny was Schrödinger's candidate for mayor.

The court had not cleared Navalny. The threat of being sent to prison hung over him like a storm cloud for the foreseeable future. A convict on bail would not be allowed to hold public office, so that even if he won the mayoral election, he would be stripped of the title and sent to jail. But, as ever, Navalny was up for a battle: 'Even if we have just a couple more months to fight, we will fight.'

And fight he did, one of his leaflets proclaiming: 'He Does Not Lie and He Does Not Steal.' Team Navalny started investigating his opponent Mayor Sobyanin and found 'a swampy quagmire'. As so often, Navalny focused on the anomaly between an official's stated salary and the vast wealth in property he and his family members held. There was a fancy 308-square-metre apartment in downtown Moscow which appeared to be used by the mayor's younger daughter, Olga. The *Moscow Times* reported: 'Navalny, who is Sobyanin's major rival in the race, sent a request to the Prosecutor General's Office to check whether the privatisation of the apartment was legal, claiming that its price is six times as much as Sobyanin's estimated income over the last ten years. The apartment on 12/1 Rochdelskaya Ulitsa might be worth about $5.3 million, Navalny said, adding that his estimates are based on the information available from open sources ... Navalny said in his LiveJournal post that Sobyanin, as a mayoral candidate, must provide transparent information on his income and property ownership and explain "how his under-age daughter came to own a huge luxury apartment in a high-end district of Moscow".'

Sobyanin's press officer later said that the apartment had been legally privatised, everything had been declared, effectively, that there was no story, nothing to look at here.

But there was a second daughter, Anna Sergeyevna Sobyanina, who bought a 116.6 million rouble or $3.5 million flat in the heart of St Petersburg in 2011. Navalny wondered: 'How could the 25-year-old daughter of a civil servant, whose maximum income over the past ten years could only have been 27 million roubles [$814,000], end up with an apartment worth 116 million roubles [$3.5 million]?'

Archly, he dismissed one deduction: 'We reject, with indignation, the very thought that this chic apartment in downtown Petersburg was gifted by civil servant Sobyanin to his daughter on her twenty-fifth birthday. That would be so unlike a civil servant! Of course, Anna Sergeyevna Sobyanina earned enough to pay for it all by herself.'

He then dissected her business career, discovered that she was one of the founders of Forus Group Ltd, a building firm specialising in historical renovation, which had won contracts for work on the Administrative Authority Building in Khanty-Mansiysk; a conference room for the president of the Russian Federation; work stations for Government International Communications; an Engineering Service Complex in Khanty-Mansiysk; the Office of the Director of the Block of Work Stations for Government International Communications and, Navalny's favourite bit, the Reception Hall for the Ministry of Defence of the Russian Federation.

'WHAT AN AMAZING COINCIDENCE,' blogged

Navalny in capitals. Rather naughtily, though, he added that the scope of Anna Sobyanina's company's interests were in Moscow, St Petersburg and Khanty-Mansiysk where her father had been governor of the region.

Navalny asked his opponent two simple questions.

'One, Sergey Semyonovich: by what means and with what revenue did your daughter, at twenty-five years of age, buy an apartment that exceeds by threefold your total income over ten years?

'Two, is the fact that your daughter's business is involved in the supply of elite furniture for government services connected to the fact that you were able to exercise direct influence over the signing of these contracts, by having been in the civil service?'

He encouraged his followers to write to the prosecutor's office and the Investigative Committee, Russia's FBI, asking these questions and to help them out, created a website to make it all the easier: 'They won't talk about this on TV, which means that we have to talk about it ourselves. We can do this and we're up for it.'

The other side did not sit on their bottoms. By the other side, I don't just mean the mayor and his supporters. In fact, the people who gave Team Navalny the hardest time were rival candidates to Mayor Sobyanin. Step forward Nikolai Levichev, an MP in the Just Russia party, also candidate for mayor. Welcome to the 'systemic opposition'. It's a rather deadening phrase for patsy pretend opponents of the Putinist status quo, who exist to confuse ordinary Russians in the sticks and useful idiots in the West that Russia is a democracy when it isn't. They have all the appearance of a political party, leaders, members, logos, rallies, conferences, attempts to win power through elections. But none of the reality. On the corruption of Putin and his goons, they sit there like so many tapioca puddings, in silence. But they come to life again when a serious rival to the Putin system breaks surface. And that was how a team from Just Russia rocked up at the flat of some Navalny supporters with an angle-grinder.

Navalny blogged on 14 August 2013: 'The police arrived and started sawing through the door with an angle-grinder and without a search warrant!!! They were sawing through the door for five hours, thus demonstrating their high degree of professionalism.

'After they cut through the door of the apartment where three of my supporters were staying, the police started an illegal search. It was carried out by police officers and politicians from the Just Russia party.'

Navalny added that a journalist was beaten up too.

The police raid was officially because there were some pro-Navalny leaflets in the flat and they were libellous, charges Navalny, on brand, pooh-poohed. He blogged that the raid 'is their response to our investigation today about Sobyanin's daughter who bought an apartment for 116 million roubles [$3.5 million]. In case Sobyanin reckoned that now we'd declare a holy war against the insignificant Just Russia party – no, we won't.'

To punch that point home, the blog was headlined: 'This Door Was Sawn by Sobyanin's Daughter'. In it, he tagged a tweet from his chief of staff, Leonid Volkov: 'Levichev is the perpetrator of the crime, the organiser Sobyanin, and the paymaster Putin' and suggested that the best retort to their breaking and entering and to beating up people would be to go online and ask the prosecutor's office and the FBI about how come the mayor's daughter had such a fancy flat: 'Print it and hang it up on your doorway. Show the rascal Sobya-nin that he can't seize all the leaflets.'

Navalny lost, polling 27 per cent to Mayor Sobyanin's 51 per cent. Of course, the vote was rigged; of course, the postal vote favoured the sitting mayor; of course, Sobya-nin's numbers went through the roof in polling stations that were not monitored; of course, Navalny lost. But being Schrödinger's mayor, Navalny also won. He could rightly claim a moral victory and, if the votes had been honestly counted in a fair election, with him and the sitting mayor getting equal coverage in the media, a real victory too. But that isn't how Putin's Russia works.

It goes without saying that there may well be perfectly innocent explanations for the rich property portfolio of the mayor and his daughters, but a credible one was not forth-coming at the time or subsequently. Navalny's forensic investigations of this or that opponent may not be compel-ling to everyone, but it does give you a flavour of his style, of genuinely how much like Terminator 2 he was and why so many people profiting from sitting inside Putin's system wanted him to hold his tongue.

Or for that tongue to fall silent.

CHAPTER EIGHT

Is This a Sausage Sandwich
I See Before Me?

Vladimir Putin's corruption engine has been built for export, although, once out of Russia, the trail of evidence is hard to follow because of the fog machine. But the evidence is compelling that the Russian dark state has funded, fuelled and supported far-right and far-left politicians across the world. Following the chain of cause and effect is tantalisingly difficult and all concerned deny any wrongdoing. That said, one has to worry about the involvement of the men with snow on their boots in the following affairs.

Donald Trump's social media company Trump Media managed to go public only after it had been kept afloat in 2022 by emergency loans provided in part by Anton Postolnikov, a Russian-American businessman under continuing FBI scrutiny, the *Guardian* reported in April 2024. The effect of this deal was to make Trump the richer by something like two billion dollars. The consigliere of the far-right Italian politician, Matteo Salvini, met Russian counterparts in Moscow and an investigation took place into allegations that there were discussions on funnelling funds. The investigation was later dropped due to lack of evidence. The French far-right presidential candidate Marine Le Pen's Front National received funding from a Russian-linked bank, only to return it. All concerned deny any wrongdoing.

And then, in a different category, there is Arron Banks. The GoSkippy car insurance oligarch of Catbrain Lane, Bristol, if oligarch he is, and I have a funny peculiar/funny ha-ha relationship. While at BBC *Newsnight* I made a series of films on Banks' business empire including the two flats he and his then Russian-born wife owned overlooking the Royal Navy dockyard in Portsmouth. I also examined his friendship with Nigel Farage and Banks' £8 million donation to the Brexit camp. At the libel trial of Carole Cadwalladr, he saw me by the entrance of the Royal Courts of Justice as he was going into court and said: 'Look, John. No snow on my boots.'

It was a warm sunny day. Arron Banks was right. It's fair to say that although he lost on some points, he did in fact come out on top of his libel action against Carole Cadwalladr. His Brexit donation was investigated by both the Electoral Commission and the National Crime Agency and they, too, found no snow on his boots.

But the Kremlin's power and influence in neighbouring Ukraine was off the scale. Time and time again, Ukrainian political leaders were found to be creatures of Ukrainian oligarchs who were subtly or not so subtly pro-Putin. Viktor Yanukovych was a former convicted robber made good from Donetsk, formerly Stalino, formerly Yuzovka after Welsh mining engineer John Hughes who founded the city on top of rich coal and iron ore seams in the east of Ukraine in 1860. There is an extraordinary photo of Hughes's Welshmen and their Ukrainian friends using great white oxen to drag a big boiler on a sledge across the snowy wastes.

Yanukovych was elected president in 2010 on a clever ticket, defending the rights of Russian speakers in his native east of the country while mouthing warm words about furthering integration with the European Union. In 2013, plans were afoot to announce closer harmony with Brussels at a summit in November. One week before that was due to happen, Yanukovych stunned Ukraine by saying that he was ditching that and, instead, getting closer to the Kremlin. A Russian bailout helped sugar his pill. The switch led to massive demonstrations in the Maidan, the square in the centre of Kyiv which continued despite police brutality on a horrific scale throughout the winter. My friend Vlad Demchenko, who arrested me on day two of the big war, was one of the many brave Ukrainians who got badly injured fighting for a free Ukraine.

On 20 February 2014, police snipers opened fire, killing around 100 protesters, who became known as the 'Heavenly Hundred'.

Ukraine revolted, Yanukovych fled to Russia and the Kremlin's sphere of influence was moved 800 and something miles to the east. The revolutionaries broke into Yanukovych's Mezhyhirya estate and found a temple constructed to the god of kleptomania. While millions of Ukrainians struggled on the poverty line, Yanukovych boasted a log cabin on steroids, a garage full of vintage motors, an exotic zoo and a ton of receipts proving his thievery. Expenses that stood out were $800 for medicines for his pet fish, $14,500 for tablecloths and $41 million on light fixtures. Other boxes of files showed how much he spent on spying on critical journalists, $5.7 million for the month of December 2010 alone. The nitty-gritty was nasty: there were files on heroic investigative journalist Tetyana Chornovol who had sneaked into the estate and wandered around for three hours before being nicked by security. On

Christmas Day 2013, she had been savagely beaten by attackers. Her most powerful enemy was Yanukovych.

In June 2015, my former BBC *Newsnight* colleague and pal, Gabriel Gatehouse, got a scoop when he interviewed Yanukovych in his Russian exile. The disgraced president defended himself, saying the hoo-hah about the Mezhyhirya follies were 'political technology and spin: and that the estate did not belong to him personally'. When Gabriel challenged him about the exotic zoo, he replied: 'I supported the ostriches; what's wrong with that?'

Politically, Yanukovych was dead before his 'I supported the ostriches' remark. After it, he was stuffed.

What the Ukrainian revolutionaries did was to expose the deep vein of corruption at the heart of Yanukovych's regime which was exactly what Navalny had been longing to do in Russia. Two days after the fall of Yanukovych, Team Navalny hit the Manezhka, close by the Kremlin, to show their solidarity for thirty-seven fellow Muscovites who had been arrested at Bolotnaya Square on 6 May and were still being dragged through the court system. Navalny was arrested but not banged up for the standard fifteen days. Instead, Putin, always a cunning sod, rearranged the legal furniture to do its best to mute Navalny's voice at a critical moment in history. Navalny was accused of violating his parole in the Kirovles judgement and sentenced to house arrest, confining him to his flat and banning him from personally using the internet.

Yulia took over but the effect was to blunt Navalny's staunch support for Ukraine's Revolution of Dignity as it was happening in real time. Down the track, this, and Navalny's own later clumsiness, was to ruin his relationship with a free Ukraine and the only beneficiary of this mess was Putin.

In the spring of 2014, Russian soldiers, stripped of the

badges that identified their units, invaded Crimea, the diamond-shaped peninsula that hangs down from Ukraine into the Black Sea, the first armed invasion of a European country since the Second World War. Blessed by nature and cursed by history, Crimea has been a weathervane of who holds power in Europe and Asia down the centuries. When the Mongol hordes swept westwards, they captured Crimea and their Tartar descendants held on to the rocky and arid peninsula long after the Mongols had fallen from grace. Owing some kind of fealty to the fading Ottoman Empire, Crimea fell prey to the rising star of the Tsars towards the end of the eighteenth century. In 1853, Imperial Russia fought the Crimean War against Britain, France and the Ottoman Empire. It was a ghastly conflict that exposed the terrible weaknesses of the great powers. Tennyson's magnificent poem, *The Charge of the Light Brigade*, highlighted the military incompetence at the top of the British army:

> *Someone had blundered.*
> *Theirs not to make reply,*
> *Theirs not to reason why,*
> *Theirs but to do and die.*
> *Into the valley of Death*
> *Rode the six hundred.*

Florence Nightingale's work cast a grim light on the primitive conditions sick and injured British soldiers had to live and die in. But after three years of bloodshed, and ferocious battles to evict the Russian fleet from its base at Sevastopol, it was Imperial Russia that had to lick its tail. The Russians were allowed to hold Crimea but they had to abandon their naval base. The Kremlin's anxiety about its asserted right to park its armoured pedalos in Sevastopol continues to this day.

After the humiliation of the Crimean War, Russia abandoned serfdom and reformed how it ran the country, establishing a strange and mostly good tradition, that three out of four times it lost a war it got better. In 1905, after the Russian Imperial navy was humiliated by the Japanese, the first great defeat of a Western power by an Asian one for centuries, the Russians created the Duma, its first parliament. After its defeat by Imperial Germany in 1917, the Tsar fell and Russia had six months of chaotic liberal democracy before the abyss. After the Soviet invasion of Afghanistan ended in a bloody quagmire, the Soviet empire collapsed. Three out of four good outcomes is progress, of a kind.

The Soviets established control of Crimea after the 1917 revolution and it became a part of the Russian republic of the Soviet state until, after the death of Stalin, his successor, Nikita Khrushchev, gifted Crimea to Ukraine in 1954. The gossip – OK, the judgement of Kremlinologist Mark Kramer, professor of Cold War Studies at Harvard University – was that Khrushchev presented Crimea as a sweetie to First Secretary of the Ukrainian Communist Party Oleksiy Kyrychenko to screw over his rival for power, then Soviet Prime Minister Georgii Malenkov. The decision didn't seem to matter very much back then when the whole caboodle was all part of the ever-lasting Soviet Union. But empires come and go, and many Russians have never properly got over the fact in law that Crimea has been, since 1954, part of Ukraine and Ukraine has been an independent country since 1991.

When Putin stole Crimea back in 2014, he ripped up the order established after 1945, secured by NATO and what became the European Union, that there would be no more land grabs in Europe. Putin, his 1970s secret policeman sunglasses blinkering his vision, doesn't get it that he is reheating

Hitler's chips. The move was hugely popular inside Russia and that caused Navalny, always with an ear for the mood of the Russian electorate, a major headache. Side with Putin on Crimea, and Navalny would keep in with the Russian public but fall out with Ukraine and the international rules-based order; side with Ukraine and, he feared, he would lose relevance back home.

Navalny took a swipe at 'the thief Yanukovych' who went from hitting his critics on the head to shooting them so he ended up in Russia. Had Yanukovych appealed to the nation and sacked a couple of cops, Navalny mused, he would still have been president.

Navalny's next question is: 'Why is Putin so furious about what is happening in Ukraine?'

The answer was: 'Loaves of gold.'

Navalny noted that photos of ordinary people gaping at the excesses of Yanukovych's estate, the exotic zoo, the sculptures of loaves in gold, the golden toilets, 'wounded our chief swindler to the very heart. After all, Yanukovych would cry like a little girl if he saw how much more Putin and his friends had stolen. They have loaves of diamonds.'

Navalny went on to say: 'Changing the borders of states in Europe using troops and force is unacceptable. This won't lead to anything good.'

But that got lost in the noise.

As 2014 dragged on, Vladimir Putin's killing machine marched into the two most eastern, most Russian-speaking oblasts (or counties) in Ukraine: Donetsk and Luhansk. Ordinary people hit the streets to protest. They were shot. Millions fled to the safety of free Ukraine; hundreds of thousands stayed to become Russian proxies and, more to the point, cannon fodder for Putin's war against Ukraine.

In July 2014, the Russians shipped a BUK anti-aircraft missile launcher across a military pontoon bridge on a river to keep it from prying eyes to help their proxies. The BUK launcher, missile and radar unit were too heavy for the pontoon bridge so the Russian commander elected to leave the radar unit on the Russian bank. When the BUK missile launcher was made ready to knock Ukrainian fighter jets out of the sky, none of the crew realised that the relatively primitive in-built radar unit in the launcher alone could not properly distinguish between, say, a fighter and a Boeing passenger jet. That's how MH17, flying from Amsterdam to Kuala Lumpur, came to be shot out of the sky and 298 wholly innocent people killed. BBC *Panorama* sent me to the crash site. The Kremlin was furiously denying any involvement and its fog machine was working full-time. They were lying. I will never quite lose the memory of the smell of aeroplane fuel, human flesh and cornfield.

The Russians managed to take Crimea with barely a shot being fired, but after a bad start, the Ukrainian army got its act together and mounted a spirited defence. The front line wobbled a bit as time went on, but essentially, by the late summer of 2014, the trenches were dug. The Russians had Crimea, great chunks of Donetsk and Luhansk oblasts but by no means all of them. The Kremlin's goal was, with the east of Ukraine occupied, to make the country's dreams of joining NATO and the European Union impossible. The dog was in the manger and wasn't going to move.

One opposition leader condemned the annexation of Crimea outright, but his name wasn't Navalny. Boris Nemtsov said that Crimea was an integral part of Ukraine, that its annexation was illegal and, in an article in the *Kyiv Post*, he lamented the 'fratricidal war' between Russia and

Ukraine: 'This is not our war, this is not your war, this is not the war of twenty-year-old paratroopers sent out there. This is Vladimir Putin's war.'

Navalny piped a different tune. In October, freed from house arrest, he was interviewed by Echo Moscow radio station. Prodded by host Alexei Venediktov on the popular Putinist slogan 'Crimea is ours', Navalny dodged the question: 'Crimea belongs to the people who live in Crimea.' Pressed for a proper answer, he added that 'Crimea, of course, now de facto belongs to Russia. I think that despite the fact that Crimea was seized with egregious violations of all international regulations, the reality is that Crimea is now part of Russia. Let's not deceive ourselves. And I would also strongly advise Ukrainians not to deceive themselves.'

Navalny went further, saying that if he were to become president of Russia, he would not return Crimea: 'Is Crimea some sort of sausage sandwich to be passed back and forth? I don't think so.'

Macbeth said something similar:

> 'Is this a dagger which I see before me,
> The handle toward my hand?
> Come, let me clutch thee:
> I have thee not, and yet I see thee still.'

The Scottish king was tortured by the lure of power gained through the wrongful shedding of blood. Navalny hated the idea of not being able to topple Putin because he might adopt too liberal a conscience. But he betrayed his better self, betrayed his ideal of being the man who 'does not lie, does not steal', betrayed the spirit of 1945, that you don't go around stealing other countries' land.

It was not his finest hour.

CHAPTER NINE

Thieves R Us

In Vladimir Putin's Russia, the crooks run law and order and the honest go to prison. To make that perversion of natural justice work, the master of the Kremlin puts a lot of thought into timing, never striking an enemy when he is strong but waiting, for example, until the demonstrations have petered out and the world has moved on.

Putin is a subtle tyrant.

The land grabs of Crimea and a great bite out of eastern Ukraine in 2014 pleased the Russian crowds and distracted the critics. A good time, then, to lock up some of the Kremlin's more annoying mosquitoes. In July 2014, three judges jailed two rebels arrested for their part in the demo staged on the eve of Putin's third inauguration two years before. Sergei Udaltsov and Leonid Razvozzhayev, both leftists, got four and a half years in a penal colony, raising the stakes and putting yet more pressure on the opposition and its uncrowned leader Navalny.

Once again, Putin delighted in the legalistic form of due process but not the substance. He liked it that his political enemies were taken off the board by judges, sometimes after trials and appeals and other shenanigans that lasted months, years, the judges having weighed the evidence, phoney, absurd and surreal as it so often was. The detailed case against Udaltsov and Razvozzhayev was based on a 2012 NTV state television 'investigation' called 'Anatomy of a Revolution'. The show was dross from start to finish, passing off murky clips with rubbish audio as proof of a plot between Georgian government agents and the two accused. Navalny blogged that the TV 'investigation' said that the clandestine meeting setting up the conspiracy took place in June 2012, but the actual protest happened one month earlier in May.

And the story behind the story of how Razvozzhayev had ended up in a Moscow court was also compelling. In 2012, Razvozzhayev had fled Russia to seek sanctuary in Ukraine and then, mysteriously, he had vanished off the face of the earth.

How come?

When he turned up in a Moscow courthouse some days later, being escorted by jailers into a police van, he managed to shout out to the waiting media: 'They tortured me.' Just as the guards were about to close the van door shut, he managed to yell out more: 'They tortured me for two days; they kidnapped me in Ukraine.'

Razvozzhayev had watched the 'Anatomy of a Revolution' TV show and knew that he was going to be framed, so he fled Russia for Ukraine. On 19 October 2012 in Kyiv, he requested asylum from the United Nations High Commissioner for Refugees. They told him to go to a local NGO that helps asylum seekers. He popped out for lunch and was promptly kidnapped.

Navalny's blog explained: 'Four Russian intelligence agents seized him right in the street, regardless of the fact that they were in the territory of Ukraine, and bundled him into a mini-van.'

The goons gave him a nasty going over, immobilising him in handcuffs and leg irons, no water, food or toilet breaks for two days. When they threatened to kill him and his children, an eight-year-old daughter and a sixteen-year-old son, he broke down and signed his 'confession'. Then they spirited him back to Russia. Remember in 2012, Yanukovych was still firmly in charge in Ukraine and his secret police must have eased the passage of their Russian brethren across the border. Yet, once back in Russia, he withdrew the confession, saying it had been extracted under torture.

Navalny's blog set out what the NTV investigators had missed, how court evidence was obtained in cells 'stained with blood' with 'tongs and bare wires', adding, 'these crooks make up fake charges and then torture people, forcing them to confess'.

The Public Observer Commission, a Russian human rights NGO, met Razvozzhayev, got his full story, then issued a statement in which they 'expressed grave concerns that Russian authorities were returning to Stalinist methods of suppressing dissent'. The opposition, forever bickering and bitching amongst itself, for once got together and issued a statement 'Against Repression and Torture'. They denounced 'the full-scale witch-hunt against dissidents', denounced torture and kidnapping and everybody who was anybody who opposed the Kremlin signed, including, of course, Navalny.

The official Russian version denied the kidnapping and asserted that Razvozzhayev had turned up back in Moscow of his own free will where he had voluntarily made his confession, backing up the NTV documentary that he and

Udaltsov and a third man were creatures of the dark Georgian state, hired to cause widespread rioting.

On 7 November 2012, a court in Moscow added two more criminal charges to the original one of organising mass riots: robbery with violence in his home town of Angarsk in Siberia, back in 1997, and, this is Kafkaesque, illegally crossing the border.

In December 2012, Razvozzhayev was secretly transferred to Angarsk in connection with the ancient alleged robbery case. For five days he vanished inside the Putin gulag, only to pop up in a remand prison in Chelyabinsk, Siberia. In March 2013, he vanished again, only to surface, as it were, in a remand prison in Moscow. And so on and so forth. The Russian state was to play exactly the same 'pass the parcel' with prisoner Navalny in due course.

Razvozzhayev had worked as a parliamentary aide for Ilya Ponomarev, a lone voice in the Duma. I mean that literally. After Razvozzhayev was jailed in the summer of 2014, Ponomarev was the only MP out of the 450 members of the Duma who voted against Russia annexing Crimea. Shortly afterwards, while on a trip to the United States, Ponomarev was charged with embezzlement on nonsensical evidence and resettled in Ukraine, never returning to Russia.

Sergei Udaltsov suffered not physical torture but a kind of legal-administrative variant of the rack. Charged with creating a mass riot, he was placed under house arrest because of concerns that he was not honouring his bail conditions. Officially, this was because Udaltsov's wife was 'living in Ukraine' even though she was sitting in court in Moscow. Navalny said: 'What we don't know is why they even bother to call it "a trial".'

The tyrant's subtlety was that, from late 2012 to summer

2014, for the best part of two years, Razvozzhayev and Udaltsov were not convicted and sentenced but moved on bail from pillar to post, so their supporters hesitated to protest for fear of making things worse. It was only after Russia invaded eastern Ukraine that Putin prodded the judges to lock them up and send them to the penal colony.

With Udaltsov in the slammer, that left the three big beasts of the opposition still, more or less, left at some kind of liberty in late 2014. They were Boris Nemtsov, Alexei Navalny and Mikhail Kasyanov, Putin's first prime minister turned enemy.

Time to tighten the thumbscrews on Navalny but this time by proxy. It is one thing fighting an enemy, knowing that you might get locked up or killed. It is quite another when the enemy locks up, not you, but your younger brother. That is exactly what happened to Navalny in late December 2014 when he and his brother were convicted of defrauding 30 million roubles, around £300,000 at the current exchange rate then, from a Russian affiliate of the Yves Rocher cosmetic company. The case was another dark fairy tale cooked up by the Kremlin goon squad. There was no serious evidence of theft; defence witnesses who could have explained that were either not called or intimidated into silence; blatant discrepancies in the prosecution case were overlooked by the judges. It was a Stalinist show trial, retuned for the twenty-first century by a subtler composer, grey smudges replacing the black of the 1930s. Navalny's sentence was suspended but his younger brother Oleg got three and a half years of real jail time. Navalny was outraged, yelling at the judge, Yelena Korobchenko: 'Aren't you ashamed of what you are doing? Why are you putting him [brother Oleg] in prison? To punish me even harder?'

On the steps of the courthouse, Navalny told reporters: 'The authorities are torturing and destroying relatives of their political opponents. This regime doesn't deserve to exist; it must be destroyed.'

Navalny headed off to the Manezhka for a demo, but the cops lifted him by the Ritz Carlton, providing the rich people with a short scene from the Theatre of Cruelty. The police officers took him home, where they blockaded him in. Three years before, Navalny had tens of thousands of people out on the streets shouting 'Putin is a thief!' Now, they were psychologically torturing him by proxy and there was nothing he could do about it.

Troubled by his brother's jailing, Navalny, to his great credit, was not cowed by the Kremlin's unremitting corrosion of what was left of Russian civic society. In 2015, his team would go on to investigate Sergei Shoigu, the Minister of Defence; Dmitry Peskov, Putin's PR man; Roman Abramovich, Putin's wallet; and Yuri Chaika, Putin's Prosecutor General. All concerned deny any wrongdoing.

Chaika means seagull in Russian which is why I found myself standing on the frozen wastes of Lake Baikal. . . OK, it was really Southend-on-Sea in January 2016, holding a chip in the air, waiting for a seagull to pounce. The truth is that turning investigative journalism into good telly is often joyously absurd and shooter-producer Nick Sturdee and I spent a small fortune on chips, laughing our heads off until we got the 'seagull wolfs chip' money shot. We were making a BBC *Newsnight* cut-down off the back of a brilliant film by Team Navalny called *Chaika*, still up on YouTube.

If you are trying to get your head around the Humpty-Dumpty world of the misrule of law in Putin's Russia, where the gangsters prosecute the good people, then Navalny's film, narrated in English by Irish corruption fighter Arthur Doohan, is essential viewing.

Human fireflies come as standard when you're launching your hotel worth €30 million. The creatures that glowed in the dark were young Russian beauties dolled up in neon firefly suits welcoming guests to the 2013 opening ceremony of the five-star Pomegranate Wellness Spa Hotel on the Aegean Sea in Greece. Cutting the ribbon was Artem Chaika, who just so happened to be the eldest son of Russia's Prosecutor General, Yuri Chaika, who at the time sat right at the top of the law enforcement tree. Russia Inc turned out for the gig, the guest of honour was Vladimir Medinsky, who once said that Russians have an extra chromosome, which makes them like Superman. He's not a geneticist but was then Russia's Minister of Culture, a United Russia stalwart and, surprise, surprise, someone who has been accused of plagiarism. Russia's Dissernet community – an informal group of academics and journalists who sniff out copycat dissertations – found that Medinsky had cut and pasted eighty-seven pages out of 120 for his first thesis and similarly 'borrowed' – that is, stole – lots of words for the second and third.

Navalny's Anti-Corruption Foundation (ACF) found out that the mystery owners of the hotel were Artem Chaika and Olga Lopatina, the former wife of Gennady Lopatin, the Deputy Prosecutor General, and Yuri Chaika's then number two. Team Navalny lodged the key points of their investigation into Chaika with a parliamentary committee at the House of Commons so it enjoys some degree of legal privilege, 'arf, arf' (as with the earlier reference to la-de-dah Gunner Graham, any international readers who can tell me the origin of this expression get a beer if we happen to meet).

The Anti-Corruption Foundation reported that Lopatina

had 'clear and questionable ties' to the wives of gangsters behind the infamous Tsapok crime gang massacre in Kush-chevskaya in 2010 in which twelve people were killed, including three children and a baby.

Not mentioned in the report lodged with parliament is that Lopatina filed a five million rouble claim against Navalny and co for the film. But a court in Moscow threw out her case because, in one account, her lawyer did not produce the right paperwork. Navalny's film is still available online. All concerned deny any wrongdoing.

Roman Borisovich organised for me in London to interview Navalny in Moscow by Zoom, not that common in 2016. Navalny told me: 'The crime shook the whole of Russia because it was a real massacre and twelve people were killed, including four children, one of them newborn. They threw him in the fire while he was still alive.'

The bulk of Artem Chaika's wealth came from his dealings in Siberia, 'where he made his fortune by illegally privatising government assets thanks to connections in the region's government,' the ACF reported. Chaika's Siberian businesses, although little known, won deals for salt mines and sand quarries and routinely got renovation tenders over state-owned firms. For BBC *Newsnight* I reported on what happened to an early critic of Chaika's business methods. Businessman Nikolay Palenniy ran a shipping company in the Lake Baikal region until it was stolen, he said, by Artem Chaika. The next day, he was found dead with a rope around his neck. 'Suicide,' said the authorities. Navalny told me differently: 'According to the papers from the coroner's office, traces on his neck showed that it wasn't a suicide. But the Russian investigative bodies just refused to do any investigation.'

Watched almost five million times in the first seven weeks after its release on YouTube in Russia, Navalny's *Chaika* was a smash hit with the public. Putin's PR flak, Peskov, said the allegations 'did not provoke our interest' because they were not related to the Prosecutor General but to his sons, who had their own business activities. Artem Chaika did not reply to our questions at BBC *Newsnight* but I did quote his dad, Yuri Chaika, who said that the Navalny film was 'a hatchet job, not paid for by those who made it' – standard Kremlin insider code for foreign intelligence services. 'The information presented is deliberately falsified and has no basis in fact,' he said.

Prime minister again Dmitry Medvedev said that the film was akin to Stalin-era repression: 'You said a certain person has been accused. If we're going to operate in such a way, we'll be going back a long way, back to the 1930s. Only law enforcement can lodge accusations.'

But if law enforcement is crooked, it's not Stalinist to say so. Chaika and sons were, of course, not the true target. That was the master of the Kremlin, or, as Navalny told me over Zoom: 'the tsar of corruption'.

It should be noted that after Navalny's film caused a scandal in Russia, the authorities did act. All of the Chaikas remained at large, and Yuri stayed in his job as Prosecutor General. But three of the Tsapok crime gang committed suicide in a few days; then Tsapok died 'of a stroke'. Fancy that. Once again, all concerned deny any wrongdoing.

After the *Chaika* film went out, Navalny emailed Marvin Rees, his classmate from Yale: 'Hi, Marvin! Thanks for your letter. I know you're running [to be Bristol's mayor] – Twitter is a sort of Big Brother. Hope you will win. I'm still not allowed to leave Russia, but when I can I hope to visit

Bristol like a boss – with a mayor friend of mine. You are right I'm out of house arrest and back to my activity.' Navalny included a link to the Chaika investigation, signing off: 'Saw your pictures on Facebook – [Rees's son] is so big! Stay in touch. Best, A.'

Team Navalny's focus on Kremlin corruption did not let up for a second. When Putin's creepy PR man, Dmitry Peskov, got married for the third time in Sochi in August 2015, at 'the wedding of the year', they spotted a photo of the groom taken by his old pal, Oleg Mitvol, who, in 2023, was jailed for corruption. Mitvol's shot showed a fancy watch on Peskov's wrist with a gold skull on the dial. It turned out to be a limited edition Richard Mille 52-01 watch, only thirty of which have ever been made, worth £397,000, more than four times Peskov's declared annual income. Navalny stuck the boot in in his blog: 'Clearly there are some details of his life that we do not know about. Because of the "wedding of the year", there were so many photos of the watch that we decided to ask these questions publicly. How could the head of state's press secretary have a watch worth more than four times his annual income?' Navalny added if the watch was a gift, Russia's anti-corruption laws would compel him to forfeit it because officials have to declare gifts that are worth more than 3,000 roubles or £30. When Mitvol said that the watch was merely an elaborate trick played on journalists, and that Peskov borrowed it from a mega-rich pal, up popped another photograph taken two weeks before the wedding, in which the watch with its oh-so-distinctive gold skull can clearly be seen on the Kremlin spin doctor's wrist.

As Navalny commented on his blog: 'How can one not recall the famous statement by Peskov that "the guts of [the anti-corruption] protesters should be smeared on the asphalt . . ."

'So, it's personal. For his beautiful Richard Mille watch, Dmitry Peskov will smash you into pieces and lie on TV as much as necessary. PS: We expect that the Administration of the President of the Russian Federation – Mr Peskov is an employee – will publish the relevant information regarding the sources of funds that were used to purchase this watch. AHAHAHA. I haven't laughed so hard in a long time.'

Not long afterwards, Navalny blogged: 'At the end of last week, a very reliable source contacted the Anti-Corruption Foundation and said: "The press secretary of the Russian President Dmitry Peskov is currently spending his honeymoon with Tatyana Navka, a small circle of friends and children on a rented yacht, *The Maltese Falcon*, off the coast of Sardinia." *The Maltese Falcon* turns out to be outstanding. We present to you 1) the largest, 2) the most luxurious, 3) the most expensive sailing yacht in the world, 88 metres, almost as long as a football field.

'Renting *The Maltese Falcon* yacht costs €385,000 or 26 million roubles [or £320,000] per week. And this cost does not include expenses for food and entertainment. Dmitry Peskov needs to cough up his entire salary for three years to allow him to spend only seven days on this yacht.'

So were Peskov and his new missus relaxing off the coast of Sardinia in a three-masted schooner? He denied the story, telling the Anti-Corruption Foundation: 'I'm staying in a hotel.'

But greed's no fun unless you flourish it. And, it turned out, Navalny was just taxiing down the runway. 'How can you prove it, apart from your "reliable source" you may ask. What if Peskov and Navka and the children are on a camping trip in Crimea and not in Sardinia on one of the most expensive yachts in the world?'

He turned to open sources: yacht-tracking services showed that *The Maltese Falcon* had been off the coast of Sardinia; Mitvol took photos of other yachts close by which he posted on social media; the two yachts were geo-located next to *The Maltese Falcon*; the geotag of the Instagram account of Sasha, the daughter of Tatyana Navka, and the stepdaughter of Peskov, says she's in Sardinia.

'And one last thing: Sasha is obviously on a yacht and the name of the yacht can be read on her robe. The name is not completely visible – "?altese Falco?" but guessing the missing letters turned out to be not very difficult. The photo was taken on *The Maltese Falcon*.'

Revving up his engines, Navalny said the Anti-Corruption Foundation demanded from civil servant Peskov an explanation as to who paid for the yacht hire or, if he paid it himself, where the money came from; for Peskov to be dismissed because of the watch scandal and the trip on a yacht which would have cost him three years' salary; and an ethics report on Peskov and his boss, Putin.

Dmitry Gudkov, an extremely rare Russian MP who dared to be openly critical of a member of Putin's innermost gang, tweeted: 'Peskov's yacht is a sign of the long-awaited split among the elites. We're stocking up on popcorn.' Later, Gudkov was kicked out of his party, lost his seat in a Duma election, was framed, he said, on fraud charges, did a spell in prison and fled to Ukraine in 2021.

Next up? A private jet to fly the corgis owned by Olga, the wife of the First Deputy Prime Minister Igor Shuvalov, to mystery destinations around the world. To illustrate that nonsense, a joyful Navalny pretending to be stern-faced addressed the camera head-on, while holding a corgi in his lap. The Anti-Corruption Foundation's film on the corgis' private jet is brilliant investigative journalism and brilliant theatre, both at the same time. Shuvalov is a smooth operator with a bouffant hairdo and fluent English, held responsible for landing the 2018 World Cup for Russia and one of Putin's favourites. He is slavish in sucking up to the boss, saying in 2015: 'If a Russian feels any foreign pressure, he will never give up his leader. Never. We will survive any hardship in the country – we will eat less food, use less electricity or, I don't know, some other things we are all used to. But if we feel that someone from outside wants to change our leader, and that it is not our will but the will that is forced upon us, we will be united as never before.'

Woof! Woof!

The Shuvalov private jet, a Bombardier Global Express, was worth around $50 million and not declared on the official register of interests of members of the Russian government. There was nothing that officially linked it to Shuvalov. Team Navalny tracked the Bombardier jet by simply putting its registration number into flight tracking websites and hey presto, found that very often, wherever Deputy Prime Minister Shuvalov went, it would go. So, on 16 December 2015, it flew to Beijing, where the DPM had a summit with the Chinese; on 18 May 2016, it flew to Sochi for some Russian government powwow; on 30 May, to Astana in Kazakhstan where the DPM was attending a post-Soviet state beano with Putin. But there were other unofficial trips too. The Anti-Corruption Foundation found that in 2016, Shuvalov made thirteen work trips and eighteen private flights to Salzburg on the jet. It just so happened that Shuvalov had admitted on the register renting a $10

million castle near Salzburg. But, when people went looking, right at the bottom of a series of matryoshka dolls of
entities, including an Austrian company and a trust in Liech-
tenstein, was a British Virgin Islands firm owned by Evgeny
Shuvalov, Shuvalov's then 24-year-old son. Its current ownership remains opaque.

But what about the other unofficial trips? Team Navalny
noted that the Bombardier jet had been to at least eight destinations, places like Riga, Prague, Cyprus and Windsor in
England and that Olga Shuvalova was a champion breeder
of Welsh Corgis with names like 'Pinkerton', 'Tsesarevich',
'Ostap Bender', 'Hugo Boss', 'I'm Your Idol' and, Navalny's
favourite, 'Fox Pack Gabby Joy of Elves'.

And then they checked those destinations for dog shows
and bingo! 'Olga Shuvalova, wife of the vice premier, has
moved her animal breeding hobby to a whole new level,'
said Navalny. 'Her corgis, accompanied by special managers, are flying to dog shows on a private jet.' Navalny
quoted one of the dog 'managers', called Rita Ehrman,
saying on social media that the corgis do not fly on scheduled
planes because 'it's not that comfortable in business class'.

Shuvalova told Team Navalny that her corgis flying hither
and yon to the dog shows helped 'defend the honour of
Russia'.

Navalny in his video hit the roof: 'We have 22.9 million
extremely poor people, 20 per cent of the population are
nearly beggars, and this man is spending 40 million roubles
[£475,000] a year on flights for dogs. It is not normal; it is
immoral; it is insane.'

The Anti-Corruption Foundation went on to claim that
Shuvalov had done up ten flats in one of Moscow's signature
Stalinist skyscrapers to make a single 'tsar apartment' for

nigh on $10 million and owned homes and flats in Switzerland and London and the aforesaid castle in Austria, worth in total $90 million.

Navalny kicked off his investigation by going back to August 2014 when the Russian invasion of eastern Ukraine was in full swing and Deputy Prime Minister Shuvalov paid £11.5 million for his London apartment. Taxes on the purchase alone would have accounted for eight times Shuvalov's official annual income. Shuvalov, on his declaration of interests for that year, made no mention of the purchase but said that he had rented an apartment in London. Navalny pooh-poohed that and focused on two flats at 4 Whitehall Court, on Victoria Embankment, which so happen to overlook the headquarters of the British Ministry of Defence. Whitehall Court forms the southern end of an imposing piece of Victorian architecture that faces the Thames; the northern end houses my club, the National Liberal.

Navalny noted that the building was very impressive, on the Thames, five minutes from Westminster, and used to be until the end of the First World War the headquarters of MI6, the British secret service. 'It's quite difficult to imagine that you can live in such a building; it's too chi-chi and pompous,' said Navalny.

The flat has almost 500 square metres of space, six bedrooms, a dining room with two fireplaces, and a living room complete with grand piano and views of the Thames. Navalny's blog said: 'For more than ten years, Shuvalov hid his apartment behind anonymous offshore companies, and now behind a Russian company, instead of openly admitting that this 500-square-metre luxury home in London belongs to him. He misled the Russian and British tax authorities, hired lawyers to manage the asset, set up blind trusts, all to hide the fact that this particular apartment belonged to the first deputy prime minister of the Russian Federation.'

Navalny's investigation showed that the ownership of the flat was shuffled through a series of anonymous entities like a deck of cards, but it ended up in the hands of Sova Real Estate, a Russian company owned by the then deputy prime minister himself and his wife Olga.

Navalny said that Shuvalov was not just a fraudster but one of the Kremlin shysters who 'promotes all this false and hypocritical nonsense that "citizens must rip off their last shirt for the party and the government." That's a bit rich, to lead us to war and quietly pay 688 million roubles for an apartment on the territory of a potential enemy.'

He announced that the Anti-Corruption Foundation would file official complaints about Shuvalov to Putin himself, to the government bodies supposedly fighting corruption and to the Duma, the Russian parliament: 'Let's wait for their answers, have a read, then have a laugh.'

What was striking about the Shuvalov revelations is that in 2018 he resigned from the Russian government. This opens up the possibility that rival power centres in the Kremlin sometimes used the Anti-Corruption Foundation to pursue their vendettas by proxy. In Russia, as one old British intelligence officer loves to tell me, nothing is as it seems. Sure, but I suspect that what really happened is that Team Navalny genuinely did its own thing and once the dirt was out there, the big players in the Kremlin manipulated the content for their own dark purposes. Clearly, anyone whose response to compelling evidence of massive corruption, the proof being that they are so rich they can ship their show corgis around the planet on a private jet, was to prattle on about the honour of Russia, is a bit thick. It's also worth noting that Putin himself is very aware that every fish in the Kremlin piranha tank, just like him, is corrupt, and there are moments when that corruption is so nakedly offensive that he deems it necessary to kill the career of an underboss. To that extent, what happened to Shuvalov was rather like the scene in the James Bond movie, *You Only Live Twice*, when Ernst Stavro Blofeld strokes his fluffy white cat and presses a pedal and the bridge over the piranha pool in his Volcano Lair breaks to deliver Helga Brandt to be eaten alive. Life inside the Kremlin must be extraordinarily unpleasant. The riches to be stolen are off the scale, but the consequences of failure are horrible too. And all the time the others are watching you, waiting for you to make a mistake.

One last reflection about a Russian deputy prime minister being so extraordinarily rich thanks to corruption that he could afford to fly his wife's corgis around the world and buy a flat overlooking the Ministry of Defence in London. Did anyone inside MI5, Britain's security service, flag this up, sending out a memo saying something along the lines of: 'I say, chaps. The Russian deputy prime minister is buying a flat overlooking our Ministry of Defence. The possibility of the Russians using this flat as a base to spy on us, to train spy cameras on who is coming and going, to use the latest in eavesdropping technology to hear our conversations is high. Are we going to stop this?' I have no idea whether such a memo was ever sent. But it is clear that Her Majesty's Government, as it then was, took the money and allowed Putin's creature to move in. One is left feeling that Navalny had a stronger sense of the danger that the Russian dark state posed for the United Kingdom than its supposed defenders.

After Shuvalov, Team Navalny then turned their

attention to the second most powerful figure in the Russian regime, Dmitry Medvedev, who owes his position in the power vertical to the fact that he is a pointlessly ambitious lawyer, like Richard Rich in Robert Bolt's play, *A Man for All Seasons*, and that he is three inches shorter than Putin. Russian journalists knew that Medvedev had a country estate on the Volga but the walls around it were eighteen feet high and no one had ever succeeded in taking a photo of it. Enter the Anti-Corruption Foundation's air force, as Navalny called its drone army in their video. The drone flies over the Volga into the massive $966 million estate, clocking its own marina, ski slope, three helipads, special communications tower, an outdoor board for giant chess pieces, and bespoke duck house. The immense amount of roubles spaffed away on ducks became a thing for the Russian opposition, with young people turning up to anti-regime demonstrations carrying little yellow rubber ducks. Medvedev's spokesman said that he has never owned or rented living space in the estate but that he had stayed there, hence the communications tower. As denials go, it was a bit rubbish.

A sea of fireflies, a watch, a yacht, a private jet for corgis, a multi-million-dollar duck house: Chaika, Peskov, Shuvalov and Medvedev and the rest have between them stolen billions of dollars of public money and diverted it to their own grubby and greedy ends. Putin's Russia is, not surprisingly, the most unequal big country on earth, where one per cent of the population own 58 per cent of its wealth, far worse than Brazil, India, the United States, Germany, China and the United Kingdom.

It's hard to convey just how poor ordinary Russians are, but I got a flavour of that in 2007 when I made a BBC TV documentary, *Vodka's My Poison*. They called it the yellow death. It started in the summer when dozens of people turned up in casualty, a vile shade of yellow. The dozens turned to hundreds, then thousands. The better cases recovered, but will die long before their time. The worst cases? Natasha was not yet thirty, she had a seven-year-old boy called Maxim and she had less than a year to live. Her whole body had gone yellow, an instantly recognisable feature of toxic hepatitis. Something had destroyed her liver and now all the natural toxins in the body were stacking up. Her own body was poisoning her and there was nothing medicine – or at least nothing state medicine in Russia – could do about it. How come? Putin put up the price of vodka threefold in one strike. Craving alcohol, Natasha and her friends had added a new brand of handwash to their moonshine. The handwash was cheap and highly alcoholic, but also lethal. I remember the gloom in the hospital basement, steel doors slamming shut, dark yellow wraiths living out their last weeks, the lack of medicine, of care, of money, of light, of hope. It made me angry; it still does; and what I felt would be a fraction of the rage that consumed someone like Navalny who had a clear grasp of where the extraordinary riches of the Russian state were being siphoned off.

It's fair to say that of the three serious opposition candidates who had the chops to run against Putin – Kasyanov, Navalny and Nemtsov – only Navalny caused this extraordinary level of grief for the Kremlin's apparatchiks. But in the long run-up to the next presidential election of 2018, Putin's opponents went down in number from three to one.

The first to be removed from the chessboard of Russian power was Nemtsov, the charismatic former deputy prime minister under Yeltsin who had been promoted, in a sense, to become Navalny's cellmate when they were locked up together for the anti-Putin Bolotnaya protests. Walking home with his Ukrainian girlfriend across the Moskva River, the Kremlin immediately to the right, about one hundred metres away, in February 2015, he was shot four times in the back.

Roughly a year before, I had interviewed Nemtsov about Putin's grotesquely corrupt Winter Olympics in Sochi, asking him about the $5 billion road–rail link resort from the coast to the mountain ski resort. Nemtsov replied that: 'It would have been cheaper to have lined this road with Louis Vuitton handbags.' Before meeting Nemtsov, I had spent time with the comically stupid Putinist mayor of Sochi. He had knocked back my question about how gay Olympians would be treated in a city where the Kremlin's homophobic laws held sway by proclaiming: 'There are no gays in Sochi.' When I told Nemtsov about this, he laughed and laughed and laughed for so long we had to trim it down in the edit. He had a beautiful sense of the ridiculous and when I heard he had been shot, I burst into tears.

Nemtsov had foreseen his death. Down the years, he had been rather rude about Putin, calling him paranoid, 'the evil dwarf-president' and 'a mental patient'. Two weeks or so before his murder, Nemtsov told the Sobesednik website that his 87-year-old mother was worried: 'Every time I call her, she wails: "When will you stop mocking Putin? He will kill you!"' Was he afraid for his life, the website asked? 'Yes, not as much as my mother, but still . . .'

He said the same thing in another conversation with Yevgenia Albats, the Jewish democracy activist who had walked with Navalny on the right-wing Russian Marches. Albats said that Nemtsov 'was afraid of being killed . . . And he was trying to convince himself, and me, they wouldn't touch him because he was a [former] member of the Russian government, a vice premier, and they wouldn't want to create a precedent. Because as he said, at some stage, power will change hands in Russia again, and those who served Putin wouldn't want to create this precedent.'

The gossip inside the Moscow beltway is that the assassination was commissioned by Putin's psychopathic quisling in Chechnya, Ramzan Kadyrov, and that Putin was furious with him for ordering the hit. I don't know whether that is true or not. It's possible that Kadyrov did have Nemtsov killed of his own volition; it's also possible that Kadyrov over-interpreted a Putin criticism, a bit like Henry II's comment, 'Will no one rid me of this turbulent priest?' on Thomas a Becket; it's possible that Putin had Nemtsov killed and his goons switched on the fog machine and pointed it at Kadyrov. Readers who find this unsatisfactory are asked to go back to the sentence in the introduction of this book: 'It's hard to check facts in Russia because if you do it properly you end up dead' and start again. For what it's worth, I suspect that the instincts of Nemtsov's mother were right and Putin had him killed. If he didn't, he was the ringmaster of the circus where the murder took place under his big top. After his assassination, the Kremlin said that Nemtsov was 'little more than an average citizen'. They have previous for disparaging the people they kill. It is a tell.

The second chess piece knocked off the board was Mikhail Kasyanov, Putin's first prime minister who had become a severe critic from within the political establishment. He wasn't killed but sex-shamed when the secret police filmed him and not his then wife but his girlfriend, Nataliya Pelevina, making love. The films were plastered over NTV and the Kremlin patsy tabloids. Pelevina told me for the podcast *Taking on Putin*: 'I was completely and utterly destroyed. My world collapsed around me and there was nothing left and I didn't want to live. And I'm not exaggerating because obviously they didn't just show me as a horrible individual. They also showed me naked. They showed me in just an unimaginable way for a woman. After that I got messages from people around the world saying that their friend killed themselves after a similar video. So people even take their own lives after something like that is exposed. For a while, I didn't want to live . . . Back in 2012 when I arrived in Russia to fight against the regime, we didn't know Vladimir Putin would become so monstrous that I would end up being shown on television naked, having sex.'

But gifting Putin the pleasure of her suicide was not an option. I told Nataliya that I felt sorry for her and Kasyanov and that the Kremlin's goons who did this were disgusting human beings. She replied: 'Thank you. I appreciate that. Yes, I agree with the sentiment that they are disgusting and they really don't care for human life, let alone human relationships and human dignity. They have none themselves. I didn't want to give them the pleasure of killing me off completely, so I had to fight through this awful, horrible reality of mine and hope that there is some light at the end of it.'

Kasyanov told Mikhail Fishman of the *Moscow Times*: 'I was prepared for the pressure but I was not anticipating them to pick the lock to my apartment and install bugs and cameras. It's something only two special forces in Russia are capable of doing: the FSB or the FSO, the Federal Security Services. I don't know which it was. It came as a surprise.'

Fishman summed up the fate of the opposition under Putin by citing a line in Kasyanov's 2008 autobiography, *Without Putin*: 'In chess, there is a term zugzwang. It's when you can't skip your turn, yet every turn makes your position weaker.'

His first downfall came in late 2004 when Putin sacked him. Kasyanov was considered to have been a good prime minister, but in the late nineties he was first nicknamed 'Misha Two Per Cent', a reference to the two per cent stake he allegedly took from government deals. Kasyanov says Putin himself brought up the nickname during their last meeting in December 2004: 'Remember that name if you ever decide to go over to the opposition,' was Putin's threat. His second downfall was the sex tape during which the couple, as every political couple does the world over, slagged off their allies, Navalny included. Kasyanov carried on for a bit, a bird with a broken wing, but his career in Russian politics was dead.

That left only one man standing: Navalny.

CHAPTER TEN

Fighting the Lizard King

In April 2017, Marvin Rees got word from an ex-con: 'Hey, Marvin, came out of jail, started to check emails and very happy to see yours. Thanks for your support, man!' A few days later, someone threw caustic chemical in Navalny's face, half-blinding him.

His blog after the attack was on brand: 'So many people are asking, "How is your eye?" and "What about the investigation?" so let me answer everyone at once. Many thanks to everyone who is worried/sympathises/suggests a good doctor. I am now being treated by one of the best ophthalmologists in Moscow, everything is fine with me. The eye itself is not so good, unfortunately. The doctor thinks that they threw a green dye mixed with something else in my face, because you can't just burn your eye with green dye that badly . . . It's unpleasant, of course, but nothing can be done. This is Russia 2017, and instead of election debates, they just throw caustic agents in your face. Old man Putin's method of doing politics means that I am going to look like this . . .'

And up popped an image of half-man, half-robot, red eye blink-blink-blinking.

Navalny's 'beautiful Russia of the future' was a long time coming. Still is.

He had been moving outside his office in Moscow when a man ran up to him, threw a beaker of something in his face and ran off. In the beaker was a green dye, zelyonka, commonly used as a medical disinfectant and not itself harmful. Being 'zelyonkered' by the Kremlin's goons is a regular occurrence for the Russian opposition, a way of suggesting to some people that, next time, it could be something worse. Navalny himself had been 'zelyonkered' in the past and that did not stop him steamrolling on, but this time the heavies had added a caustic agent that, for a time, cost him 80 per cent of his vision in one eye. He travelled to Spain for special treatment, recovered and carried on.

CCTV is everywhere. Cameras caught Navalny's attacker in April 2017 but no one was arrested because, for no obvious good reason and for obvious bad reasons, the police doctored the video before they released the tape to the public, blobbing out the face of the attacker and a second man, slowly walking away from the scene, mobile phone in hand. Why on earth did they blob the attacker and the second man?

Team Navalny started to investigate and found another version of the CCTV footage where the blobbing of the second man glitched for a few frames. The second man walking away slowly with a mobile phone in his hand was Aleksei Kulakov, a former major in the Moscow police. Even though the face of the attacker was blobbed, Moscow's finest did not blob his clothes and shoes so it was relatively easy to identify him as Aleksandr Petrunko. All concerned deny any wrongdoing.

Both men were members of a strange group of creepy

weirdos called SERB. The letters stand for the South East Radical Block, an acronym in English not for a group based in the Home Counties but Russian-occupied Ukraine. Its goal was to promote 'traditional Russian family values and put an end to the moral decay of society being forced upon us by the West and America' and it spent its time disrupting pro-democracy rallies, echoing the Kremlin line and, in particular, harassing Russians loyal to the memory of Boris Nemtsov who stood guard at the makeshift shrine made up of candles, wreaths and framed photographs at the spot where he was assassinated on the bridge over the Moskva just by the Kremlin.

From his murder in 2015 onwards, pro-Kremlin thugs had repeatedly attacked the guardians who manned the Nemtsov shrine around the clock. In August 2017, an unknown attacker beat up a 35-year-old volunteer who later died in hospital. There's no evidence that SERB had anything to do with that death. I suspect that the Kremlin wanted to keep up the pressure against the Nemtsov activists while exercising better control over the harassment, turning it into a kind of street theatre of repression. And for that kind of work, there's no one better than a failed actor. The leader of SERB is Igor Beketov; profession: failed actor.

In September 2018, ten activists from SERB attacked two Nemtsov guardians with pepper spray in the face, threw shit at them, stole flowers and portraits of Nemtsov, then fled the scene, Radio Free Europe reported. The guardians called the police but they didn't show up. Remember, this is a stone's throw from the Kremlin and Red Square. I have been arrested within ten seconds of being filmed there. It is one of the most heavily policed areas on earth. The Nemtsov guardians identified Beketov among the attackers.

The mindset of people who make some money by desecrating a memorial to a dead hero is hard to fathom, but one has to realise that this activity was driven by the moral degenerate in the Kremlin.

Andrei Soldatov and his partner Irina Borogan are world experts on the Russian secret police, and are now living in exile in London as they are wanted by the Kremlin. Soldatov told me that SERB were effectively licensed by 'Centre-E', short-form for Russia's 'Centre for Combating Extremism', the counter-terrorism police. But, in this case, you can drop the counter-. Studying how 'counter-terrorism' functions in Putin's Russia is worth the substantial effort. In March 2024, 144 Russians were massacred by members of Islamic State-Khorasan Province in the Crocus City Hall shopping mall in Moscow. The authorities tried to shift the blame on to the Ukrainians with absurd and unbelievable evidence. It turned out that the United States intelligence community had warned their Russian counterpart that IS-K were planning an attack in that very shopping mall, but the Moscow authorities were caught napping. Quite how the IS-K killers could succeed in killing so many innocent people becomes less puzzling when you understand how Russian counter-terrorism officers spend their time: not infiltrating extremist organisations but planning the blinding of the leader of the opposition.

The SERB activists were not as ghastly in the flesh as I had expected. They were much, much more ghastly. In early 2018, BBC *Panorama* producer Jon Coffey, Seamas McCracken and I went to Moscow to shoot 'Taking on Putin' in the run-up to the March presidential election about Navalny's great fight against the lizard king. Coffey thought me hanging out with SERB would make good

telly, in the same way that adding lithium to water does.
Our fixer Zagit Akchurin made the calls and, lo, we met up
by the Marshal Zhukov statue close to the Kremlin. There
were four of them. Beketov was strikingly tall, noisy and
boring. Once again, it's hard to get across how tedious servants of dictatorship are, how monotonous and unreasonable
their conversation. To protect his bonce against the snow,
Beketov wore a bright red woolly hat with SERB on it and,
underneath his winter clothes, a stab vest. Odd. Ex-police
major Kulakov, the second man blobbed in the video of the
blinding attack against Navalny, hung back, filming everything on his phone mounted to a selfie stick, creepy,
uncommunicative, wall-eyed, and not a little mad; and two
others who were less vivid members from secret police aux-
iliary central casting. Navalny's attacker, Petrunko, didn't
show up, presumably because his minders in Centre-E reckoned that would be too provocative.

Beketov took us to the spot where Nemtsov had been
assassinated and started mouthing off at an old chap, single-
handedly guarding the shrine. The old fellow was having
none of it: 'All the leaders I wanted to vote for were killed.'
Beketov then attacked him for using the phrase the 'Nemtsov Bridge', rather than its official name, yet another iteration
of the preference for administrative propriety over common
human decency by the enforcers of the regime. I challenged
Beketov about the allegations that they were controlled by
Centre E. He denied it.

Beketov suggested that we go to a second site, where
there was another 'illegal' shrine to Nemtsov. Zagit whis-
pered in my ear that this smelt to him like some sort of trap.
Thing is, traps make good telly, so off we went. At the end
of the Nemtsov Bridge we headed to an apartment block

where he had been living when he was killed. The owner of that block had refused permission for supporters to put up a photo of Nemtsov on the wall, but the owner of the next block along, just a few feet away, had said yes. There was a photo in a frame of Nemtsov, a handsome fellow, and a floral wreath hanging on it. Beketov wrenched the picture and wreath off the wall and threw the wreath away while I stood back, appalled. The whole scene was caught by Seamas and ex-major Kulakov via his selfie stick. On video, you can clearly hear me say: 'Aren't you desecrating a shrine?'

We said our goodbyes to SERB and went about our lawful business, but not for long.

The next day we interviewed Soldatov about the FSB in our van driving around the Lubyanka, the headquarters of the FSB, being followed by the FSB, as you do. Like Mary's little lamb, the FSB followed us everywhere we did go. Seamas and I had fun shouting out the number plates of the goon cars, as they kept on popping up. Circling the Lubyanka, I asked Soldatov how many people had been killed in the basement: 'Thousands. We are doomed in a way. You have fear installed in your memory. You cannot get people interested in freedom because you have this disaster in the past and nobody wants to talk about it. We are still in fear of Stalin's secret police.'

That last sentence is the essence of Russia's continuing tragedy, of this book, of what Navalny was fighting against his whole life, in nine words.

Coffey, our violin-playing Northern Irish producer, wasn't out on the road being followed by the secret police but relaxing in his dressing gown sipping a vodka Martini in his hotel suite, claiming he was wiring back our rushes, the film cards we had already shot, to the edit house back in the UK. Coffey's story was that he was using an encrypted system to keep our rushes safe from prying eyes, but the process was time consuming because the hotel internet was slow. It just so happens that on this particular occasion the producer was telling the truth. Coffey had been using the faster internet at the BBC bureau in Moscow, but they had asked him to leave for unexplained reasons.

Back to the chase: for security reasons, I had left my normal phone back in London and was using a burner. It was on that that I got a call from Coffey, saying that four Russian coppers had arrived at the hotel asking to talk to Seamus, Zagit and me.

The bad news was that we still had Soldatov in our van and the film card of his unedited interview in Seamas's camera. The van pulled up bang next to a metro stop, we wrenched open the door and Soldatov legged it down into the Moscow tube before our tails could follow him. I decided that we would go to the BBC bureau, drop off the film card there to protect our source Soldatov, then go to the hotel and face the music.

Our colleagues from the BBC Russia service at the BBC Moscow bureau listened to our request to hide our film card with incredulity, then anger, then fear. They didn't get it. I explained that I had been filming a highly sensitive inter-view with an expert on the FSB, that we were being followed by the FSB, that we needed to lose the film card while we were being interviewed by the cops. Did I have a Russian press card? No, I said, the guy at the Ministry of Informa-tion pretended he had flu. They never give me a press card, I added, using administrative regulations to break the spirit of an open media. To me, they seemed to be enforcing the Kremlin's rules against a BBC reporter. Can you look after the film card – it was no bigger than a first-class stamp – while we go to the police station, I asked? They said no.

Be it noted, a friendly Russian hid our film card which is just as well as Zagit, Seamas and I were taken to a Moscow police station and isolated in separate rooms, so we couldn't tip each other off as to the line of questioning. Cop shops eat time. They asked for my passport. Within twenty minutes, I got a text from the BBC in London saying that my passport details were all over a Russian secret police-friendly Telegram channel. I was told to cancel it, lest it be used for fraud. Nice thought but I had to get out of Russia first. London also texted me details of stories on Russian state media, accusing me of desecrating a shrine to Boris Nemtsov, with video of SERB, not me, doing exactly that the day before. It was maddening.

Left to my own devices in a first-floor room of a Moscow police station, realising just how hand in glove SERB and the authorities were, I began to share a glimmer of the righteous anger that drove Navalny to stick it to these fuckers. The other side were stupid and banal and they clunked. True, I was detained in a police station with a compromised passport and a false allegation against me out on the airwaves, but the idea that I should be intimidated by Putin's goons was an abomination unto God, if, that is, such an entity exists.

When the cop led the way to the police interview room on the ground floor, I took out my camera phone and secretly filmed his back, a tiny clip that made it into our *Panorama*. Resistance may be futile but that little 'fuck you' was extraordinarily satisfying. They let us go in the dark, only for us to be doorstepped in the snow by some useless Herbert from Russian state TV and his cameraman pal. Seamas can be intimidating when he sets his mind to it – did I mention that he is from the north of the island of Ireland? – and he switched on his camera phone with light on and I went into the attack: 'Are you some part of the police state?' The Herbert flunked it, going: 'Er?' so I hit him again: 'Are you some part of the police state? Can you answer the question?' The reporter and his rubbish camera-man started to go backwards so I pivoted to Seamas's phone camera and said: 'These colleagues here from Russian state TV have come to doorstep us but they have done this so incompetently they're now walking away.'

Sweet.

Zagit, our fixer, was born in one of the stans back during the days of the Soviet Union. He had a right to live in Moscow but, in the aftermath of our *Panorama*, that was revoked. Worse, he was deemed a 'terrorist' and was forced to flee Russia for good. His Russian wife did not want to go into exile so his marriage fell apart and he lost access to his three-year-old daughter. The BBC declined to give him a job and I had to push very hard simply for BBC manage-ment to write letters on his behalf explaining why he had ended up stateless and jobless.

There's a clip of Tony Blair from May 2022 enjoying a soft-soap interview with CNN's Fareed Zakaria about how Putin had transformed himself over the years. The former British prime minister kicked off with a little self-deprecating patter about how he had aged since his first meeting with Putin in the spring of 2000, to which Zakaria clapped like a sea lion being fed fresh mackerel at the zoo, and Blair was off the hook. Putin, Blair said, had insisted on meeting him in St Petersburg because it was 'West-facing' and so, back in the day, was Putin. Blair went on to argue that Putin had sought to change Russia but found that too hard a project,

so he ended up reverting to banging the nationalist, auto-
cratic drum and then, during COVID, he lost the plot
completely, cutting himself off from all but the most syco-
phantic courtiers. I buy the last bit but Blair's analysis of
young Putin being 'West-facing' is for the birds. Blair would
have read the MI6 Top Secret profile on Putin, how he had
been the 'Mayor By Night' in St Petersburg in the early
1990s, easing the mafiya's control over the city for a slice of
the action, how he got the keys to the Kremlin by surfing
on the back of the sex kompromat operation against then
Prosecutor General Yuri Skuratov, how he made himself a
nationalist superstar on the back of the Moscow apartment
bombs of September 1999 – bomb outrages planned and
controlled by the FSB. By the way, I haven't read the MI6
reporting on Putin but I know some of the people who used
to write it and we think the same thoughts and drink the
same drinks, shaken not stirred.

Putin's war against the Chechens was barbaric, utterly so.
I went undercover to Chechnya in 2000, twice, and saw
with my own eyes evidence of the Russian army attacking
white flag refugee convoys, of using banned fuel aid bombs
against civilian targets, of an industrial use of torture. The
particularly horrible thing the Russian army did was the
'Slon', Russian for 'The Elephant' from the Soviet issue gas
mask which has a corrugated tube hanging down from the
face mask to the filter which looks like an elephant's trunk.
They would tie a Chechen captive's arms behind his back,
place him on the chair, fix 'The Elephant' over his face,
unscrew the filter and then squirt CS gas up the tube so the
victim would start to drown in his own tears, vomit and
snot. One Chechen victim told me for our BBC Radio 5
documentary, *Victims of the Torture Train*: 'Once the gas mask

was on, they would choke you, so you were gasping to breathe. And they would let go and you would breathe in deeply. And then they would squirt CS gas down the breathing hole. It was so bad just the sight of the gas mask in the room would make people confess to anything.'

Imagine my horror when I went to a police station in newly liberated Kherson in Ukraine twenty-two years later which had been used as a torture chamber. And there, in the basement, was an Elephant gas mask, without the filter.

Reporting torture is beyond grim. Inside Russia in 2000, based in Ingushetia, next door to Chechnya, I found it hard to sleep, getting through bad nights by re-reading *Code of the Woosters* while downing half a bottle of vodka. The Russians' use of torture, for me, isn't a kind of 'Government fiddles economic growth statistics' story; it's personal.

I first called Putin 'a war criminal' in the *Observer* on 5 March 2000. Yuri Felshtinsky, the Russian-American historian who co-wrote *Blowing Up Russia* with the late Alexander Litvinenko in 2002, later told me: 'Many other Western journalists got it, but when you called Putin "a war criminal", you were the first one.'

Reader, forgive my pathetic insecurities, but I like to remind myself of Felshtinsky's words when I get a parking ticket.

Just to make sure that Number Ten got the drift, I followed the first story up with an investigation into the FSB's murky involvement in the Moscow apartment bombs on 12 March, helpfully entitled for Number Ten: 'Take care, Tony, that man has blood on his hands'.

If Blair didn't quite work that out, the sub-heading spelt it out: 'Evidence shows secret police were behind "terrorist" bomb'.

Blair's team was acutely aware of what I was up to. In 2023 his former spin doctor, Alastair Campbell, confessed all in an article in the *New European*: 'In the spring of 2000, the early days of his presidency, Putin visited London, where he was warmly welcomed by Tony Blair. We had met him prior to his ascendancy to the top, and his calm, mild-mannered style, and Western-leaning analysis of the geopolitical landscape had persuaded TB that Putin, to quote Margaret Thatcher on Mikhail Gorbachev, was a man we could do business with.

'Sweeney had already decided otherwise. Putin's visit coincided with a period when, trying to dispel some of the media mythology developing around our so-called "spin machine", I had invited in the documentary-maker Michael Cockerell to make a film, *News From Number 10*.

'The film had interesting behind-the-scenes footage ahead of a joint press conference at the Foreign Office. Putin and Blair both looked nervous. There was a clip of John Sweeney saying he expected to be prevented from asking a question because I knew that it would be hostile to Putin for his actions in Chechnya, and hostile to Blair for his refusal to condemn the Russian actions more vigorously. And he was right. Right that I made sure he wasn't called. Sorry John. And right that Putin was not the leader we hoped he would turn out to be. That being said, the calm, mild-mannered, "saying the right things about the West" Putin remained the Putin we mainly saw for some years. It was around the time of the war in Iraq, at a bilateral meeting at one of his private dachas, complete with a stable full of stallions and an Olympic-sized pool only he could use, that we saw a very different Putin close up. Swaggering. Sneery lips curling. Dismissive of the arguments of others. Insulting of

TB. He didn't call him "Bush's poodle", as anti-war posters back home did. But he got close. Even then, however, did we seriously think he might become the Putin of the murder machine we see now, blowing friends turned enemies out of the sky, waging war not just in Ukraine but across different parts of Africa and the Middle East, and against liberal democracy wherever he can undermine it? I am not sure we did. John Sweeney would argue we should have seen it coming. Maybe he has a point.'

Luke, 15:7: 'I say unto you, that likewise joy shall be in heaven over one sinner that repenteth, more than over ninety and nine just persons, which need no repentance.'

It is, of course, highly entertaining to get an apology from Alastair Campbell, but to be fair to him and Blair we should not rule out the possibility that Putin really did change, that the man they first met in 2000 was emollient, vulnerable and needy, just like Oliver Quick, the protagonist in the movie *Saltburn* played by Barry Keoghan who, having taken over the country house and poisoned the rightful heir, gets to do the dirty on top of Russia's grave. Putin needed Blair in 2000, to give him a cosmetic makeover from secret policeman to democratically elected politician. Three years down the track, Putin was ruling Russia's *Saltburn* so could afford to switch off the poor little fellow impression and be his real self: 'Swaggering . . . sneery . . . dismissive.' That does ring true.

Yet the evidence is compelling that Putin's record was murderous from the get-go. What I suspect happened is that the Blair government didn't want to examine his scoresheet by February 2000 – the Skuratov kompromat, the Moscow apartment bombs, levelling Grozny – too closely because it was so depressing. They were hyper-focused on the immediate geo-strategic nightmare in front of their eyes, that posed by radical Islam, not realising that another, greater threat to Western security was sitting in the Kremlin. Like Jack in the panto, Blair and Campbell traded the cow for some magical beans and realised, too late, that they had been taken for a ride by a psychopathic conman. Putin played the Americans too, tricking George W. Bush who famously said of Putin that he 'looked into his eyes and got a sense of his soul'.

Russia and the true nature of Russian power is fabulously hard to read. You can watch the Bentleys swish by and drink cocktails in the Metropol Hotel and not get it that you are living inside a twenty-first-century kleptocracy which will crush you if you choose not to accept its crooked rules. All becomes much clearer, much faster, close to light-speed fast, when you challenge the source of that power, the secret police state within a state. But even I was shocked at the dark majesty of Russian fascism dealt out to supporters of Navalny and the wider opposition in the six months running up to Putin's fourth coronation in March 2018.

Vladimir Ivanyutenko was a street cleaner from St Petersburg with an unusual hobby. He liked to go to anti-Putin marches wearing a Vladimir Putin mask and a T-shirt proclaiming in Russian 'Putin is a dickhead'. One morning at 6am in December 2017, he was on his way to work when one man tasered him. He fell down, helpless from the massive electric shock, whereupon a second thug knifed him twice. The two attackers then ran off, leaving him to bleed to death in the snow. Fortunately, citizens nearby came to his rescue. Ivanyutenko told me: 'I can only connect it with my opposition activities. I back the critics of the Putin regime and I think he is a kleptocrat. He is not a legitimate president.'

Months later, Ivanyutenko read an article in a newspaper and realised that someone photographed in it was one of the two men who had attacked him, a single piece of information that unlocked a whole web of poisoning, torture and murder stretching from Russia to Ukraine and Syria and the spider at the heart of that web was Yevgeny Prigozhin, Putin's cook. I will do my best to describe that web in a later chapter.

In January 2018, Team Navalny organised a 'voters' boycott' in St Petersburg to protest against the fact that the electoral commission had banned Navalny from standing, owing to criminal convictions based on trumped-up charges. Documenting police harassment of these demos was an important and dangerous task for volunteers, in no way risk-free. Dinar Idrisov is a human rights activist in Russia's second city who took on the job, live-streaming a video feed of the police going in heavy on his mobile phone. The problem was the live stream made him an easy catch. Local cops could watch his output and use their knowledge of the area to geo-locate his position and then tip off their friends in the heavy mob.

The best way for Idrisov to monitor what the cops were up to against the demonstrators was not at street level, where you would be open to a quick arrest, but from up high, looking down on the hey-nonny-nonny. Idrisov got himself into a block of flats and went up to the top floor, knocking on doors at random so that he could ask the owners whether he could film from their balconies. He had no luck and was back at the ground floor when he saw three men in plain clothes coming at him. When he tried to walk on by, one of them punched him in the gut, and then the others went to work, knocking the living daylights out of him, but silently:

'These people were emotionless.' That, to Idrisov, meant that he was being beaten up not by random thugs but trained professionals. The beating came to an end when locals opened their doors to see what all the screaming from Idrisov was about. The silent muscle broke a rib, a cheekbone and his left arm and smashed up his face into blackberry pulp. Idrisov took us back to where it had happened and flashbacks were not good. There are no other candidates for beating the crap out of a pro-democracy live-streamer that day other than the Russian secret police or their friends and relations.

Towards the end of our 'Taking on Putin' shoot, we went to Team Navalny's HQ in Moscow, a buzzy place full of young activists typing furiously or staring into space. There we interviewed Nikolai Lyaskin, Navalny's campaign chief in Moscow, young, hard-working, driven. In September 2017 he was on the street when a man hit him over the head, twice, with a steel pipe or iron bar wrapped in a news-paper. He told me: 'At first, I actually thought that something had fallen off a roof, maybe the building is collapsing. I turned around and saw a man hit me on the head again with an iron bar.'

The cops arrested a local career criminal with a history of psychiatric problems. And along came the twist. Lyaskin got a text saying: 'Done' and then found himself being interrogated by the police because the local psycho had told them that Lyaskin had said he would pay him $2,500 to attack him.

Lyaskin told the independent Russian website Meduza – motto: 'Make the Kremlin sad' – that he recognised his attacker, that he had visited Navalny's Moscow headquarters: 'He said that he had come on a business trip from St Peters-burg and wanted to help. I spoke to him for about fifteen minutes at the office, in front of multiple witnesses, and it was immediately clear that he was there to stage a provocation. He had no idea what the campaign was about, what it was doing, or what it aimed to do. During our conversation, he even mentioned that he'd been in prison. As for me, I thought this was just another crazy guy.'

But this lunatic was working hand in glove with the authorities. Summoned to a police station, Lyaskin explained: 'There were a lot of questions and explanations from the suspect, and everything indicates that they're trying to drag out this provocation even further, saying that I hired him to bash me in the head with a steel pipe.'

Lyaskin told me: 'It was completely absurd. I got hit on my head with an iron bar and they just confiscated all the flyers, all the stickers, all the stuff with Navalny's name on it from our office.'

Navalny came out of a meeting room and said hello. His charisma exuded its own force field, turning the unremarkable office space into something quite different. I have been inside the Kremlin, to challenge Putin's PR man Peskov about the poisoning of Alexander Litvinenko, in 2007 – 'can you buy polonium in a shop?' – and the Russian parliament or Duma, to chew the fat about the state of Russian democracy with MP Vyacheslav Nikonov – the grandson of Stalin's foreign minister, Vyacheslav Molotov, who signed the Nazi–Soviet pact back in 1939, what George Orwell called 'the midnight of the century' – and neither the Kremlin nor the Duma sizzled with anything like the same level of energy as Navalny's office in Moscow. I don't make a habit of gushing in front of power and money, but Navalny's HQ genuinely felt like an alternative power centre. I wasn't there for a long interview, just a good strong ending to our *Panorama*. We had documented the blinding attempt against Navalny, the cars spying on us; interviewed Solda-tov: 'We are still in fear of Stalin's secret police'; the nonsense of our detention in the police station after SERB, the blind-ing team, had desecrated the shrine to murdered Nemtsov; two doorsteps by the Kremlin media; the taser-stabbing of the street cleaner; the silent beating up of the live-streamer; the attack on the campaign manager investigated as if it was self-harm by proxy.

Was Russia a police state, I asked Navalny? 'Absolutely, one hundred per cent,' he replied.

'Police state' didn't do Putin's Moscow justice.

It felt like Berlin, 1938.

CHAPTER ELEVEN

The Man Who Rose from the Dead

The unlikely messiah looks straight down the barrel of Daniel Roher's camera for the *Navalny* documentary: 'They splashed a toxic liquid into my face and my first thought was, "Jesus, I will be kind of a monster until the end of my days."' But the green dye soon cleared and Navalny was not disfigured and, after a time, his sight got better. His calculation was that his status as the single best-known critic of Putin's fascism was a life insurance policy of an unusual kind: 'As I became a more and more famous guy, I was totally sure that my life became safer and safer because I am a kind of famous guy and it would be problematic for them just to kill me.'

'And boy, were you wrong,' Roher replies.

'Yes, I was very wrong.' Something rather pleasing about a messiah who is happy to own up to his mistakes.

'So, we went to Siberia to make a nice movie about local corruption,' Navalny continues. 'I expected a lot of police. I expected a lot of people who'd try to prevent our filming, confiscate our cameras or just break our cameras or try to beat us. I expected that sort of thing and I was very surprised, like, "Why is nobody here?" "Why is there a kind of . . ." I even have this strange feeling like, like a lack of respect. Like, seriously? I'm here and where is my police? The whole trip was the smoothest trip I ever had in the regions. I am a kind of slave of Thursdays, because on Thursday I have my online YouTube show. And then weekend, I can spend with my family before another trip to another region. I was going home and then I died.'

Team Navalny were flying home from Tomsk in Siberia to Moscow on 20 August 2020, when he fell ill. Mobile phone cameras captured the chilling sound, like a fox caught in an iron trap, of Navalny howling out in piteous agony. The pilots of the S7 commercial jet called Omsk for an OK to land. Five minutes later, someone called in a bomb threat to the airport terminal. When the plane landed, the pilots asked for an emergency medical team and were told not to let anyone off the plane because of the 'evacuation'. The bomb threat was a hoax.

The airport medics jabbed him with atropine, a drug which slows down messages to and from the brain, which is the standard emergency medical treatment for anyone who has fallen into a coma the world over and just so happens to be the best possible thing to give someone who has been poisoned with a nerve agent.

Poison, said his supporters; poison, thought anyone who has tracked what happens to so many of Putin's critics; poison, thought anyone with half a mind. Not poison, but Navalny 'drank moonshine last night'; hallucinogenic drugs had been taken; there was something wrong with his blood sugar level, said different generators of the Kremlin fog machine. Doctors at the local hospital did not, at first, rule out poison, but soon did an about-turn and said exactly that. Coincidentally, it was flooded with police and the FSB. The open-minded medics fell silent.

Yulia Navalnaya arrived from Moscow and tried to gain

access to her unconscious husband. Or his doctors. One of the most emotionally powerful scenes in the *Navalny* documentary is her, grim-faced, hurrying through a gaggle of reporters asking whether her husband had been poisoned. Inside the hospital, she punches the lift button to get to the floor where he is being treated and a security guy, towering over her, blocks entrance to the lift and says: 'You are not allowed in here. You need a COVID mask.'

The security goon has such a mask but it is tucked in under his nostrils rendering it wholly useless.

'What about your mask?' asks Navalnaya, quietly.

'I am wearing a mask,' says the goon.

'Not really,' replies Navalnaya.

'I'm wearing a mask, you're not, let's go,' says the goon, raising his arms to shepherd her to the exit. Navalnaya dodges him and a second goon, in blue police military-esque camouflage, also wearing his mask below his nostrils, blocks her path. Navalnaya tells the camera-phone: 'They're not letting us see the doctors.' The first and second goons block the corridor as Navalnaya, her phone filming, says with quiet desperation: 'We're not getting access to the doctors.'

A third goon, his mask on brand below his nostrils, joins the blocking duo: 'Go sit quietly over there.' He moves close in, Navalnaya's camera filling up with a blurred rushed image of his chest.

'Stop pushing me. Have you lost your mind?' The anxiety in her voice screams out at you.

There are two other women with Navalnaya. One calls out to the masks-below-nostrils trio: 'Don't you understand? We're with her.'

'Who is she?'

'No need to get hysterical.'

'She's his wife.'

Later, to Roher's camera, Navalnaya reflects that she feared that Putin and the FSB would use the situation, of her husband lying comatose in hospital, to have him killed off for good.

The sight of the three goons menacing a woman who fears that she may soon be a widow is sickening and yet another edition of a familiar trope, of Putin's security officers of the absurd using administrative law, this time about wearing COVID masks in hospital, to prevent natural justice, of a wife seeking to talk to the doctors treating her husband who had just been poisoned by a different but like-minded set of fascist operatives.

Navalnaya turns away from the goon who has accused her of being hysterical and talks to a phone camera, first swallowing a sigh, and then saying: 'We demand the immediate release of Alexei because right now there are more police and government agents than doctors in this hospital.'

And soon the goons nobbled some of the doctors, or so it would seem. Alexander Murakhovsky, the chief doctor at the Omsk hospital, gave a press conference to a mass of reporters on 24 August. The boss medic boasted a walnut whip hairdo, sported a cheap suit, shirt and tie, and read slowly and, if I may say so, moronically from a piece of paper in front of him: 'We have come to the conclusion that judging by the fact there were no poisons found in his blood, or other biological materials, that he had a disorder of the metabolism, lowering blood sugar levels to be specific.'

It just so happens that Murakhovsky is a member of Putin's United Russia Party – of course he is – and, down the track, was promoted to be health minister for the Omsk region. Fancy that. To be fair, it is worth noting what happened to three other doctors at the hospital, all of whom are believed to have treated Navalny. In October, the deputy head of the hospital, Anatoly Kalinichenko, initially responsible for his medical care, resigned. In December, head of trauma Dr Rustam Agishev 'suffered a stroke', dying the following March. In February, senior anaesthetist Sergei Maksimishin died 'from a heart attack'. He was fifty-five.

For the avoidance of doubt, there is every suggestion that one doctor could have lost his job and two others could have been murdered because they honoured the Hippocratic oath and put saving a patient above being a creature of Putin's fascist state. Vladimir Putin has not been blessed with eternal life. At some point he will die and his regime will fall. If I am still alive, I plan to go to Omsk and sit down with people who knew the two dead doctors and, if possible, read the FSB files on what the goons were up to and talk to them too. If I die before this is possible, I invite young journalists who like poking crocodiles in the eye with a stick to pick up the challenge. If I prove to have been on the money, they must knock back a slug of vodka and toast the old fool who told them so.

One more thing on the doctors of Omsk. In May 2021, following the two deaths and the resignation, Dr Murakhovsky vanished for three days in the wilderness. When he popped up again, he was taken to a local hospital for a health examination. I wonder what was going on inside his head because, by May 2021, the whole world knew that when he had so very publicly ruled out poison, he had been telling yet another Kremlin dark fairy tale.

The odd thing is that Putin let Navalny go. Germany's then Chancellor, Angela Merkel, is believed to have lobbied hard on behalf of the comatose politician, but the decision was down to the Kremlin. My working hypothesis is that in 2020, Putin was up for trying to kill Navalny while free range but did still not feel strong enough to have him murdered while in the tender care of the Russian medical system. So, he let the man in the coma be flown to Germany, his calculation being, I suspect, that it would cause him less political grief to do so, hoping that he would stay in exile and then be quickly forgotten. But there was a downside, too, that the best doctors and scientists in the free world would work out what, exactly, had happened. And, lo, that came to pass.

When Alexei Navalny emerged from his induced coma in Berlin's Charité Hospital, his old mucker Leonid Volkov was one of the very first people to see him. Volkov recalled in the *Navalny* doc: 'When you come to a room of a comatose patient, you are starting to just tell him the news. Telling him his story: "Alexei, don't worry. You were poisoned. There was a murder attempt. Putin tried to kill you with Novichok." And he opened his blue eyes wide and looked at me and said, very clear: "*Blyat shto*? What the fuck?"'

For Volkov, it was a great moment: 'Like, he's back. This is Alexei.'

Navalny had risen from the dead.

Once again, one is left wondering at just how thick the supposedly super-cunning killer in the Kremlin can be. To use Novichok against his number one enemy is an extraordinary schoolboy error; poison his calling card, his favourite, signature method of killing; Novichok, created and made in Russia, the most infamous example of that method. Hands up who had Navalny poisoned? Vladimir Putin. But could Team Navalny prove it beyond reasonable doubt?

The view from the spire of Salisbury Cathedral is one of the most beautiful on earth. Towering above the green and pleasant land of Wiltshire one takes in blue sky, white fluffy clouds and green pasture as far as the eye can see, thanks to the very latest in fourteenth-century hi-tech. Constable backs that up. The added fun, for Kremlinologists like me, is that from the spire you can espy the centre of Salisbury, the railway station, the neighbourhood where former GRU – that is, former Russian military intelligence – spy Sergei Skripal lived and know that the two 'sports health technicians' who visited Salisbury to admire the famous '123-metre spire' were morons sent by morons.

The two poisoners, GRU officers, Anatoliy Chepiga and Alexander Mishkin, were filmed arriving at the airport, at Salisbury railway station, crossing the bridge over the River Avon, walking past a petrol station, proving a route that took them nowhere near Salisbury Cathedral but directly to the neighbourhood where Skripal lived. They were not spied on in any particular sense. The United Kingdom has the most CCTV cameras per capita than any other country apart from China. Did no one in the Kremlin, the Lubyanka or 'The Aquarium', the head office of the GRU in Moscow, understand that their poisoners would be clocked, again and again, on candid camera? Did no one close to Putin have the courage to say to him, 'Listen, Boss, if we use Novichok against Skripal there is a very good chance that the British will work it out.'

Clearly no one had. Perhaps Putin doesn't care. Perhaps showing that he is willing to take extreme risks to kill people he considers traitors is the point.

After Sergei and Yulia Skripal were both found unconscious on a bench by the Salisbury Avon in March 2018, their eyes lolling, their mouths frothing, they were jabbed with atropine by paramedics, thus, just like Navalny, saving their lives. In hospital in Salisbury, someone googled 'Sergei

Skripal' and discovered that he had been in a spy swap. He and other Western spies caught and locked up in Russia were traded for 'The Americans', Russian sleeper spies caught by the FBI, including the ultra-glamourous Anna Chapman. Once they had worked out that Skripal was a Kremlin target, the Salisbury medics called in the poison experts.

Like all nerve agents, Novichok buggers up the chemical triggers in the body's nervous system which switch muscles on and off. Novichok jams all the muscles on, so the eyes flutter uncontrollably, the voice box howls, the whole body goes into a massive spasm and that leads to a heart attack. But every contact leaves a trace and that goes for the chemistry of the body's nerve system. The precise mechanics are complicated but Novichok 'inhibits' or jams an enzyme, Cholinesterase, that switches muscles off. But Cholinesterase inhibitors change the structure of a specific protein in the nervous system and that allows unambiguous identification of the poison.

To the layman, to someone like, say, Vladimir Putin, Novichok is famously untraceable, being lethal in tiny amounts, clear and smelling of nothing. That is so to the naked eye and, er, naked nose. But a good chemistry prof with a very good lab can detect the presence of the modified protein in parts per billion, so, actually, if you know what you are doing, Novichok is not untraceable at all. If you are on the case with your protein structures, it is like following a burglar's footprints in the snow.

Back in Berlin, the doctors at the Charité Hospital called in the boffins from the Bundeswehr Institute of Pharmacology and Toxicology who found a new type of Novichok. Their findings were backed by scientists in other labs working for the Organisation for the Prohibition of Chemical

Weapons. They found Novichok in Navalny's blood, urine, skin samples and his water bottle. But the precise method of how the poison was delivered eluded the boffins.

Enter a new figure to Team Navalny: Christo Grozev – the Plovdiv Sherlock Holmes. Famous, when at the Bellingcat website, for cracking the true identities of the Salisbury poisoners, Grozev is the greatest open-source detective of our time. What's fascinating about him is that he had serious doubts about Navalny because of his flirting with the far right back in the day. Originally, what became the *Navalny* documentary had started out as a profile of Grozev. Navalny was poisoned while Daniel Roher was filming him so the documentary turned into something quite different. Grozev set out his anxieties: 'For the longest time, I wasn't sure what to make of Navalny. I always wondered how much of an independent figure he is or is he one of the many fake opposition figures created by the Kremlin. I've criticised him on Twitter.'

In July 2017, Grozev tweeted: 'Navalny is hopeless as a presidential candidate. Such a pity if this is indeed the best opposition candidate Russia can offer. (Hint: it is not.)'

Grozev told Roher: 'He walked side by side with some pretty nasty nationalists and racists. Had he moved beyond that? Had he actually become a reverse dark knight?'

The film doesn't actually go into what made Grozev change his mind, although the poisoning must have been the key factor. At the start, finding out who poisoned Navalny seemed to be impossible: 'We all were very sceptical about investigating Alexei's poisoning,' he told Roher. 'As opposed to previous cases, this poisoning took place on Russian soil, so no one is going to share security footage with us. They're not going to have fancy videos from the airport where the poisoners fly in and out. And as much as it hurts to admit, while Putin is in power, we'll never find out the truth.'

But nothing will come of nothing. It became clear that the Russian media had discovered zero and the German authorities did not have legal agency. Grozev did something rather beautiful. He used Russia's corruption engine against the tsar's poisoners. Grozev explained: 'Traditional journalism implies you meeting with a source and that source telling you a story. In today's world of fake news, we don't trust sources because we don't trust humans. We trust data. Bellingcat is an organisation of digital nerds. Most of us have an almost autistic-like fascination with numbers. Every time you use your email, you make a phone call, you make a doctor's appointment, take a plane or a train, any time you use the ATM, every time you actually look at the screen of your phone: that leaves a trace. In a place like Russia, imagine the person who works at the travel agency that has access to the flight manifests. They're getting like, what, $25 a day as a salary, and then for another $25 they would be able to sell that flight manifest to anybody who asks for it, just because it'll double their income for the day. This is a whole industry. Data brokers are on the dark web. You negotiate the price and within a few minutes they say, "Yep, I can get that data for you by tomorrow." And then you have to send Bitcoin.'

When Grozev was at Bellingcat, he couldn't bill them for his purchases on the dark web. He estimated that he, personally, had spent $150,000 on buying Russian data, adding: 'My wife has no idea about this.'

The team started with the Signal Institute in Moscow which officially develops 'sports nutrition drinks', but is in reality a poison factory employing twelve scientists whose background was not in fizzy drinks but chemical weapons. Grozev went shopping on the Russian black market, buying the phone records of the Signal Institute. They scanned in the numbers that popped up just before 20 August 2020, the date of the Navalny poisoning, and matched those with a peculiarly helpful Russian app that allows you to see how those numbers are listed under what name or nickname in other people's phonebooks.

The first, non-routine and therefore suspicious number calling into the Signal Institute Grozev looked up showed on the 'Name in Other People's Phonebooks' app – not its real name – was 'Alexei, doctor from FSB'. They squared that off against a third database, this one holding car registration numbers, the names of their owners and their mobile phone numbers. And in that database he dialled in: 'Alexei, doctor from FSB' and out popped 'Alexey Alexandrov'. Then Grozev put that name into a fourth naughty database, containing the details of Russian passport holders, and he had a prime suspect, his name, photograph, car number plate, place of work. And then he could really start digging, looking into Dr Alexandrov's CV, university, career records. He did the same with other dodgy-looking numbers, came up with names, then he put those men into yet another dodgily acquired database, that of flight manifests to Siberia, at the same time as Navalny was there.

Bingo: FSB goons, Dr Alexey Alexandrov, thirty-nine, Dr Ivan Osipov, forty-four, and Vladimir Panyaev, forty, travelled alongside Navalny to Novosibirsk and then followed him to Tomsk where he was poisoned. Five more FSB goons were very definitely in the frame.

'So,' Grozev told Roher: 'We found a nest of wasps we didn't know existed. It's a domestic assassination machine on an industrial scale. I was absolutely shocked that this was so fast and the whole plot disentangled so quickly, so I just reached out by Twitter and said, "Alexei, I think we may have found who poisoned you."'

In December 2020, Bellingcat, The Insider, *Der Spiegel* and CNN set out their goodies. The journalists dug up evidence showing that the Russian secret police had had another go at poisoning him in Kaliningrad, one month before he was poisoned in Tomsk, that the goons reported to a chemical weapons expert, that their cover was that they all belonged to FSB Criminology Institute or Military Unit 34435.

Aka the Poison Squad.

Shortly after Navalny had declared his intention to run for president in 2017, the Poison Squad had started following Navalny around Russia, shadowing him on thirty-seven overlapping flights: thirty-seven coincidences. Most often, the Poison Squad flew out one day ahead of Navalny, so as not to be seen on the same plane. Once, in April 2017, two goons, Dr Alexey Alexandrov travelling under the fake identity as 'Frolov' and Vladimir Panyaev, using his real ID, flew from Moscow to the southern Russian city of Astrakhan. But Navalny didn't make it. He was planning a trip to Astrakhan but changed his plans when one of the SERB crew threw green dye and the caustic agent in his eye, blinding him for a time. The Poison Squad flew back, their tails between their legs.

Unit 34435 had originally been set up back in 1977 as a secret scientific bit of the then KGB, doing the same kind of work as Q branch in the Bond movies – 'Don't touch that 007, that's my lunch' – working on lie detectors, face recognition programmes and robot bomb disposal. But very quickly Russian Q went to the dark side. Bellingcat in its superb long report on the Navalny poisoning noted that one of Unit 34435's first jobs was, according to former KGB general Oleg Kalugin, preparing the ricin poison for the umbrella tip that killed Bulgarian exile Georgi Markov in London in 1979. The unit's HQ was so secretive that it was used, the story goes, by the KGB hardliners who staged the coup against President Gorbachev in 1991 which led to the fall of the Soviet Union. Since Putin took power, Unit 34435 'investigated' the September 1999 Moscow apartment bombs, the Nord-Ost Theatre siege in 2002 and the Beslan school siege in 2004, all three of which have long been suspected of being black operations part-controlled or stage-managed by the Russian secret police.

The investigative journalist Anna Politkovskaya worked on all three and found the official accounts unbelievable. For example, she got herself into the besieged Nord-Ost theatre at one stage and saw one of the supposed leaders of the hostage-taking terrorists, Khanpasha Terkibayev, also known as Abu Bakar. The authorities used some unknown poison gas to subdue the terrorists, but it had the effect of killing more than 100 hostages and all forty terrorists, apart from Terkibayev, who managed to slip back to the safety of Azerbaijan. There, Politkovskaya tracked him down and concluded that he was an agent provocateur for the secret police. Terkibayev later died in 'a car crash' in Chechnya.

Politkovskaya was on her way to Beslan in southern Russia when she was poisoned, preventing her from being a neutral negotiator between the terrorists and the security services. She survived but her stomach was wrecked and she could not eat proper meals again until, of course, she was shot dead on 7 October 2006, which so happens to be Vladimir Putin's birthday. Three hundred people were killed in the Moscow apartment bombs; 132 hostages at the

Nord-Ost theatre siege; 334 people in Beslan, of whom 186 were children. Unit 34435 has a lot of blood on its hands.

In early July 2020, Navalny took his wife Yulia for a romantic getaway to Kaliningrad, the Russian enclave on the Baltic, formerly the Prussian capital, Königsberg. They were walking along the beach when Yulia, without any warning of her symptoms, 'felt sicker than I had ever felt in my life'. She said she could hardly control her legs as she walked the mere 300 metres back to the hotel, went to bed and slept deeply, waking up the following morning. The Navalnys decided not to seek medical help because whatever had pole-axed Yulia was non-specific.

But track the flight and phone traffic of the Poison Squad and a very specific explanation comes to mind.

On 2 July 2020, three members of the FSB Poison Squad – Alexandrov, travelling as per usual under his fake name 'Frolov', Mikhail Shvets and Panyaev travelling under their real names – bought tickets to Kaliningrad, a day before the Navalnys flew in. Alexandrov's flight arrived on 2 July, 'Frolov' and Shvets flew in the same day as the couple but on a different flight from a different Moscow airport to the one the Navalnys used.

The phone traffic is equally damning.

Just before their flights, all three Poison Squad goons had lots of phone calls with Colonel Stanislav Makshakov, the day-to-day boss of the unit who looks like Mr Potato Head from *Toy Story*. He in turn had lots of phone calls with his bosses, Generals Kirill Vasilyev and Vladimir Bogdanov.

On the day that Yulia Navalnaya fell ill, the phone traffic went through the roof. Bellingcat reported a crossfire of calls between the three goons who had just come back from Kaliningrad, Mr Potato Head and his bosses, Generals Kirill

Vasilyev and Major-General Vladimir Bogdanov. They, in turn, got on the blower to Artur Zhirov, the boss of the Signal Institute who, in turn, called Oleg Demidov, a chemical weapons expert formerly from the Shikhany-based 33rd Military Institute.

Fancy that.

In the morning of 12 August 2020, the Anti-Corruption Foundation's star investigator, Maria Pevchikh, bought a ticket to Novosibirsk in Siberia after Team Navalny had discussed its plans for its next road trip. At 1.39pm that day, three Poison Squad goons – Alexandrov, Panyaev and Ivan Osipov – booked their tickets to Novosibirsk. Alexandrov would fly as 'Frolov' and Osipov as 'Spiridonov'. Panyaev would use his real name. Just before their trip east, another member of the squad, Oleg Tayakin, who looks like Uncle Fester from *The Addams Family* and appears to be Mr Potato Head's sergeant-major, phoned the three agents who would fly the next morning. Call records show that Tayakin stays in Moscow but communicates via an unknown burner phone back and forth through a secure messenger.

Another flurry of phone calls between members of the Poison Squad, not just Mr Potato Head and the agents on the road but also to and from people staying back at the office, including Shvets, Oleg Tayakin, Alexey Krivoshchekov and my favourite backroom boy, Konstantin Kudryavtsev. Log that name.

As standard practice, the poisoners on the road would use burner phones to make everything more secure. But they could also be a bit thick. The next day, 14 August, Alexandrov briefly switched on his own phone, pinging its geolocation. His nearest phone mast was at 2, Dimitrova

Prospekt, very convenient for the hotel where Maria Pevchikh had booked a room and a second hotel where Navalny and his team would check in a few hours later. Months later, a Russian state TV channel broadcasts a fake investigation into the poisoning, showing secret camera footage of Pevchikh in Siberia. The goons were following her.

On 19 August, everybody, that is the key players in Team Navalny and the Poison Squad, were now in Tomsk. At 4.21pm Moscow time, 8.21pm Tomsk time, Vladimir Panyaev texted Mr Potato Head. Navalny went for a swim in a local river, leaving his hotel room in the Xander Hotel unattended. Back around 11pm, Navalny met his gang in the hotel's Velvet Bar and ordered a Bloody Mary. The barman said he didn't have the right stuff but counteroffered a Negroni. Navalny later told Bellingcat: 'The cocktail tasted like the most disgusting thing I've had in my life,' and he only took one sip. Then he went to bed around midnight.

At about the same time, Krivoshchekov called Mr Potato Head four times. Then Alexandrov made his second booboo, turning on his own phone, again. He only did it for a brief second but that was long enough for it to be geolocated to a mobile phone tower in central Tomsk, just a short drive from the Xander Hotel.

The next morning Team Navalny go to the airport, check in, begin the long haul back to Moscow and then democracy's champion in Russia starts to howl like an animal.

CHAPTER TWELVE

Moscow4, Moscow4

Five days later, Konstantin Kudryavtsev, one of the scientists in the Poison Squad, a chemical weapons specialist, flew from Moscow to Omsk. The phone metadata shows that he stayed in the city for less than ten hours. He drove from the airport to the centre of town and left for Moscow in the evening.

How come?

Would what Kudryavtsev did in Omsk unlock the mystery of how they applied the poison? When Team Navalny published their investigation, the world had a thorough understanding that a top secret Russian chemical weapons unit had tracked Navalny for years, that three members of the team had flown to Siberia at the same time as he had done, had made a series of urgent phone calls up to and after the poisoning, and that one of them had geo-located himself within a few blocks of the place where Navalny was staying. All of these events were absurd to write off as a series of coincidences, but the final chapter of the whodunnit was missing. How had the poisoners administered the Novichok?

Team Navalny and the journalists from Bellingcat, The Insider, *Der Spiegel* and CNN were due to publish their joint efforts on 14 December 2020. The night before,

Navalny, Yulia, his daughter Dasha and Grozev were filmed for the *Navalny* documentary going through the plans for the sting.

Navalny stands in front of a wall of the kitchen in their rented flat in the Black Forest in Germany covered with a map of Russia overlaid with red cotton thread leading from where key figures have been geo-located, Tomsk, the Signal Institute, back to mugshots of the Poison Squad. The names and faces in the frame start with the three who flew to Siberia: Alexandrov, Panyaev, Osipov; then the other team members: Shvets, Tayakin, Krivoshchekov, Kudryavtsev and others; then the immediate boss, Colonel Makshakov/ Mr Potato Head, his boss General Kirill Vasilyev, and his boss Major-General Vladimir Bogdanov and his boss, FSB director Alexander Bortnikov, obliquely, a little above and to the left, Nikolai Patrushev, the former head of the FSB and the head of the National Security Council, and above them all, the poisoner-in-chief, Vladimir Putin. The diagram looks as though it has come from the set of the Russell Crowe movie *A Beautiful Mind*, about the brilliant but paranoid mathematical genius John Nash, but it is all too real.

Time for one last chore. Navalny stands up and says: 'Hold my beer while I make a TikTok.' He gets Dasha to film a video for TikTok of him mouthing OMC's hit 'How Bizarre' in front of the mugshots of the Poison Squad. He tells Dasha to make an edit on her phone.

Dasha: 'I don't know how to do that.'

Navalny: 'Who's 19?'

Dasha: 'You apparently.'

Yulia looks on, her eyes lit up with joy. The film plays a brief clip of Navalny lip-synching the hit. This is investigative journalism for the twenty-first century.

Dasha goes into the kitchen to role-play General Bogdanov. Navalny calls up and Dasha immediately notices that there is one digit not showing up on the screen of her mobile. Grozev has worked out how to patch the phone so that the number that pops up appears to be a landline at the Lubyanka, the FSB headquarters. He declares it's not a problem. This is Happy Families, the Russian version.

First thing in the morning, Navalny is to make a series of calls, some straightforward, some pretending to be a Kremlin insider to see if one of the Poison Squad goons will react or, even better, spill the beans. The night before, Navalny is the most sceptical, suggesting that there is no way the FSB killers would fall for a prank, but then he recalls Grozev's mantra: 'Moscow4'. This stems from a fabulous but true story that anti-Kremlin hackers managed to get hold of the password of a senior figure in the GRU, Russian military intelligence, discovering that it was 'Moscow1'. Having been hacked, the Russian George Smiley changed his password to 'Moscow2'. He was hacked again, so he changed it to 'Moscow3'. On the fourth hacking, he changed it, yet again, to 'Moscow4'. Navalny sums it up: 'So Moscow4 is the explanation of the stupidity of the system.'

Just before going to bed, Navalny reflects that tomorrow the great investigation will be published. And his TikTok: 'We'll have a kind of fifteen minutes of shame with it. OK, see you tomorrow!'

Navalny, Grozev and Pevchikh are all present and correct at sparrow fart, 4.30am, German time, to prank call the Poison Squad members in Moscow. The investigation will be published at noon so they have a few hours to put the frighteners on the Poison Squad. For the Navalny documentary, a sound mic is attached, the technician hiding the leads under his jumper.

'Now I totally feel like I am an undercover agent wired up,' jokes Navalny.

'Are you not nervous?' asks Pevchikh, playfully for her, playfully for anyone at 4.30 in the morning. She is normally stern-faced, a female Professor Snape.

'Sorry?'

'Are you nervous?'

'No.'

'Come on.'

'A little bit.'

While in a coma, Navalny has lost a fair bit of weight and looks leaner, far more handsome than his time back in the day when he was on the far-right Russian Marches. He is wearing a blue hoodie, in command, but occasionally his face lights up with boyish glee; Pevchikh in a big blue fisherman's jersey, her dark hair done up, glasses, pearl earrings, forever watchful; Grozev in a black jumper with red and blue armbands, his demeanour that of a bloodhound sniff-sniffing the air, worried that the prey might escape.

There seem to be five slightly different translated versions of Navalny's phone conversations with the Poison Squad from Bellingcat, The Insider, CNN, *Der Spiegel* and the *Navalny* documentary, although the gist is the same. This last is the fullest and the stand-out best but, once again, to my perhaps too fastidious ear, where it may not quite get the true flavour of the Russian original across into English-English I have, in a few places, come up with my own translation.

What Roher managed to capture on film is incontrovertible evidence of a crime. Navalny gives a tour-de-force performance where his quick-wittedness and guile are there for all to see, teasing out the testimony of how the poisoners went about their business. It is important, to understand Navalny's story, to follow every twist and turn of these events.

The first calls are to the team who flew to Siberia, shadowing him. The team have worked out that these people will know Navalny's voice very well so he doesn't prank call them, just asks: 'I'm calling to ask why you wanted to kill me?'

On a personal level, these calls must have been rather satisfying, but journalistically they don't work, the members of the Siberia Poison Squad hanging up.

'Maybe try the prank way?' suggests Pevchikh. She is, of course, absolutely right and Navalny is being a bit silly.

'OK.'

For the prank calls, Navalny plays 'Maxim Ustinov', a senior aide to Nikolai Patrushev, a former boss of the FSB, now secretary of the Security Council of Russia, a fascist and a hawk. Patrushev paints the clouds for Putin's castle in the sky. Navalny's manner is abrupt, overbearing, insistent, pitch perfect for 'Ustinov', the fake Kremlin insider.

He calls Shvets, who recognises Navalny's voice, and says: 'I'm done with your game. I know who you are. Goodbye,' and puts the phone down.

Grozev: 'That was a freaking scared guy.'

Pevchikh: 'He recognised your voice?'

Navalny: 'Yep, yep. Mikhail's not stupid.'

Grozev: 'I really think a scientist might talk to you. A one per cent chance.'

Navalny calls Kudryavtsev, the chemist who went to Omsk five days after the poisoning. Kudryavtsev sounds befuddled, his voice nasal, thick. The legend is that Patrushev's aid, 'Ustinov' – Navalny – has to write a report about what went wrong with the operation. He tells the chemical weapons expert that he got his number from Bogdanov. The two voices are strikingly different. If I was casting them for a movie, Navalny plays the arrogant patrician, Kudryavtsev a servant with a bunged-up nose.

Navalny: 'I apologise for calling so early but I need ten minutes of your time.'

Kudryavtsev: 'Yeah, yeah, right.'

Navalny: 'So I must get a statement from each unit member about what went wrong in Tomsk. Why did the Navalny operation fail?'

Kudryavtsev: 'I will gladly help but I am at home with coronavirus.'

Navalny, lord to serf: 'That is why I am calling you.'

Kudryavtsev: 'And what about Makshakov [Mr Potato Head]? Have you considered calling him?'

Navalny: 'Of course I will call Makshakov. This is a simple process. I'm calling Alexandrov, Makshakov, Tayakin, and I will ask each of them to briefly explain what went wrong. And what should be done next time to succeed.'

Kudryavtsev: 'I have been wondering about the same thing myself.' Pevchikh, filming the sting on her camera phone, raises a hand to her mouth, her eyes lighting up with delight.

Kudryavtsev, continuing: 'I would rate the job as well done. We did it just as planned, the way we rehearsed it many times. But in our profession, as you know, there are lots of unknowns and nuances. We try to take everything into account, as best we can. But when the flight made the emergency landing, the situation changed and not in our favour. If the flight had lasted longer, then I think things would have gone our way.'

Grozev rests his head in his hands, not quite believing his ears.

Navalny: 'If he was in the air longer?'

Kudryavtsev: 'The medics on the ground acted right away. They injected him with an antidote of some sort. So if they were in the air longer, things would have gone as planned.'

Navalny, silently, lifts his arms in the air in 'We are the Champions of the World' mode while Grozev still hides behind his hands. But there is more, much, much more.

Navalny: 'So it seems the dose was underestimated. How come?'

Kudryavtsev: 'Our calculations were good. We even applied a bit extra.'

Navalny: 'Good. Now please tell me about the specific mechanism. How was the poison administered?'

Kudryavtsev: 'Well, this should be communicated via a secure channel.'

Navalny, firmly: 'No, that is not necessary. You need to realise who this report is being written for. At this level, there is no need for secure channels. This high up, they don't want technical details. How can I explain the delivery mechanism? Just tell me in the simplest terms possible.'

Kudryavtsev, a little surprised: 'You don't know?'

Navalny, riffing rather nicely: 'I know some of it but not all of it. Nevertheless, I have to ask you. These are the questions I have to ask so that's why I am asking them.'

Kudryavtsev: 'Well, I can't tell you that on this phone.'

Navalny: 'OK. What happened to his belongings?'

Kudryavtsev: 'The last time I saw them they were in Omsk. We left them there after we had worked on them.' Grozev has emerged from behind his hands and pumps his thumb in the air, repeatedly. 'I have no idea where they finally ended up. I can only say that when we arrived they were given to us by the local guys from the Omsk police force. What's their name again?'

Navalny, laughing noiselessly: 'Transport police?'

Kudryavtsev: 'Yes, yes.'

Navalny: 'So the clothes have been sorted. All good with that?'

Kudryavtsev: 'When we finished working on them, everything was clean.'

Navalny, pouncing: 'What piece of clothing did you focus on? Which item had the highest risk factor?'

Kudryavtsev: 'The underpants. The inside, where the crotch is.'

Navalny: 'The crotch of the underpants?'

Kudryavtsev: 'The codpiece, they call it. On the seams.'

Navalny: 'OK, this is important. Who told you to work on the crotch of the underpants? Makshakov?'

Kudryavtsev, fingering Mr Potato Head: 'Yes.'

Navalny: 'Do you remember the colour of the underpants?'

Kudryavtsev: 'Blue.'

Navalny, in taking notes voice: 'Blue, blue. And the trousers?'

Kudryavtsev: 'There was a chance of some residue there, so we cleaned them too, so there would be no traces left.' Pevchikh again puts a hand to her mouth, aware that the poisoner has dug his own grave; Grozev, the digital bloodhound, gives a twitch of his tail.

Navalny: 'So how did the Germans detect it?'

Kudryavtsev: 'Maybe they have special methods of detection.'

Navalny: 'Which part of the body could they find traces?'

Kudryavtsev: 'There was nothing on the body. It was in the blood. We cleaned up his body in the hospital.' At which Grozev, not a demonstrative fellow, grips his head with his hands lest it fall off, grinning from ear to ear all the while.

Navalny: 'I have a rather strange question. You travelled with Navalny several times, for example to Kirov in 2017. What is your assessment of him as a person?'

Kudryavtsev: 'He never makes any unnecessary moves, in my view. Careful and meticulous at all times. Maybe he had a hunch our boys were following him. You still there?'

Navalny: 'Yes, I am all ears. I'm writing. Is there anything else you want to add to my report?'

Kudryavtsev: 'No, I've said it all. Probably too much. Honestly, I am shocked by the questions. I hope you understand why.'

Navalny: 'Konstantin, we are all shocked. Imagine how shocked I am.'

Kudryavtsev: 'OK.'

Navalny: 'Thanks. Bye.'

At which Grozev leaps up and high-fives Navalny, the executor of the best journalistic sting of the millennium. The boy in Navalny erupts with glee. Pevchikh buries her face in her enormous sweater, trying to come to terms with the poisoner's professional suicide and what it will mean for him.

'How did you do that?' says Grozev.

'So now we got everything. Moscow4,' says Navalny.

'Oh my fucking God.' Grozev is awestruck. 'He has spilt the whole story. This is unbelievable.'

'Poor guy,' says Navalny. 'They will kill him. They will kill him.'

'Literally,' says Grozev. 'I think you'll be president, seriously, after this.'

'After this,' Navalny can't stop chuckling, 'they will definitely kill me.' He's joking but this prediction does, in the course of time, come true.

'Poor Kudryavtsev,' says Pevchikh.

'Poor Kudryavtsev, yes,' the men echo.

'He's a dead man,' says Grozev. 'Let's offer him to defect. Let's arrange for him the whole thing.'

'Seriously,' says Pevchikh.

'Cos I think that's a humanitarian thing to do.'

'He will be in a ditch by tomorrow,' says Pevchikh.

'They will kill him. They will kill him,' says Grozev.

Kudryavtsev has never been seen again.

The team agree to Pevchikh's suggestion that they will hold their scoop back until after Putin's annual telethon which is happening in a few days' time.

On 16 December, CNN broadcasts its chief international correspondent Clarissa Ward going up to a dingy flat with a green door somewhere in Moscow's unfashionable suburbs and knocking on the door. For this book, Ward explains what happened when CNN targeted Uncle Fester from *The Addams Family* or, more correctly, Oleg Tayakin, the sergeant-major of the Poison Squad: 'The building itself was a classic old-school Soviet apartment block. I was a pile of nerves before, not really so much because of the fact that I was about to doorstep an FSB operative and confront him for his role in the attempted assassination of Alexei Navalny, but more because, as you know, with a doorstep, there's eight hundred things that need to go right. And if any one of them goes wrong, just all the dominoes suddenly collapse. And so you spend ages going through what could go wrong: "OK, what if he grabs the camera? Well, maybe we'll be already streaming into Atlanta, so that even if he grabs the camera, the material is already in-house. Let's not even use a camera. Let's use a phone. And where does Jeff the camera operator stand? Is he behind me? When does he reveal himself? When do I go up? And who rings the first doorbell and what do we tell them? And what time do we go?" We ended up knocking on his door before seven in the morning which was crazy. But he lived on the outskirts of Moscow and it struck me that this guy may well leave for the office at 0730 in the morning, I don't know. Or he may be at home all day because of COVID. Like, there's so many moving parts. He was one of three people that we were trying to doorstep that day. My colleague Dasha rang the first doorbell, at the entrance to the apartment building, three times and then he had answered and she just sort of babbled, like, "Hi! Can we come and chat to you?" and I think he was so irritated by us ringing the doorbell before seven in the morning that he opened the first door just so that when we came up, he could just give us a piece of his mind and say: "What the hell do you think you're doing ringing my doorbell like a madman at 0645 on Monday morning?"'

Uncle Fester is wearing double camo pyjamas. 'Never in his wildest dreams did he think that the chief international correspondent of CNN was going to ask in broken Russian: "Was it your team that poisoned Navalny, please?"'

Ward continues: 'There was this extraordinary moment because when he saw me, he was ready to give me what for, then he saw the camera, and he closed the door, but he didn't close it all the way. He just closed it to hide himself from the camera. And then the minute he heard the word "Navalny", the door slams shut. You can't quite believe what's just happened, especially because I've been studying photographs of him for over a month, looking at his mug every day, and then to suddenly see him there in his double camo pyjamas.'

It is a classic doorstep, beautifully done, and super-ballsy because of the timing and the place.

The next day, Putin sneers at Team Navalny's joint investigation with Bellingcat, The Insider, *Der Spiegel* and CNN, telling his audience of zombie journalists that it represents a type of 'information warfare . . . a dump where everything is being dumped, dumped, dumped in the hope that it will make an impression on the citizens, instil mistrust of our political leadership'. As is his funny peculiar custom, Putin cannot bear to mention Navalny by name but calls him the 'Berlin patient' who 'has the support of the American intelligence services'.

Putin mocks the team's methods: 'You don't think we know that they're tracking geolocations? Our intelligence agencies know that. Agents of the FSB and other special agencies know this. And they use their telephones where they think it's necessary, not hiding their location.'

What's so pathetic about Putin's world view is that anything that makes him look weak can only be the work of the CIA. The possibility that Russian citizens working with free-spirited Western journalists and a Bulgarian Sherlock Holmes could get the better of him and his goons is not allowed. That flows from him having a closed mind inside a closed world. Putin does not get open-source investigation, where Grozev and co show their own homework for all to see. He does not get it that this is a new way of doing things, that, for example, the CIA would never dream of explaining to the world in the way that Grozev does in *Navalny* how he cracked the names and numbers and flights taken of the Poison Squad. Putin does not understand the twenty-first century. He asked the zombies: 'Who needs to poison him?' adding that if Russia had wanted Navalny dead, 'they would've probably finished the job.'

Team Navalny lays a trap for Vladimir Putin. They put out the poisoning investigation – the names of the Poison Squad and the telephone metadata showing them tracking Navalny across Russia to Tomsk but held back the clincher – Kudryavtsev's confession. After Putin sneers at their evidence during the Kremlin's telethon, they break the story of the poisoner explaining exactly how the Poison Squad secreted the Novichok on Navalny's blue underpants and all. They make Putin look like a common murderer.

And a fool.

CHAPTER THIRTEEN

The Temple to Cupid Stunt

Navalny dared Putin not to kill him when he made his great and terrible decision to return to Russia in January 2021. It was a great decision because it showed Navalny's raw courage for all the world to see, that his idea of 'the beautiful Russia of the future' was something he was prepared to risk his life for, that the idea of a democratic Russia was something worth dying for; it was a terrible decision because Putin, his domestic political position strengthened immeasurably by the big war against Ukraine, did end up killing him, three years down the track.

In the immediate aftermath of the poisoner's confession, the Russian fog machine went to town, doing its utmost to follow up on the lead from Putin, that if the Poison Squad had wanted to kill Navalny before, they could have done so. This Kremlin riff rules out any consideration of the political risk to Putin, that the reason that he didn't have the leader of the Russian opposition poisoned before 2020 was that he was grievously afraid of the consequences for his grip on power. Navalny had succeeded in getting more people protesting on the streets of Moscow about yet more years of Putinism than anyone else since the fall of the Soviet Union.

The reality was for a long time that Putin, when facing off against Navalny, felt fear. People forget that before the 'swaggering . . . sneery . . . dismissive' strong man Putin, witnessed during the time of the Iraq War by Alastair Campbell, there existed a weak man Putin, who carried the bags of Anatoly Sobchak, the mayor of St Petersburg; who meekly said 'yes, boss, no boss' to Boris Berezovsky when the oligarch was fishing around for a replacement for Boris Yeltsin; who conned the Yeltsin family too with his subservient act; then did the same thing for Blair and George W. Bush. The tricky thing to get your head around is that weak man Putin was a performance but it was also part of the truth, that when up against an unflinching enemy, he has history of backing down, of being far more fearful than the far better understood sneery side of his character would suggest. Navalny turned out to be wrong but it was not inevitable that he would be killed.

He was always going to go back to Russia. His great Tonto, Volkov, explained in the *Navalny* documentary that they were worried that after he woke up from his coma he would go straight back: 'Our expectation was once he's released from intensive care, he will have a desire to go to Russia immediately. To our great relief, he told me: "I'd better spend several months here. I want to go back to Russia strong and fully recovered."' From late September 2020 to mid-January 2021, Navalny was in a village in the Black Forest getting stronger every day.

Shortly before his return, he explained his logic in a video, seen by almost two million people on Instagram. 'And now Putin, who gave the order for my murder, is screaming in his bunker and ordering his servants to do everything to keep me from returning. His servants are acting like they usually do: inventing new criminal cases against me.' But he was going home: 'Russia is my country, Moscow is my city. I miss them.'

The return flight from Berlin on 17 January 2021 was a media carnival with reporters filming everything on their camera phones. Navalny and Yulia were model passengers, their faces half-hidden by COVID masks. Navalny watched his favourite cartoon series, *Rick and Morty*, a US sci-fi romp featuring Rick, the classic mad genius with a hole in his immortal soul, and his fearful but humane grandson, Morty. They travel through space and time, having silly adventures in their bubble-capsule 1950s-style flying saucer. One time-line is that Rick makes Morty a love potion that has a hideous side effect; the antidote to that leaves humanity monsters, their genes spliced, half dinosaurs, half praying mantises, not a bad metaphor for the Poison Squad. Yulia, as so often, wore a severe expression behind her COVID mask, her face doubly impossible to read. One could only guess at the anguish in her heart, but she had been married to him for twenty-one years at this point. Showing fear was not her thing; nor his.

Navalny told the reporters on the plane that he was 'very happy to be back', adding: 'This is the best day in the last five months. I'm home.' He joked that he was more concerned by the icy weather awaiting him in Moscow than what the authorities could come up with: 'What bad things could happen to me inside Russia? I have every right to come back.'

Hundreds of Navalnyites had gathered at Moscow's Vnukovo airport to cheer his return when, at the last minute, the airport was suddenly closed and dozens of beetle-like Ministry of the Interior 'OMON' riot police entered the terminal, nicking his supporters, among them his younger brother, Oleg. There were cries of 'fascists' as the supporters were marched off to police cells. Navalny's flight was diverted to Sheremetyevo, thirty-five miles away: shades of Omsk airport being closed by a 'bomb threat'. His PR spokesperson, Kira Yarmysh, tweeted that the diversion was proof of the Kremlin's fear: 'Until recently, it was impossible to believe they [the authorities] were so scared. But here's the confirmation.'

The moment he rocked up at passport control, the cops lurched towards him. He kissed Yulia and gave her a last hug and then the police pounced and that was the end of his time as a free man as he disappeared into the Kafkaesque hell of Putin's criminal justice system. The reason for the arrest was his failure to attend parole hearings from the Yves Rocher case while he had been in a coma caused by the Novichok poisoning.

Welcome back to Absurdistan.

Why did he go back to the certainty of a long time in prison? The best explanation came from one of the few other surviving members of the real Russian opposition, Vladimir Kara-Murza who said: 'You can only be a Russian politician from within Russia. Outside you lose relevance.'

Navalny's lifelong goal from 2000 was to unhorse Putin. To live in exile was to give that up, to surrender to the brute force of the regime and that wasn't in his character. There's also something about the very nature of people who strive for political power. Reflecting on a very different politician indeed, the former British Tory MP, Matthew Parris, did his best in a column in *The Times* in April 2024 to explain the psychology of Tory MP Mark Menzies who lost the whip because he had been accused of begging an elderly

Conservative aide for help after being locked up by 'bad people' demanding money for his release. Menzies denies the allegations. Parris wrote: 'People who want to be MPs are not normal. They are not representative of the general population, but a very distinct personality type: a minority whose nature disposes them to take stupid risks. The word "risk" is key, and it is here – in their calculations, not their propensities – that they are unusual. They think they can wing it. And often enough they do. Always have.'

Navalny took the risk because he thought he could get away with it. He was, of course, a far greater man than Menzies would ever be. I don't wish to insult his memory by making a direct comparison between the two, but to be hungry for power makes you a risk-taker extraordinaire. To try to get power in Russia is to enter a different universe of risk. To be fair to Navalny, he had something in his back pocket, something he knew would hurt the lizard in the Kremlin. Two days after he got locked up, a new Anti-Corruption Foundation movie hit YouTube, the biggest and boldest and funniest yet: *Putin's Palace: The Story of the World's Biggest Bribe*. It's stonkingly good, a great watch, funny and grimly fascinating on just how naff Putin's taste in home decor is: one billion dollars naff.

The film opens with the presenter – 'Hi, it's Navalny' – sitting on a bench somewhere nondescript in Germany but immediately getting into the thick of it. Once again, various chunks have been differently translated online. Where necessary, I've fiddled with the translation to capture the tang of the original Russian.

'We came up with this investigation when I was in intensive care,' says Navalny, 'but we immediately agreed that we would release it when I returned home, to Russia, to

Moscow, because we do not want the main character of this film to think that we are afraid of him and that I will tell the story of his darkest worst secret while I'm out of the country. He's one of our viewers, the most devoted admirer of our work. On his orders I was poisoned. It's Vladimir Putin.' Navalny looks around, circumspectly as if Putin is hiding in the shrubbery: 'He is definitely watching this now and his heart is filled with nostalgia. This is not only an investigation, but also, in a sense, a psychological portrait. I really want to understand how an ordinary Soviet officer turned into a madman who is obsessed with money and luxury and literally ready to destroy the country and kill for the treasure chests of gold.'

Navalny explains exactly where he is: 'I am in Dresden, and this unflashy apartment building is where first corruption schemes were drawn up by the gang who would later pull off the greatest robbery in Russian history . . . Their leader, then 33-year-old Volodya Putin, the future richest man in the world, lived here.'

Team Navalny took apart Putin's KGB career in Dresden, in then East Germany, emphasising how the official Leninism and secret police skulduggery masked epic corruption, as was the Soviet way: 'Neither his methods nor his circle of cronies have changed. It's just that back then, they were into tape recorders, and now they're into megalithic state enterprises. They took part in the ceremonies, read speeches. It's just that in those days, they praised grandfather Lenin and swore their allegiance to Communism, but now they cross themselves in churches and teach us holy conservatism . . . We will go where no one is allowed. We will pay Putin a visit and see with our own eyes that this man, by his craving for luxury and wealth, has gone completely bonkers.'

Navalny sets out that Putin came to Dresden as a petty KGB officer in 1985. He mocks the Kremlin legend: 'He wants us to think of him as a cool operator. But in fact, he was an ordinary employee.'

Up flashes a photo from 21 November 1987, with a suited and booted Putin at a beano dedicated to the friendship between the KGB and the Stasi, the East German secret police. It's hard to convey the biting edge to Navalny's commentary, but this was a year and a half after the Chernobyl catastrophe when the boy Navalny was banished from his Ukrainian childhood idyll for ever by the sickness of Soviet secrecy and here is Putin glorifying that very darkness. Boy has the boy Navalny got skin in this game: 'Throughout the evening, Putin and his colleagues make interminable speeches, drink Soviet brandy, watch slides and quiver with pride at the ideas of Marxism–Leninism. In less than two years, not a trace of this will remain. The Berlin Wall will fall. East Germany, along with the Stasi and KGB offices, will cease to exist. The system built on lies and repression collapses, but it will leave behind one very important legacy: the archives.'

Navalny puts on white gloves and with a German archivist pores over the file on Vladimir Vladimirovich Putin. In a photo of Putin picking up some gilded Soviet gong is a fellow KGB officer, Sergei Chemezov, now head of Russian defence conglomerate Rostec, billionaire and owner, according to the Pandora Papers leak, of a $600 million superyacht.

Navalny's biting tone gets even bitier which is not, I suspect, permissible English-English: 'So, in this photo, we see two of the richest people in Russia. Putin is probably the richest man in the world and Chemezov is definitely in the top five richest people in our country.'

Navalny riffs on how carefully the Germans record everything – 'Typical Germans . . .' – before going on to point to a second KGB man in the photos, Nikolai Tokarev, the head of Transneft, who had hitherto covered up his career in the Soviet Gestapo. Attentive readers will recall that in 2010 while at Yale, one of Navalny's first investigations showed how a fiddle at Transneft had led to £2.5 billion going missing. The moral of the story, Navalny leans into frame, is that: 'It was here, in Dresden, that Putin defined his main life principles, which would later become the basis of the Russian state. One, always say one thing and do another. Lying and hypocrisy are the most effective methods. Two, corruption secures trust. Your best friends are the people who have been stealing and cheating with you for many years. Three, the most important of all: there is no such thing as too much money.'

The story moves to St Petersburg in the early 1990s where Putin, broken by the collapse of the Soviet Union, becomes the night mayor to the daylight holder of the office, the late (and probably poisoned by Putin) Anatoly Sobchak. Navalny shows how Putin approved export licences for oil, timber, aluminium, copper and cotton to be swapped for much-needed food. The beneficiaries were offshore companies, some of which Putin and his friends secretly controlled. The catch was the food never arrived. In a nut-shell, Navalny's allegation is that Putin sat above a criminal gangster network in Russia's second city that fenced indus-trial amounts of the country's natural wealth to foreign buyers for massive profits. Putin's critical role was to sign off the paperwork so everything looked official and square off the cops. If nosy journalists or politicians got in the way, then either Putin would switch on the cops or the gangsters, or both, and the problem would end up in the morgue.

Navalny runs through just how many of Putin's cronies in St Petersburg made it to become titans of Russian capitalism. For example, he says that Putin made a killing out of gangster control of St Petersburg's docks. Ilya 'The Antiquarian' Traber was a major crime boss at the time and ran the waterfront, along with Gennady Petrov, head of the Tambov gang, and Putin. Navalny reported that Alexander Dyukov was the then head of the port terminal; he is now the billionaire boss of Gazprom Neft, one of the world's biggest oil companies. One of the biggest oil traders in the port was Gennady Timchenko, the future billionaire and one of the most famous of 'Putin's friends', said Navalny, in wink-wink mode.

The big point, implicit in all of this, is that down the track, Putin copied and pasted the St Petersburg docks racket and applied it to Russia: as president he would sign off the paperwork, to make it look official, and the dirty money would flow to secret accounts controlled by his cronies; if nosy journalists or politicians got in the way, then either Putin would switch on the cops or the gangsters, or both, and the problem would end up in the morgue. (Reader, please note: the repeat of the wording from the last but one paragraph is ever so deliberate.)

In *Putin's Palace*, Navalny sets it out in fine detail: 'When Putin became president, four out of five of our country's major oil companies did not sell their oil abroad directly, but through the Swiss intermediary Gunvor. Thus, Timchenko, without doing anything, earned incredible money. Throughout the entire existence of Gunvor, it was believed that Putin had a secret share there; even the US Treasury officially claimed that Putin had access to Gunvor's money. But it was not clear to whom this share was registered for many years. And then it was found out. All this time there was a secret shareholder in Gunvor: Pyotr Kolbin. No one understood where this amazing shareholder came from and how a person who says himself that he is not engaged in business could have millions of dollars to invest in Gunvor. Until 2016, when journalists discovered that Pyotr Kolbin was Putin's childhood crony – they grew up in the same village, went to discos together and were old family friends. And it became obvious that Kolbin was the holder of Putin's share all this time. You're probably thinking now: "Wait, does that mean Putin was directly paid bribes? In envelopes?" Yes!'

How did that work? Navalny quotes one of the players in the St Petersburg crime scene in the nineties, Maxim Freidzon, saying in an interview: 'If it was necessary to formalise something, they needed to come to the Foreign Relations Committee [run by Putin], listen to a ceremonial speech about the importance of economic partnership and then Putin simply wrote on a piece of paper the required amount of kickback, a small one, $10,000 or $20,000, and added that the money needed to be "registered", that is, brought to his assistant, Alexey Miller.' That assistant is now the boss of Gazprom, and a multi-multi-billionaire.

Navalny adds one more mega Russian corporate into the mix: the story of Rossiya Bank, created by the Leningrad Regional Committee of the Communist Party of the Soviet Union. In 1991, Mayor Sobchak ordered Putin to reorganise Rossiya Bank for post-Soviet times. Putin put his placemen in key positions. Navalny goes on to allege that Putin's cronies at St Petersburg City Hall back in the day now run Russia PLC: Alexey Miller at Gazprom; Medvedev became prime minister and president; Viktor Zubkov, one-time prime minister, now at Gazprom; Igor Sechin, now head of Rosneft: 'It's like an unofficial Forbes list,' cracked Navalny. There's more: Vladimir Churov became head of the Russian Electoral Commission, 'assigned to falsify elections so that unwanted candidates would not be elected and would not interfere with stealing'; Marina Entaltseva became the head of Putin's protocol; German Gref, now the head of Sberbank; on and on it goes.

All concerned deny any wrongdoing.

Navalny takes Putin's shtick and shoves it back right at him: 'For more than thirty years they have been in power and they like to tell us how they stand against the cursed nineties. But they are the personification of all the worst things that happened in the nineties.'

That's just the prelude. Navalny's message is that Putin's cronies from back in the day are allowed to keep their ill-gotten wealth so long as they owe fealty and pay tribute to their master. His underlings are expected to cough up. Hence, they must contribute to the billion-dollar bung, a bribe written in marble and gold: 'The world's largest construction project, the most secret and best-guarded facility in Russia, without exaggeration. This is not a country house, not a dacha, not a residence, but a whole city, or rather a kingdom. It has impregnable fences, a dedicated port, guards, church, no-fly zone and border checkpoint. It's a state within a state. And in this state there is a single and unchanging tsar: Putin.' He added that the palace's grounds were thirty-nine times the size of Monaco. 'Looking inside, you will understand that the president of Russia is mentally ill. He is obsessed with gold.'

To quote the late Kenny Everett's drag queen, Cupid

Stunt, Putin's Palace was done up: 'All in the best possible taste!' Not. Navalny's documentary is gripping because it reveals both the immensity of the tsar's wealth but also the shabbiness of his soul.

Dictators murder decor like they murder people. Idi Amin's sordid bungalow, Saddam's pre-cast cement palaces in Northern Iraq, Kim Il Sung's waxwork house, I've seen them all and they smack – how can I put this diplomatically? – of Cupid Stunt. One striking memory of Nicolae Ceausescu's great cement barn in Bucharest is that no toilets were provided for the 15,000 workers building 'The House of the People' so they sneaked into dark places for a shit. One summer day, The Conducator stepped out of the carefully constructed pathways, marked by white tape, into the gloom to get a closer look at something and came back having stepped in a monstrous turd. A builder told me: 'The workers started to laugh but then the Securitate [the Romanian Communist secret police] looked at them so they shut up. A Securitate man rushed over and started to clean the shoe but there was so much on it, it was impossible. Normally, he would stand around giving orders, but this time he said nothing and just walked off to his car. With every other step you could see the tidemark the shit left on the floor. Nobody spoke. Nobody dared laugh. It was as if an atomic bomb had gone off.' The builder who told me this story for my book, *The Life and Evil Times of Nicolae Ceausescu*, shuddered at the memory of the Securitate investigation into which saboteur had done the bad thing. A colleague was the supervisor for the area where the shit had been shat and was ordered by the Securitate never to talk about the shit or talk to Ceausescu. One day the dictator returned and, not knowing about the secret police's ukase, asked the man a series of questions. He had to run away. Later, he came to my friend's flat, put his head in his hands and said: 'That shit. It's going to be the death of me.'

Stories like that only get told when dictators die. What was so extraordinary about Navalny was that he chose to mock the dictator when he was locked up inside his machinery of fear, when the dictator was not just alive but kicking him. Team Navalny's investigation into the tsar's new palace on the Black Sea only succeeded thanks to Russian workers like my Romanian friend leaking plans and photos and extraordinary drone shots. But Putin's Palace was super secure. How on earth did they get the drone footage?

Cut to a fat man at sea in a rib: 'Hello everyone, this is Georgy Alburov.' The *Putin's Palace* documentary shows Alburov, Team Navalny's Friar Tuck, bobbing up and down on the Black Sea, not far from the southern Russian resort city of Krasnodar Krai. (Once again, I have fiddled with the translation.) Alburov explained that he was 'literally three kilometres from the famous Putin's Palace. We came here in a very roundabout way. We switched tickets, got off at the wrong stops, swapped SIM cards and phones. We carried out a whole special operation to get here. All this has been done so that we don't get followed by the police, FSB officers and agents from Centre-E' – the counter-terrorism police who managed the SERB team that half-blinded Navalny.

'We managed to do it,' Alburov continued: 'Right now, we are a few hundred metres from the shore and not a single policeman for tens of kilometres around knows what we are up to. This is great because right now we are going to launch a drone and get legendary footage of Putin's Palace which has never been seen from a drone.'

Alburov's camera follows a tiny drone lifting above the

waves, on its mission. The area, Alburov said, 'is so classified that it is guarded by the Federal Security Service', the FSB.

The drone closes in on a vast dazzlingly white palazzo on a handsome tree-covered bluff overlooking the Black Sea. Navalny takes over the translation: 'Everyone said that it was impossible to film this. Yes, we thought that ourselves, but then we went ahead and had a go. It didn't work, so we tried again, four times in all. And then we got away with it. We present the most secret palace in Russia, Putin's Palace at Gelendzhik. This is it, right in front of you, the largest private residential building in Russia, its size officially confirmed by documents: 17,691 square metres . . . This is the new Versailles or the new Winter Palace, a truly royal place.'

Then the tone switches to a close-up of a tarpaulin, of blocked-off windows, a swimming pool closed, of mounds of builders' rubble here and there, even tiny figures of builders dotted around: 'Huh, what's going on here?' asks Navalny. 'What is happening? Why is there a construction site if six-year-old satellite images showed that the palace was finished? The builders explained it to us. Everything was completed a long time ago, but then disaster struck. Its name is mould. And sloppiness. The palace was badly designed from the get-go. The ventilation did not work, the ceiling leaked, the humidity seeped in. They decided to do the whole thing all over again, stripping off walls, stripping out the marble, literally threw billions on to the rubbish dump and started all over again. What a waste! But this headache for Putin is a chance for us to learn more about his palace. After all, a lot of people were involved in the reconstruction and they were happy to tell us about literally every square metre of this grandiose object. For example, here's the arboretum, where they've collected rare species of trees.

And for those plants that don't like this climate, there's a 2,500-square-metre greenhouse. The trees and plants are tended by a small army of around forty gardeners.'

Solipsism plus a billion dollars doesn't look good.

The drone moves on, picking out naff sculptures dotted around the shrubbery. The drone is too high to make out the detail of whom the statues depict, but Navalny speculates that one might be to the goddess of theft. There's a church, a helipad, a rink, an oyster farm, a church, a teahouse and an underground hockey rink: 'The owner loves a bunker. He likes hanging out underground. He probably imagines himself as a gnome from the *Lord of the Rings* movie, guarding his gold.'

The palace estate stretches out for 70 million square metres, is owned by the FSB, fully leased until 2068 for 'research and educational activities', boasts state-of-the-art communication towers, its own gas station and boilers. There is an almighty fence to keep out the riff-raff, an amphitheatre, a secret tunnel leading from the palace to the beach, a window cut in bare rock so that the dictator can admire a sea view just like a Bond villain from his lair.

Out to sea, there's a two-kilometre exclusion zone so fishermen have to chug the long way round to avoid any trouble and there's a no-fly zone, officially designated 'URP116: just like for nuclear power plants or secret military facilities. Why would the FSB establish a no-fly zone over a private palace?' asks Navalny. 'There can be only one answer. This is the palace of the very person for whose safety the FSB is responsible.'

The original planning application for the palace, Navalny explains, was for a children's recreational facility. Throughout the film, clips of Putin himself pop up every now and again, appearing to endorse Navalny's message. Here Putin says: 'They say one thing and do another.' It's laugh out loud funny: once again, you are left thinking just how much Putin would have hated being mocked so, how much he detested Navalny, how much he wanted him shut up for good.

'No one can have the slightest doubt that this is Putin's palace,' continues Navalny. Actually, after the release of the film, Arkady Rotenberg, one of Putin's favourite buddies, said he owned the gaff, a move widely interpreted to cover up the embarrassment of the tsar of tackiness.

The documentary moves from drone footage shot from above to architects' plans and sneakily shot photos, supplied to Team Navalny by the thousands of builders sickened by the grandiose excess and the secrecy enforced on them. The viewer clocks gold and marble, Louis XIV sofas and couches, mosaics, frescoes, stained-glass windows, a home cinema and an aquadisco. In the basement, there is a huge swimming pool, a spa area, a massage room, a beauty salon, some kind of spa capsule, saunas, hammams, plunge tubs and bathing pools.

Above ground, the team find fabulously expensive Italian sofas and furniture, a gym, a drama theatre, bars, a hookah room, sofas, tables, dim lights: 'The perfect atmosphere to discuss budget issues,' says Navalny, his voice laced with scorn: 'Lying among soft pillows, the president and his guests can also enjoy a show. This room is also equipped with a small stage and surprisingly there is a special plinth with a pole coming out of it. We just can't even imagine why a pole is needed on the stage. Maybe for a Christmas tree? Or a giant kebab? Or maybe for performances in support of the constitution?'

There's a casino with all the trimmings and then Navalny

leads up to tiptoe inside the boudoir, the personal bedroom of the 'crazed emperor: gold, velvet, canopies, but also an obligatory TV opposite the bed, so as not to miss the important news on Russia's Channel One.'

On and on and on it goes, the Russian ecologist who came to investigate who was knocking down protected forest and got beaten black and blue, the exquisite vineyard, the toy cars, the real cars, the gold Italian toilet brush costing €700.

Watch *Putin's Palace*. More than one hundred million people have. Think of the money squandered on dross while ordinary Russians live in poverty. Think, too, on Putin's taste. Get inside Alexei Navalny's head. Why did he go back to Russia to face near certain death? Because he was sick of Putin the thief, sick of his great robbery of Russian wealth and sick of Putin's fouler robbery of the Russian soul. Navalny went back to Moscow because the other tsar, while controlling perhaps the greatest accumulation of private wealth in human history, built himself a temple to Cupid Stunt.

CHAPTER FOURTEEN

A Brave but Terrible Mistake

Navalny's patriotism drove him back to Russia. That and a profound loathing of Vladimir Putin and his thievery. Hatred or, better, contempt governed fear. Besides, remember his quote at the very beginning of this book, that kowtowing to the Kremlin's power and corruption was not for him because 'first of all, it's boring'.

In February 2021, Navalny was tried for not complying with his parole conditions while in a coma caused by his poisoning by the Russian secret police. The trial was a black farce tipped with Novichok. Back in 2014, the authorities had staged the Yves Rocher corruption trial. Subtle as ever, Putin had sensed that the evidence against Navalny was threadbare so the actual sentence against him was suspended, but his brother Oleg was jailed. Navalny called it 'a stitch-up', based on such thin air that he and Oleg appealed to the European Court of Human Rights, the ECHR, in Strasbourg, of which Russia was a member state. The ECHR ruled that the trial had been 'arbitrary and unfair . . . and manifestly unreasonable'. Still, Russia used it and other legal shenanigans to ensure that Navalny had a criminal record, useful when ruling him out of the running for the 2018 presidential election.

Now that he had come back to Russia, the authorities dug up the Yves Rocher case to provide some kind of legal reason for keeping him off the streets.

In the meantime, the Kremlin rounded up the usual suspects. They came for the press officer of the Anti-Corruption Foundation, Kira Yarmysh, on 1 February, placing her under house arrest so that she couldn't cover his trial proper the next day. Navalny once blogged about Yarmysh: 'It is important for us that the press secretary has a weird surname,' but she was a brave and good soldier for Team Navalny. In the run-up to the 2018 presidential election, sorry re-coronation, Yarmysh had retweeted a post mocking Putin. She was arrested and held for five days for her effrontery, officially because her action 'formed a negative opinion of another candidate'. That May, two days before the re-coronation had formally taken place, she tweeted: 'He's not our Tsar.' For that she got twenty-five days in the slammer, an experience she turned into a novel, *The Incredible Events in Women's Cell Number 3*. It opens: 'If you asked Anya which day in prison had been the most trying, she would say the first. It had seemed both insane and endless. Prison time was elastic: it stretched out interminably, only to then fly like an arrow.'

Read it. If you have an idiot relative who thinks that Donald Trump is right about Putin, give it to them for Christmas.

After Navalny was arrested on his return to Moscow in January 2021, Yarmysh and fellow Team Navalny members – Georgy Alburov, the tubby, brave guy in the rib who went boating on the Black Sea to get the drone shots of Putin's Palace, lawyer Lyubov Sobol and Navalny's doctor, Anastasia Vasilyeva – called for people to protest. Yarmysh, Vasilyeva and Alburov were jailed for more than a week, Sobol fined

$3,000 but not sent to prison because she was a single mother. Sobol, while she waited for sentencing, read Aldous Huxley's *Brave New World*. Vasilyeva, while her home was being turned upside down by the police, played 'Für Elise' on her piano, a clip that went viral on social media. As a poignant statement of the contrast between the civilised aspirations of Team Navalny and the uniformed thuggery of the Putinist state, it was hard to beat. In the past, the Kremlin had harassed members of Team Navalny but in a low-key way; now, it was cranking up the volume, viciously so.

The account of Navalny's trial speech that follows is drawn mainly from The Insider, a website providing brave and good journalism which, back then, was still reporting honest news from inside Russia. It has since been banned by the Kremlin and now works out of Riga, Latvia, just like the independent press did before the Second World War in Stalin's day.

Same old, same old.

On 2 February 2021, Moscow's Simonovsky District Court sits to hear the Federal Penitentiary Service's case that Navalny's 'parole violations' mean that he should do time. There is a mass of TV cameras outside which captures the first moment of the day, when a young woman in a woolly bobble hat lifts up a sign saying 'Free Navalny' and is led away by two cops almost immediately to a police van. It's bitterly cold, minus 20 degrees C, the weather killing Team Navalny's call for mass protests.

Navalny appears in the glassed-in dock, which the Russians call 'the fish tank', wearing a blue hoodie, his blond hair swept back, his energy level high. He is chock-full of vim. If you were writing a screenplay for a movie about a resistance leader fighting an evil dictator, Navalny would get the part.

In the afternoon, Navalny makes a speech from the fish tank, appealing over the heads of the judge, the prosecutor and the inspector from the Federal Penitentiary Service. It is striking that the judge let him talk. But, once again, Russian judges are simple puppets when it comes to a political show trial. The puppet-master in the Kremlin holds the strings and he has a strange regard for the semblance of the rule of law but not, of course, the reality. On a practical level, Navalny was a big fellow and still hale and hearty after his recovery in the Black Forest, so if the judge had ordered the goons into the fish tank before he had finished saying his piece, the odds are he would have fought back and that would not have looked good. So, they let him have his say. Remember, the Western media and his supporters would listen to every word; the Kremlin patsy media would not report a single breath of it. Still, it's a fine speech and an antidote to Putin's poisoning of the Russian soul.

'All of this is weird,' Navalny opens his address. 'So, two people [a police inspector and a prosecutor] sit and decide: let's put Navalny in prison because the first one says: "He came to the police station to report not on Mondays, but on Thursdays." And the second one says: "Let's put Navalny in prison because, after waking up from a coma, he did not send us something on paper." But I would like everyone to pay attention to the fact that they want to imprison me after a trial that has already been recognised as illegal and made up. The European Court of Human Rights is part of the Russian judicial system and its decisions are binding, and after going through all stages of the trial here, I turned to the ECHR, and it issued a decision that there was no crime.

The trial which leaves me here, in this strange cage,' – he eyes the fish tank, mockingly – 'is a fabrication. The Russian government has even recognised this fact, paying me compensation. But, despite this, my brother served three and a half years in prison and I served a year under house arrest. When my probation period ended, I was arrested, brought to court and my sentence extended for another year . . . I have already been found innocent. There is no evidence of a crime. But with the tenacity of a maniac, the state demands that I be imprisoned. Well, no matter what, there is no shortage of criminal cases against me.'

Navalny introduces some sums in the court or, as he puts it, 'a little bit of mathematics'. In December 2014 he got a suspended sentence of three and a half years. That would hang over him until the summer of 2018.

Navalny, his logic biting like a chainsaw into the nonsense of the prosecution case: 'It's now 2021. Someone really did not want me to take a single step in our country as a free person. And we know why. The reason is the hatred and fear of one person who lives in a bunker. Not only did I survive, not only did I not become afraid and run away, I helped investigate my own poisoning. And we proved that Putin tried to kill me. And this drives the little thieving man in his bunker crazy. And his offence lies in the fact that he will go down in history as Vladimir the Poisoner.'

Remember, he is saying this from inside the fish bowl, his life totally at the mercy of prison guards inside a notoriously brutal system ultimately controlled by the man he is condemning so very nakedly.

Lonely are the brave.

The judge rules this out of order.

Navalny: 'Your Honour, this has a direct bearing on this

case. They want to intimidate everyone. The country is impoverished; the people are having to go without. They are trying to silence the people with show trials like this one. To put the frighteners on millions of people. But the big thing I want to say is that this trial will not be accepted by people . . . This is not a demonstration of strength, this is a demonstration of weakness. You can't jail millions. And when they realise, and such a moment will come, you can't lock up the whole country . . . I'm telling everyone, "Don't be afraid!"'

Before he is sent down, he draws a heart on the fish bowl, looks at Yulia, looks away, and then looks back at her with a sheepish expression on his face '*as when the young bird-catcher swept off his tall hat to the Squire's own daughter, /So let the imprisoned larks escape and fly /Singing about her head, as she rode by.*'

That poem by Robert Graves is called 'Love Without Hope'.

Navalny gets two and a half years. Everyone knows that this is just the start, and the show trial play actors will be back on stage, fish tank and all, to lock him away for longer and longer.

Putin's revenge against his tormentor was as cruel as it was entirely predictable. Navalny was sent off to the Pokrov correctional colony or IK-2, in the Vladimir Oblast, about seventy or so miles east of Moscow, infamous for its harsh regime. For a time, he shared a cell with a man who whiled away the midnight hours by masturbating.

Funny peculiar I know, but being banged up with a sexual pervert is a story I have heard before. It brushes against one of Putin's best-known admirers. In 2016, for a BBC *Newsnight* piece about Donald Trump and the Mob, I interviewed

Wayne Barrett, an investigative reporter for New York's *The Village Voice* for thirty-seven years and a great hero of mine. Wayne told me that, on Trump's case for his links with the murderous New Jersey mob, in 1984 he managed to get himself smuggled into the gala opening of a Trump casino in Atlantic City. Many of Trump's security staff were officers of the Atlantic City Police Department, moonlighting. Barrett told me, off camera, that, as a very unwanted guest, he was detained and led away by Trump security, handed over to the ACPD who locked him up for the night, chaining him to a radiator with another prisoner who spent the night masturbating. Perhaps that story never got back to Trump. Perhaps Navalny's ordeal with the masturbator in IK-2 never got back to the Kremlin. All concerned deny any wrongdoing.

Within a month, Navalny complained that he was tortured by sleep deprivation, that his jailers, on the pretext of him being a flight risk, were waking him up eight times a night by shoving a camera in his face. Physically, he started to suffer partial paralysis: 'He has terrible back pain and his right leg is in an awful state. He's losing feeling in it. He can't use his leg,' his faithful lawyer Olga Mikhailova told the Dozhd independent television network, adding: 'Everyone is worried about his life and his health.' Navalny ascribed his pain to a pinched nerve after standing 'crookedly' in cages going to and from court appearances inside police wagons.

In early April, six doctors, including Navalny's personal physician, Anastasia Vasilyeva, and two CNN correspondents, were arrested outside IK-2 when they tried to visit the prisoner whose health was deteriorating. On brand, he announced a hunger strike to ensure proper medical treatment. The goons at Russia's Federal Penitentiary Service rejected his complaints, insisting he had 'all the necessary medical assistance in accordance with his medical symptoms'. Dmitry Peskov chimed in, saying that Navalny was 'responsible for his deeds under the law' and no different from any other Russian, an interesting fairy story but not a true one.

As ever, Navalny was simply asking for the Russian authorities to follow Russian law: 'I have declared a hunger strike demanding that the law be upheld and a doctor of my own choosing be allowed to visit me. I have the right to invite a doctor and receive medication. But they are simply not allowing me to do either. The back pain has spread to my leg. I've lost sensation in parts of my right leg and now the left leg too. Jokes aside, this is getting worrying.' By way of response, the prison authorities had given him two tablets of the painkiller ibuprofen.

Navalny used his Instagram to get this message out. Of course, he was not allowed a phone in prison but, under Russian law, his lawyers were allowed to visit him and when they did so he passed over handwritten notes setting out what was happening to him. It might seem puzzling that these legal visits were permitted but, once again, Putin really does crave legalistic legitimacy and Navalny was facing a whole new slew of legal cases against him and, for form's sake, he had to have legal representation. I also suspect that the Kremlin wanted to know what was going on inside his head and that much or all of the interactions between Navalny and his lawyers were secretly spied on. Cutting off his access to the lawyers would also kill this intelligence-gathering operation.

The paralysis started to spread to his hands. Navalny's lawyers said he had suffered from two spinal disc herniations and had lost feeling in his hands. Agnès Callamard, Secretary General of Amnesty International, accused Putin of

'slowly killing Alexei Navalny through torture and inhu-
mane treatment in prison'.

Somehow, his doctors managed to get hold of a sample of
Navalny's blood which painted a grim picture. In mid-
April, the man who had been as fit as a fiddle in January
was – his personal doctor Anastasia Vasilyeva and three
other doctors, including cardiologist Yaroslav Ashikhmin,
said – in grave danger: 'our patient can die any minute'. The
threat was an increased risk of a fatal cardiac arrest or kidney
failure 'at any moment'. The blood tests showed too high a
level of potassium, which can cause heart attacks, and sharply
elevated creatinine levels, pointing to problems with the
kidneys. A group of brave liberal politicians wrote an open
letter to Putin spelling it out: 'We regard what is happening
to Navalny as an attempt on the life of a politician committed out of personal and political hatred. You, the President
of the Russian Federation, personally bear responsibility for
the life of Alexey Navalny.'

President Joe Biden, US National Security Adviser Jake
Sullivan, Ursula von der Leyen, the President of the European Commission and celebrities like J. K. Rowling and
Jude Law called on the Kremlin to act to save Navalny.
Peskov sneered, but in late April, Navalny was moved out of
IK-2 to a hospital for convicts. Navalny sensing victory, of a
kind, ended his hunger strike. But his agonies inside the
gulag were only going to get worse and worse, ageing him
beyond his years, until the only end of age.

There can never be any doubting Navalny's courage. The
great question is, was he beyond foolish to go back to Russia
in January 2021? The people around him were ferociously
smart. Why didn't they tell him that he was going back to
certain jail time and nigh on certain death? I suspect that

they did. The people closest to him, Yulia, Leonid Volkov, Maria Pevchikh and, at the end, Christo Grozev had no illusions about how cruel, how pitiless Vladimir Putin can be. Telling that story, getting into the detail of the Kremlin's machinery of sadism, had been the life's work of all four of them. If they did warn Navalny, why didn't he listen to them?

Clarissa Ward reflected on this question and the wider relationship between Team Navalny and their leader with me. She had interviewed him for the CNN story on the Poison Squad investigation in Germany in November 2020: 'My first impression of him was that he had a tremendous presence. When he walked into the room, you really could feel his presence, you could feel that he was someone who had such clarity and conviction and self-certainty of his mission and his purpose, which is a relatively unusual thing to see. First of all, he is very charismatic, very disarming, but also remarkably down to earth. So, you have the sense with him almost immediately that you can be quite casual, that you can joke around. And it's a very unusual thing to be able to straddle that degree of certainty of purpose and mission and belief in yourself while also being a relatively grounded, very human, relatable character. And particularly in the Russian context, it's almost unheard of. In Russia, you assert power and authority through force, through formality, not through humour.'

Navalny, face to face, was a different story: 'He didn't have such a level of self-regard that you couldn't joke around immediately and feel comfortable. I've met plenty of people who are charming, charismatic, funny, persuasive, articulate, forceful, but very few of them beneath that also have the courage to get on an aeroplane and go back to certain imprisonment and likely death and do it with grace and with dignity. And with optimism. That is a very unique mindset.'

Exactly like Ward, I found Navalny to be unique, a career-long one-off. Professional pride and a natural abhorrence of Uriah Heepery has always led me to be democratic in my loutishness, challenging figures of power and money whoever they may be, but in Navalny's presence I turned into a teenage groupie.

What did Ward make of the unease in many circles in the West about Navalny's flirtation with the far right back in the day? 'Alexei Navalny was not trying to win over the Davos set, right? He was trying to mobilise and galvanise support from within Russia. You have a limited number of options within the spectrum of the Russian opposition. I don't think it was purely opportunistic but he saw an opening. And he inserted himself there. He grew from that place. He distanced himself from it later. It just comes back to this thing of us only seeing people through the prism of our own values. You have to see people within the context of the system that they're operating in. At the end of the day, he never tried to hide from it. He was open about it. He talked about it. And he was very clear that he answers to the Russian people. I find it sort of ridiculous that we would even seek to judge him or to minimise his courage or his bravery or his self-sacrifice, just because of some stupid stuff he did fifteen years ago to get his foot in the door and build up some support within Russia. It is a deeply racist society. And if he had gone out on the streets and started talking about micro aggressions and white fragility, I can assure you, you never would have even heard of Alexei Navalny.'

Clarissa Ward is on the money. Navalny could be alive

today, working the Western liberal circuit, writing op eds for the *Guardian*, returning to Yale, hanging out in Aspen: 'If you were looking to Navalny to be politically correct, or articulating the kinds of positions that we're used to hearing from Western politicians, then you were missing a trick, and you were misunderstanding what his *raison d'être* was. And I have a lot of respect for that. He wasn't interested in pandering to the West; he could have made a career out of doing the Davos circuit and going to fabulous conventions and parties and flying on private jets and persuading them of how terrible Putin is and how great he is. Instead, he opted to get on a budget airline and be arrested and spend years in a penal colony before being killed. So he is cut from a different cloth.'

If I had been born in Russia, I would, I hope, have wanted to work for the Anti-Corruption Foundation and have been part of Team Navalny. The idea of arguing with him about not returning home, critical, as he saw it, to the great mission of his life, to get the Russian people to overthrow Putin, would be nigh on impossible.

Thinking back to the time with Team Navalny's HQ in 2018, I recalled a degree of respect for the main man which bordered on reverence. Did Ward think that there was something cultish about Team Navalny? 'Cultish is a heavy word. It wasn't like your friends in the Church of Scientology,' – she was joking – 'or anything like that. But they absolutely adored him. They worshipped him. By the way, Navalny could be arrogant, stubborn. If you saw the way he operated with his group, with his closest people, he was the one in charge. But that said, in private, the people closest to him would let him know what they were thinking.'

A screenwriter for the Navalny Hollywood movie 'based

on a real story' biopic might have a female staffer, let's call her Dasha, having a go at him, one-to-one, in an office, the blind down, everyone in the big office pretending not to be listening in:

Staffer: 'You're fucking insane. You will be serving them up what they have wanted all these years, your head on a plate. Don't you dare get on that plane. It's way too early. If, when, they lock you up, we will call for street protests. It's minus 20 degrees in Moscow right now. Don't even think about this.'

Navalny, tense, uncomfortable: 'No, Dasha, this is what I'm doing. Get on board.'

The woman walks out of the office and closes the door behind her, softly. Another staffer catches her eye. She shakes her head.

Many in Team Navalny, I suspect, knew that their hero, the champion of another Russia, was making a brave but terrible mistake.

Navalny's calculation was that Putin would not dare have him killed. But, once he had gone back to Russia and was locked away inside the gulag, two facts changed that materially altered that calculation: one, Western liberalism recalibrated its position on Navalny, selling his stock, making it easier for the Kremlin to have him snuffed out; two, Putin started Russia's big war against Ukraine, blurring focus on the fate of one prisoner so much so that he began to be forgotten, that he was in an oubliette from which there could be no return.

CHAPTER FIFTEEN

'The Cook Likes It Spicy'

Two days after a comatose Alexei Navalny arrived in Germany in August 2020, Yevgeny Prigozhin promised to ruin his Anti-Corruption Foundation and him personally, enforcing a libel suit awarded in a Moscow court for $1.2 million: 'I intend to strip this group of unscrupulous people naked,' adding, 'if Comrade Navalny kicks the bucket, I personally don't intend to go after him in this world.' But if he survived, Prigozhin warned, he would be liable 'according to the full severity of Russian law'.

Prigozhin knew all about that. As bald as a hard-boiled egg, Prigozhin was an ex-con, getting banged up in 1981 for a decade for a nasty street robbery. His Russian was crude and demotic and sometimes darkly funny, him once saying: 'War comes at you hard, like a cock up your arse.'

He became the Kremlin's court jester, but beside the jokes he was, in essence, the psychopath's psychopath, Putin's personal cook and personal sadist, a killer, torturer and hot-dog salesman turned multi-billionaire, troll farm boss and mercenary warlord. So, no surprises that he had no time for the normal human respects due to a desperately ill patient in a coma. Prigozhin was, in fact, just the sort of person that

Team Navalny would poke in the eye with a sharp stick. The Anti-Corruption Foundation published a series of highly damaging and damning investigations into how Prigozhin had cooked so many books feeding Moscow's schoolchildren and then the Russian army that he had ended up with a palace, a private jet, a yacht and a string of multi-billion-rouble Russian state government contracts. The ex-con acquired this immense wealth while making a mockery of Russian laws forbidding monopolies and the awarding of state contracts without proper process, ensuring open and competitive tenders. Instead, companies controlled by Prigozhin or his mother, Violetta, gobbled up state contracts like there was no tomorrow. One such entity got a billion-rouble contract despite registering only a table and a chair as its assets.

For a time in 2023, Prigozhin even threatened Putin's vampire squid-like lock on the Kremlin. The grim truth is that Prigozhin came much, much closer to evicting Putin through force than Navalny ever did via the ballot box. The fact that Prigozhin, a psycho, did so much better than Navalny is a bleak-as-bleak-can-be commentary on the state of Russian democracy and civilisation, or the lack thereof, in the twenty-first century.

Like so many courtiers in Putin's court, Prigozhin came from St Petersburg. He hailed from a good Soviet family, Jewish, but went to the bad very quickly. In 1981, when he was still a teenager, he and his gang mugged a woman, Prigozhin half-strangling her until she lost consciousness, the thieves making off with her purse, earrings and boots from her prone body. Sentenced to thirteen years in prison, Prigozhin celebrated his nineteenth birthday behind bars and many more. At some point in the penal colony, he lost the tip of his left ring finger, maybe due to a fight, but probably because of an industrial accident, the injury making the task of his body double down the track all the more tricky. This detail and more in this chapter, by the way, comes from reporting by Proekt, an independent online Russian news magazine, led by Roman Badanin, one of the most brilliant Russian journalists of his generation. In 2021, I arranged to Zoom him for my podcast *Taking on Putin*, but he didn't pick up. It was only when I glanced at X/Twitter that I saw the reason for the no-show: he had been dragged off to a police station. We did connect eventually for him to talk about his great investigation into Putin's mistresses: Svetlana Krivonogikh (her surname can be roughly translated as 'Lady Crooked Legs') and Alina Kabaeva, the Olympic gymnast. Worried about his safety, Badanin fled Russia and now lives in exile in the United States.

Out of the nick, Prigozhin says he sells hot dogs at the Apraksin Yard market in St Petersburg, then flogs dodgy motors. One unhappy customer was a young Soviet army officer, Andrei Bakonin, just returned from Libya. He used his foreign earnings to buy a used car off Prigozhin only to discover that he'd been sold a pile of junk on wheels. Bakonin and his tough army mates tracked down Prigozhin to his flat, where the young car trader went to his desk and pulled out a wad of notes to settle the dispute. Prigozhin is then taken up by two mid-level gangsters who run a chain of supermarkets and with their help he starts up his first proper business, the Old Customs House restaurant. Foie gras, oysters, strippers not stripping – it's a classy joint – what's not to like? Soon Mayor Sobchak is a fixture, and then along comes the Night Mayor, and the rest is bad history.

Prigozhin becomes Putin's chef. The new president brings

world leaders to the ex-con's New Island restaurant on the former pleasure boat, the Moskva-177, such as Japanese Prime Minister Yoshiro Mori, the French President Jacques Chirac and US President George W. Bush. That's fine and dandy, but Prigozhin must have been providing other services to Putin and his circle because when the ex-con fell out with his old gangster backers, they discovered that he was untouchable. And they were out of pocket.

What other services might Prigozhin have to offer Putin? Intellectual excitement? One of Proekt's sources suggests that Prigozhin hid a real appetite for the life of the mind behind a thuggish sensibility. 'What? Machiavelli? Dick-a-valley!' he once said, riffing on a crude Russian wordplay and the surname of the famous Italian cynic. But he wrote down the name of the philosopher. The source also spotted that a book by Antonio Gramsci popped up on Prigozhin's computer which explained a previous instance when Prigozhin cited the Italian Marxist's thinking on the West's weaponisation of cultural hegemony. The source said: 'He was transforming from a savage to an intellectual savage right before our eyes.'

Another service he provided was spying on his distinguished guests, and they, funnily enough, included Putin himself. Anonymous International got hold of emails from Concord, Prigozhin's firm, which shows a pattern of his waiters spying as they handed out the prawn cocktails and Black Forest gateaux. Or whatever. For example, in 2010, Prigozhin's restaurant staff were bussed in to Putin's Novo-Ogaryovo estate near Moscow when he had a powwow with the lounge lizard crooner and Italian prime minister, the late Silvio Berlusconi. The waiters reported how Putin told Berlusconi that US presidents had to be conformists because of the term limit of eight years. Prigozhin himself took notes of a 2011 natter with Putin, of how the president of Russia ordered Moscow Mayor Sergei Sobyanin and Defence Minister Anatoly Serdyukov to order the cook's ready-to-eat meal packs from his factory outside St Petersburg. Once again, I have fiddled with the translation.

Putin: 'I spoke to Sergei [Sobyanin, Mayor of Moscow]. He's in a good mood. He says that the main thing is that you keep going.'

Prigozhin: 'I am. He's really doing everything, and next year he's giving me all three hundred schools.'

Putin: 'What are the problems there then?'

Prigozhin: 'Vladimir Vladimirovich, the whole system is based on graft, and a lot of people are in it up to their eyeballs, so there's a load of shenanigans going on.'

Putin: 'And you stopped the racket. Good on you.'

Prigozhin notes: *Putin laughs and claps him on the arm.*

Prigozhin: 'Yes, at first, I stopped the racket, but now I'm giving them a little bit of the action, just for the time being. You know, I thought I'd calculated everything, but I didn't take the main thing into account. It's just how much the system fights you.'

There's a similar riff with Prigozhin moaning about graft at the Ministry of Defence, with Putin egging him on. Another time, Prigozhin delivered a cake and champagne for a birthday party in the Kremlin for Dmitry 'Dima' Peskov, Putin's mullet-haired PR man, thrown by 'The Boss':

Prigozhin notes: *I brought out the champagne and cut the cake.*

Putin: 'Does it taste good?'

Prigozhin: 'Yes, I think so.'

Putin: 'And who made it, was it you?'

Prigozhin: 'Yes, it was my cooks.'

Putin: 'Playing it safe, huh?'

Prigozhin notes: *He laughed.*

Putin, to everyone: 'I asked him, the cake, was it yours? And he said it was his cooks. Well done, he played it safe.'

What a jolly little tyrant Putin is, joking about a cake not being poisoned. The truth is that the hacked Concord emails don't give us a deep insight into the relationship between Putin and Prigozhin. The chef is far too sly to put down what he really thinks in an email. But compared to what happened at the end, these were indeed happier times. The best takeaway from them is that Putin runs his machinery of fear by having a number of machines smashing into each other, to see who comes out on top. It is government by *Robot Wars*, the British TV show first compered by Jeremy Clarkson, then Craig Charles, where toy robots play gladiators against each other.

The stand-out service Prigozhin provided to Vladimir Putin was the provision of violence. Proekt gives us a clue to Prigozhin's true character by publishing a photograph, found framed in his house. The soil is cracked, bone-dry, and on it rest the freshly severed heads of seven Africans. The blood on the ground is still bright red so the cutting off of heads happened shortly before the photograph was taken. The fact Prigozhin got this photo framed and placed it in his home is clear evidence that he was a psychopath. Over time, he worked his way up to become the master of the St Petersburg bot farms and the head of the Wagner mercenary army, the latter almost certainly responsible for the severed heads shot. But one thing is consistent: Prigozhin loved to hurt people.

In the early 2000s, Prigozhin started building a naff palace of his own, modestly titled the 'Northern Versailles'. Proekt reported that two workers fitting windowsills, cheated of their due, some 200,000 roubles, complained to Prigozhin. He listened to their story, 'then called security to beat the shit out of them. Then they were dragged out of the office and into the basement where they fucked them up one more time,' Proekt was told by a source. Prigozhin ruled through 'fear and money' said another source. People who worked for him knew that if you made a mistake, they would literally 'cut your balls off' or 'kick you down the stairs'. Once, the story goes, a chauffeur irritated Prigozhin so much by driving too slowly that he kicked him in the head, no mean feat in a car, however spacious the limousine might be. In 2004, Prigozhin found that a 25-year-old man, Dmitry Sokolov, had gatecrashed his floating restaurant after a nearby corporate party. 'The Chief' – Prigozhin – beat up the gatecrasher so badly that when he fell into the water, he drowned.

Oftentimes, the violence would be franchised out to minions. One Prigozhin employee 'misbehaved' at a business meeting, then vanished. Two weeks later, he reappeared, covered in fading, yellowing bruises. His story was that he had been taken down to the basement and beaten severely over several days by another employee known as 'The Teacher'.

In late October 2018, extraordinary evidence of Prigozhin's methods surfaced in a brilliant piece of investigative journalism called 'The Cook Likes It Spicy' by Denis Korotkov in *Novaya Gazeta*. A wall-eyed Prigozhin hitman, 61-year-old Valery Amelchenko, walked in and spilled the beans. He was thin, elderly, sipped apple juice and detailed his part in a string of kidnappings, tortures and murders at the behest of the Prigozhin organisation, several of which targeted people in or close to Team Navalny. Amelchenko did not work directly for Prigozhin but a sub-contractor, Andrey Mikhailov, who, in turn, reported to Yevgeny Gulyaev, a former Interior Ministry operative who was Prigozhin's head of security.

One day, Amelchenko called to say that he was being followed by mystery characters, one of them in a Panama hat.

And then a passer-by answered his phone, explaining that he had just picked it up on the floor. The journalists hurried around to the spot and found, lying on the ground, a second phone and a single shoe just like the pair Amelchenko was wearing when they had last met him. Where was the missing shoe? And its owner?

When Korotkov from *Novaya Gazeta* started asking questions of Prigozhin's security people, he got two unusual answers: one, a funeral wreath decorated by a photo of the reporter; two, a basket, and in it the severed head of a sheep.

Korotkov had checked out Amelchenko's stories and found him never to have told a lie. *Novaya Gazeta* went ahead and published, still not knowing what had happened to their source or why, exactly, he had come clean or where his other shoe was.

In 2013, the hitman said that he had been sent down to Sochi on the Black Sea to rough up Anton Grishchenko, a blogger from Sochi who 'wrote bad things about Putin'. To make a living, the blogger flogged second-hand car parts. Under a fake pretext of buying a gasket for a Mercedes, or whatever, Amelchenko said he left the blogger with a broken collarbone and the blog died. Korotkov checked the story out and found that Grishchenko had indeed tweeted a crude caricature of Putin by a French satirical newspaper and that, shortly afterwards, the blogger's social media accounts had been wiped. Amelchenko next turned up in Kyiv in late 2013 and early 2014. 'How come?' asked the reporter. 'I'm not rich enough to travel there on my own initiative,' came the gnomic reply. His boss, Mikhailov, suggested to the newspaper that Amelchenko was funding fake 'demonstrations' in favour of the corrupt and murderous Yanukovych regime. From 2014 to 2016, Amelchenko worked mostly in Ukraine, including in the Russian-occupied 'Luhansk People's Republic'. He hinted at using a 9-millimetre PB 'silencer pistol' in a 'talk' with a man he knew as 'Plotnitsky's right hand' in a stairwell of a nine-storey apartment block. Dmitry Karagaev, a personal aide to Igor Plotnitsky, then the leader of the Luhansk People's Republic, was found on the second floor of a stairwell in a Luhansk block of flats on 16 March 2016. He had been shot dead.

That summer, Amelchenko's group went to Pskov, a city in Russia's far west, just across the border from Estonia. One of Amelchenko's partners and a friend was Oleg Simonov, originally from the Amur region in the far east of Russia, just above China. Simonov was a trained pharmacist and, it turned out, a likely poisoner. The target was a blogger whose name Amelchenko could not remember. But he did tell Korotkov that there was a garage at the target's address on Fomina Street, Pskov; on the wall of the garage was a painted billboard for a glazier's with a phone number. Amelchenko was hazy as to who did the actual poisoning. His job was to watch the area; Simonov was 'to drive the getaway car'. The blogger was injected and fell ill.

To prove job done, a few days later, Amelchenko phoned the number on the garage. The blogger's son picked up the phone and said: 'Daddy died.'

That wasn't enough. Amelchenko phoned back a second

time and found where the blogger was buried. He then went to the cemetery and photographed the gravestone.

In Pskov, reporters found the house on Fomina Street with 'Glaziers' painted on the wall and a telephone number. They found that a blogger, Sergey Tikhonov, who wrote under the pseudonym 'Skobars' had died 'of a heart attack' on 29 June 2016. His death had not been seen as suspicious so there had been no investigation.

That November, Sergey Mokhov was attacked. At that time, he was the husband of Lyubov Sobol, the lawyer for the Anti-Corruption Foundation and its primary investigator into Prigozhin's rackets. That evening, Mokhov, the publisher of a magazine called *The Archaeology of Russian Death*, was on his way home when he passed by a young man with a beard standing at the entrance of his Moscow apartment block, holding a bouquet of flowers. Mokhov felt a sharp sting in his leg, after which he started to have a fit. He was rushed to hospital and eventually recovered.

Mokhov and Sobol were, at first, unsure as to the motives of the attacker. Mokhov suspected the attack could have been related to his work, as he had previously written stories about the gangsters who run rackets, charging grieving relatives over-the-top prices for funerals. Sobol thought that the poisoning was Prigozhin's revenge. At the time, Navalny thought that the most likely explanation, adding that he 'can't be 100 per cent sure that Prigozhin and his people are behind the attack'.

The image of the bouquet poisoner was caught by CCTV, but his identity was a mystery for two years until an anonymous source led reporters to the likely Pskov poisoner, Oleg Simonov. Simonov had died in the summer of 2017, six months after the poisoning attempt on Sobol's husband, in fishy circumstances. Simonov did not do drugs but was found dead in a bathtub, cause of death: drug overdose.

By tracking Simonov's contacts, Korotkov came across Amelchenko. The hitman was not at all happy with the official story of how Simonov, a good friend, had died and signed a deal with the reporter saying that if anything untoward happened to him, they could publish. When he vanished, leaving only one shoe and two phones, Korotkov pressed the 'publish' button.

On the Mokhov poisoning, Amelchenko explained that one of the tools of Simonov's trade was a veterinary tranquiliser dart. Amelchenko told Korotkov how Simonov tracked his target: '[Mokhov] used to go to some gym in the evenings . . . [Simonov] followed him for several days . . . he said he had bought a bouquet of flowers and waited for him outside his house. His task . . . was simply to seriously scare the guy. He pricked him with some medicine . . . [Mokhov] came up and said [to Simonov], "Are you waiting [for someone]" . . . [Simonov responded] "I am. I've been waiting. Nothing personal." Then he pricked him, threw the flowers away and left.'

Amelchenko confirmed that he was not a player in the job against Mokhov and had only heard the story secondhand from Simonov. The goal? To scare both Mokhov and his wife, the Anti-Corruption Foundation lawyer.

In February 2017, Korotkov reported, Amelchenko flew to Syria with Simonov and four others in the Prigozhin organisation, their mission to test poisons on unsuspecting prisoners. They flew to Beirut where they were met by Lebanese Mukhabarat military intelligence service, who took them to Damascus. There, they connected with soldiers from Prigozhin's Wagner Army who were helping Syrian dictator Bashar Al Assad kill off democracy in the country. The group's task, in Amelchenko's words, was to test various poisonous substances on 'prisoners of war' captured by the Syrians, perhaps Islamic State militants or other fighters.

Things went wrong from the get-go. 'They just threw us into Syria,' said Amelchenko. 'They said, "You'll have prisoners, they're waiting for you. Go." Then, when there turned out to be no prisoners, they phoned us . . . and said, "Do what you want . . . It's easier to leave you there than to get you out . . . If there are no prisoners there, then try it out on whoever you want."

'Eventually we were disguised as military prosecutors. And there was a militia there . . . guys who didn't want to fight at all. Freaks. We interrogated them through a translator. Or rather, we pretended to interrogate them . . . [really just] asking them why they refused [to fight],' remembers Amelchenko.

In Homs, Simonov handed out local Syrian fruit juice in sealed glass bottles to the conscientious objectors. Amelchenko did not know what happened to the men, but after the Poison Squad left Homs, a high-ranking Syrian Mukhabarat officer was fatally poisoned, or so he heard. Did the spook drink the poison juice by mistake, not knowing what it really was? Another Russian Wagner officer also fell ill, suffering fits of vomiting and diarrhoea, but recovered.

Shades of Moscow4, Moscow4. The story of how the Prigozhin poisoners killed a Syrian secret police chief by mistake is a classic of the genre, proving, once again, just how moronic some of the operatives of Russia dark state are or were.

Korotkov tracked down Simonov's widow, who confirmed

that it was her late husband with the poison bouquet on the CCTV and, looking back, that he had been clearly up to no good. Twice, he had left St Petersburg without explaining what he was doing. The first was shortly after they met, the second time when Amelchenko said he was with him in Syria.

Simonov's widow said that it was only after his death that she began to understand that she 'didn't know the person she had lived with'. The journalists showed her some photos. One of them was of Amelchenko. 'Ah, yes,' she said, 'that man came to the funeral.'

Three days after Amelchenko's story was published, he resurfaced to deny everything he had told Korotkov and accuse the reporter of making up the whole thing, then vanished again and has not been seen or heard of since.

There is one more name I wish to add to the roll call of people who had fallen foul of Putin's cook. Max Borodin was a 32-year-old reporter in Yekaterinburg who called up a pal in April 2018, and told him: 'There was someone with a gun on my balcony and people in camouflage and masks on the staircase landing.' Later, his pal got a text saying that he'd got it all wrong. A day later, his corpse was found on the ground. He'd fallen out of the window of his fifth-floor apartment, drunk.

Or had he?

The Wagner Army, named after Hitler's favourite composer, didn't just cut off the heads of Africans. Prigozhin picked Dmitry Utkin, who had Nazi SS flashes tattooed on his collarbones, to lead it. They fought in Ukraine and also operated in Syria, trying to capture oil wells from the anti-Assad, anti-Russian Free Syrian Army. In February 2018, around two hundred Russian mercenaries were killed by

American bombs after they had been warned to stop advancing. Some of the dead Wagner mercenaries came from near Yekaterinburg, Borodin's beat. Wagner widow Elena Matveyeva called up her late husband's unit commander on the phone: 'In one battalion there were two hundred people killed right away. We only had AK-47s, nothing in the way of anti-aircraft weapons. They beat us, they gave us hell. The Yanks said, "Russians, we're coming." '

The Wagner commander didn't know that Borodin was videotaping the call. Borodin's story set out the evidence that the generals in charge of the mercenaries had been criminally incompetent to advance having been warned not to by the Americans. I believe that Borodin did not fall out of his window but was pushed by the Wagner Army and I dedicated my novel about Stalin's great famine of 1933, *The Useful Idiot*, to his memory.

Amelchenko is probably dead now but nevertheless he provided an insight into the real Russia that Team Navalny was fighting: poorly paid and often incompetent low-lifes crippling or killing people for slights that in the West, political actors would just accept as part of the rough and tumble of ordinary democratic politics. Insights, too, into how petty Prigozhin and Putin could be when it came to taking revenge on those who mocked them. Sergey Tikhonov, the blogger in Pskov, was so below the radar that no one, as far as I can tell, publicly said that he might have been murdered. It was only the poisoner's accomplice, Amelchenko, who alerted the world to the poisoning after the fact. How many other Russians are out there who have said: 'Daddy's dead' without knowing the truth?

Remember Vladimir Ivanyutenko, the St Petersburg street cleaner, who was tasered, then stabbed because he used to go to demonstrations wearing a Vladimir Putin mask? He told me in early 2018 that he knew why he was attacked: 'I can only connect it with my opposition activities.'

When Korotkov's article in *Novaya Gazeta* appeared, Ivanyutenko recognised one of the two men who had attacked him: Amelchenko. When he started to get vocal about this, Ivanyutenko was tried and convicted for his part in an assassination plot to bomb Prigozhin, using a remote-controlled car carrying the explosives under the cook's limo, and sentenced to three years in prison. Ivanyutenko said that he was framed by a police agent provocateur. If so, all of this – the stabbing, the tasering, the prison time – all because he had the temerity to wear a Vladimir Putin mask.

One is left in awe of Alexei Navalny, Lyubov Sobol, Denis Korotkov, Roman Badanin, Max Borodin, Vladimir Ivanyutenko, Sergey Tikhonov, Anton Grishchenko and all the others for daring to challenge the cook and his master. There is another Russia and too many of the names of its heroes are written in blood.

CHAPTER SIXTEEN

Big War, Little Clout

In the summer of 2021, Russia's two tsars wrote two very different tracts. The tsar in the Kremlin knocked out a very long and very boring bad history essay, 'On the Historical Unity of Russians and Ukrainians', setting out his reasons why Russian fascist imperialism was tinkerty-tonk. The tsar in the gulag wrote a much shorter, far funnier piece on bits of paper smuggled out through his lawyers about the failure of the free world to fight corruption and what that failure could lead to. The tragedy was that Putin used his D– homework to justify his murderous big war the following February against Ukraine while the West, sensing that Navalny's clout was weakening by the day, ignored his A++ message, wise and true though it was.

Life is too short to wade through Putin's legalistic guff, but I have attached a link to it in the Notes section of this book for intellectual masochists, insomniacs and others who want to read it in full. The gist of it is that the compact made in 1945, that nations should not seek to invade other nations to seize their land, is secondary to the brotherly love imposed by Russia on Ukraine. That Russian fascism conquers all. My advice is that if you can't sleep, read *The Code of the*

Woosters by P. G. Wodehouse. Aunt Dahlia nicking Pop Bassett's cow-creamer is genuinely funny; reading about how in 1918 'Hetman Pavlo Skoropadskyi was brought to power, proclaiming the Ukrainian State instead of the Ukrainian People's Republic, which was essentially a German protectorate' makes your teeth ache.

Navalny's essay is a different kettle of trout. It's rather good. Once again, I've fiddled with the translation in a few places. As ever it starts punchily and keeps on punching: 'Exactly one year ago, I did not die from poisoning by a chemical weapon, and corruption played no small part in my survival. Having contaminated Russia's state system, corruption has also contaminated the intelligence services. When a country's senior management is preoccupied with protection rackets and extortion from businesses, the quality of covert operations inevitably suffers. A group of FSB agents applied the nerve agent to my underwear just as shoddily as they incompetently dogged my footsteps for three and a half years – in violation of all instructions from above – allowing civil investigating activists to expose them at every turn.'

Nice.

Navalny goes on to protest that the fight against corruption plays second fiddle to the 'big agenda' issues the great leaders ostentatiously battle with: 'wars, poverty, migration, the climate crisis, weapons of mass destruction'. Navalny then delivers his knockout blow: 'Amazingly enough, though, corruption nearly always merits a mention when the world's leaders are describing failures – whether their own or, more commonly, those of their predecessors. We spent years, hundreds of billions of dollars and thousands of human lives in Iraq (or Afghanistan, you name it) – but the corrupt government of al-Maliki (or Karzai, you name them) alienated the people with its thieving, opening the path to victory for radicals armed with slogans about honest, fair government and RPGs. This leads to an obvious question. Guys, if corruption is preventing us from finding solutions to the problems of the "big agenda", has the time perhaps come to raise it to a priority on that agenda?'

Navalny riffs on a powwow with Putin on the issue of corruption: 'The richest leader in the world, who has fleeced his own country, is being invited to discuss how to deal with the problem of himself. Very tricky, very awkward.'

From his prison cell in IK-2, Navalny was able to watch Russian state TV and that summer, the West's retreat from Afghanistan and the return of the Taliban was the Kremlin's favourite story: 'It is precisely the fact that the West "failed to notice" the absolute corruption in Afghanistan that Western leaders preferred not to talk about a topic they found embarrassing, which was the most crucial factor in the victory of the Taliban (with the support of the population). The West did not want to discuss the plundering of the budget; it was much better to focus on people being stoned to death or execution by beheading.'

Navalny argues that after the fall of the Berlin Wall and the implosion of the USSR, corruption – its classical definition, 'the exploitation of an official position for personal gain' – became the universal, ideology-free basis 'for the flourishing of a new Authoritarian International, from Russia to Eritrea, Myanmar to Venezuela'.

His overarching point is that dark money drives dark politics: 'Religious extremists of all stripes find it easier to conduct propaganda when their opponents are driving Rolls-Royces through the streets of penniless countries.

Migration crises are caused by poverty, and poverty is almost always caused by corruption.'

Where the West needs to pay attention is that the tsunami of corruption in the poor countries is washing into and being washed by the rich: 'An important aspect of corruption in authoritarian countries is the use it makes of the West's financial infrastructure – and in 90 per cent of cases, what has been stolen is banked in the West.'

Too true. Navalny sets out five steps that the West must take.

One, identify groups of countries that are peculiarly prey to corruption.

Two, enforce transparency: 'You work for a state-owned company in a country at high risk of corruption and want to buy a villa on the French Riviera? Fine, go ahead, but you should know that all the information about the deal will be publicly available.'

Three, sanction oligarchs: 'Any anti-corruption rhetoric from the West will be perceived as game-playing and hot air . . . At present, alas, the Western establishment acts like Pavlov's dog: you show them a colonel of the intelligence services and they yell, "Sanction him!"; you show them the oligarch paying the colonel, and they yell, "Invite him to Davos!"'

Four, jail the corrupt: 'Guess how many cases have been brought following reports by our Anti-Corruption Foundation?' he asks. 'That's right: none.' He goes on: 'The sad fact is that even Western law enforcement agencies treat corrupt foreign officials with kid gloves. With a little political will on the part of the government (and pressure from public opinion) that situation can be put right.'

Five, create an international anti-corruption commission:

'By investing relatively small sums of money, Putin is buying up extreme-right and extreme-left movements throughout Europe, turning their politicians into his creatures. Legalised bribery is flourishing, often in the form of board memberships at state-owned companies. A former German Chancellor [Gerhard Schroder], or a former Italian prime minister [Silvio Berlusconi], or a former Austrian foreign minister [Karin Kneissl], can act as strippers for the Russian dictator, normalising corrupt practices. All contracts linking former or current Western politicians with business partners from corrupt authoritarian countries should also have to be open to public scrutiny.'

Summing up, he says: 'No money, no soldiers, no reconfiguration of industry or world politics are needed in order to start taking action.'

The problem was that Navalny was locked away in IK-2 and his clarion call fell on deaf ears. Meanwhile, the Kremlin had declared the Anti-Corruption Foundation an extremist organisation, like Al Qaeda. Team Navalny headed for the hills, well, Lithuania, the United States and the United Kingdom. Navalny's candle did not die out exactly but it had started to flicker.

As early as February 2021, one month after his return to Russia and immediate arrest, Amnesty International stripped Navalny of his prior 'prisoner of conscience' status after it says it was 'bombarded' with complaints highlighting xenophobic comments that the man – who some said was 'a vile white supremacist' – had made in the past and had not renounced. The moment that happened, a huge row broke out as the Russian branch of Amnesty argued that head office in London was being played by the Kremlin's bot farms. One of the people who had been calling for

Navalny's status as a prisoner of conscience to be revoked was Katya Kazbek, a pseudo name for a 'feminist, LGBT researcher and citizen of the world'. Funnily enough, some of her previous posts had praised Stalin. Fancy that. Others echoed Kremlin fairy tales. Amnesty HQ had failed to smell a rat and, after a bit, reversed their foolishness, re-recognising him as a prisoner of conscience.

In October 2021, Navalny suffered a crueller blow when his team's hopes that he would win the Nobel Peace Prize were dashed when it was jointly awarded to Maria Ressa, a brilliant and richly deserving Filipino human rights activist, and Dmitri Muratov, the editor of *Novaya Gazeta*. Muratov was a great editor and seven of the paper's reporters had been murdered, but as time passed, *Novaya Gazeta* seemed to many Russia-watchers to be a little too accommodating of the Kremlin. Navalny was tougher, braver, had been poisoned and had returned to dare Putin to have him killed. The Amnesty revocation and the Nobel snub felt like too many comfortable people worrying, as they walked with their flat white to the break-out area, that by standing full square by troublemaker Navalny they might get criticised. Better him suffer horribly than they suffer performative abuse. When the Nobel decision came out, I remember thinking that this is the kind of thing the jellyfish at BBC management would have done. There can be no greater insult.

To be fair to Muratov, he told a press conference in Moscow that Navalny should have won the gong: 'If I had been on the Nobel Peace Prize committee, I would have voted for the person whom the bookmakers bet on. I mean Alexei Navalny.' But the damage was done. I suspect that Putin treasured the moral failures by Amnesty and the

Nobel committee, and that it made his decision to have Navalny snuffed out all the easier.

And that, in the fullness of time, is what Putin proceeded to do.

On 24 February 2022, Russia sent its heavy metal to seize Ukraine and the plight of the other tsar became less and less of a story.

That same day, while being tried for new junk fraud charges, that he had embezzled his own Anti-Corruption Foundation and insulted the dignity of a judge, Navalny managed to get his thoughts on the big war into the trial papers: 'I am against the war,' he said, adding that Putin and his bellicose supporters were 'gangsters and thieves . . . The war between Russia and Ukraine is being waged to cover up theft from the Russian people and divert their attention from the real problems that exist inside the country . . . [The war would] lead to a huge number of victims, destroy futures and continue the impoverishment of the Russian people.'

For Ukrainian critics of Navalny, his reaction to the big war was good, no, excellent, but in the middle of the country's existential battle for its survival, what he had to say got nothing like the coverage of Crimea being like a sausage sandwich back in the day. When he had been wrong, he was standing in the spotlight; when he was right, he was in the wings, cast in gloom, the audience's attention horrified by what was going on centre stage.

The Kremlin kept on cranking up the pressure. The fraud charges carried with them an extra ten to fifteen years in prison. They alleged that he had stolen £3.5 million or $4.7 million and insulted a judge to boot. But the evidence against him was – how can I put this diplomatically? – a crock of shit. One of the key witnesses against him was Fyodor Gorozhanko, a junior member of Team Navalny, who when it came to the crunch refused to testify against his boss, saying that he had been 'pressured' by the prosecution to say what they wanted to hear. He told the court that Navalny had followed the law and that the charges against him were absurd: 'Despite the fact that I am a witness for the prosecution, I act as a witness for the defence. I believe that Navalny spoke in accordance with the law as it stands.'

Before the trial, Gorozhanko had leaked a list of Navalny's supporters registered on his website. What had started out as a stupid quarrel with the team led to him being targeted by the prosecution. Gorozhanko, at great risk to himself, discovered his true moral compass before it was too late. But the frame was in place and Navalny was always going to be found guilty. What is striking is that even this late in the day, his personal charisma could still turn a prosecution witness.

In March 2022, when the Battle of Kyiv was at its height, Navalny was found guilty of fraud and contempt of court and given nine years. Amnesty International called the trial a 'sham'. In May he was hit with new charges, that he was an 'extremist' and they carried a possible further fifteen years in prison. The following month he was moved from IK-2 to IK-6, another harsh penal colony in the Vladimir Oblast, roughly one hundred miles further east of Moscow, not far from the town of Melekhovo. Why the move? What is weird about prisons is that the prison officers also get locked up, hour after hour, day after day, with the prisoners. They hate some inmates; and some, over time, they grow to admire, even love. This is what happened to William Joyce, Lord Haw-Haw, in the last few weeks before his hanging in

1946 at Wandsworth nick in London, to Nelson Mandela in Robben Island, to Saddam Hussein under American captivity in Iraq. If Navalny's electricity could have a striking effect on an old hoofer like me or a sassy journalism star like Clarissa Ward, the same would be true of the jailers at IK-2. All the Kremlin's spy cameras and audio tapes spooling in the gloom couldn't alter the fact that on a human level Navalny was funny, upbeat, brave. I can't prove it but suspect he might have got moved because the surveillance on him revealed he had won over his day-to-day jailers. Some day, the truth may out.

IK-6 is bleak. Navalny described conditions in his tiny dog kennel isolation cell, where he spent the vast majority of his time, how small it was, how cold, a puddle of water on the floor, airless, hardly any ventilation: 'The iron bunk is fastened to the wall. The handle that lowers it is on the outside. At 5am, they take away your mattress and pillow and raise the bunk. At 9pm they lower the bunk again and give you back the mattress. Iron table, iron bench, sink, hole in the floor. There are two cameras under the ceiling.'

Four years before, *Novaya Gazeta* had carried a long piece about the grim fate of Gor Hovakimyan, aged thirty-three. He had got eight years for 'drug trafficking' but he denied it and kept on writing complaints, objecting to his verdict. The prison authorities at IK-6 hated him for that. His sister, Anya Simonyan, wrote a letter describing how he would normally call his mother once a month from a prison payphone but had been unusually quiet: 'There was no news for a long time. We were very worried. Mum panicked; she had a premonition. On the evening of 11 July, we called the prison, and they told us that he was alive and well. They said: "What could possibly happen to him?" But my mother was very worried and in the morning she and my brother went to the prison and asked for a meeting. And then they were told that he had died on 6 July, that is six days before. The colony had not told us, the family, about his death. The day we arrived at the prison turned out to be the last day when the body could be removed. They wanted to hide my brother's death. After seven days, they can declare the corpse unclaimed and simply bury it. This is what they had planned. If we had come a day later, they would have told us: "Sorry, your son is dead and buried." '

The prison authorities said that a prosecutor had been present at the autopsy and that no crime had taken place. The body was already in the city morgue in Vladimir. The family made a video of the corpse: 'There are puncture wounds under the armpit from a stun gun, fingers and toes are broken, the genitals are torn, there is a huge bruise on the thigh, a huge black scar on the lower back, all the buttocks are covered in puncture wounds from the stun gun . . . Only the face is untouched. At the morgue we asked for the autopsy report, but they didn't give it to us. They said that the prosecutor and the pathologist had signed it. The cause of death was double pneumonia.' Anya's brother had been a healthy young man.

The family recorded a conversation with the pathologist on video.

Georg Hovakimyan, brother: 'He died of pneumonia?'

Pathologist: 'He died of pneumonia.'

Georg: 'And these wounds, the bruises, the scars?'

Pathologist: 'Well, I don't know, but he died of double pneumonia.'

Georg: 'Come on. These wounds didn't happen of their own accord. Look at them.'

Georg Hovakimyan said that before his death, his brother had told him that he had been targeted by the authorities because he would not conform: 'My brother was in this prison for four years, out of an eight-year sentence. We were supposed to have a long visit once every four months and shorter visits too, but in four years, only one visit was allowed. When we asked him why they didn't let him have more visits, he said that "they allow them for those who work for the administration and help them. But I don't cooperate with them, so they beat me and don't give me visits." They constantly put him in the cooler, in solitary confinement. They would beat him up and send him to the cooler.'

Gor once told his brother that previously he had been beaten with the buckle of an army belt on his genitals. His corpse 'had injuries to the groin. The pathologist wrote that there was "redness and dry, parched skin" on the genitals. But he didn't write anything about the fact that the genitals were swollen. Gor once said that they had put an empty steel bucket on his head, put a speaker into the bucket from below and turned on the music, loud, deafening him. They had also sprayed CS gas into the bucket so that he couldn't breathe. They also handcuffed his hands behind his back, and then hung him from bars as if from a rack for ten, twelve hours. Why did they do all this to him? Because he refused to cooperate with the administration, to frame someone.'

Officially, Gor had received his injuries in a fight with a fellow prisoner although, of course, his face was untouched. He had been sent to the punishment cell, got his feet wet and died of pneumonia. The family suffered threats if they dared to continue with their campaign.

This, then, was IK-6. This was Navalny's new home.

Team Navalny published a photo of him taking part in a

video conference to a court hearing around this time. The two standout observations are that the shot from the prison is green: green light, green shadow, green face; and that all the fat has gone from his face and he looks dangerously thin, the skin of his cheekbones taut, his neck standing apart from his prison clothes. They were starving him, no question.

Even so, his Twitter feed kept on poking the Kremlin crocodile in the eye with a stick. On 7 September 2022, his team tweeted a thread from his account after receiving notes smuggled out of IK-6 via his lawyers:

'1/7 Whoa, I've just hit the jackpot. As soon as I got out of the SHU [solitary confinement cell], they sent me back there for another fifteen days and labelled me as a "persistent offender".

'2/7 This means that I will now be placed under STRICT conditions inside a STRICT regime penal colony. I wonder if these conditions will be closer to those of Hannibal Lecter or those of Magneto from X-Men . . .' This tweet was illustrated by photos of the aforesaid cannibal and the shape-shifter.

'3/7 In short, the Kremlin's reaction to me not "settling down", continuing to call for sanctions against Putin's elite (the 6,000 list), and announcing once again the "Smart Voting" so hated by them, was predictable.' Team Navalny had called on people to vote for any party but United Russia.

'4/7 I hope our tsar was yelling: "Let him rot, let him rot!" and throwing stuff at his courtiers.

'5/7 By the way, you gotta admire the pettiness of these crooks. My wife and parents had been waiting for a visit to me for four months, and now it's coming up, and they're moving me to strict conditions, where visits are only allowed every six months. Tough luck for me.

'6/7 Well, I guess my starship was attacked by some nasty monsters. It got damaged, and in order to survive I have to move to a tiny surviving compartment, where there'll be less food and more cold, but also more time for thinking. Maybe I'll think of something interesting 😊

'7/7 By the way, here's what occurred to me. It seems that only two of the political prisoners in Putin's Russia have been recognized as "persistent violators" so far. The second one is me. And the first was my brother Oleg. What a family we have.'

The next day he was sentenced to yet more time in the cooler because he was held to be such a bad prisoner.

His energy, his enterprise, his level of activity considering where he was is, in hindsight, amazing. That summer, Navalny launched the Anti-Corruption Foundation International as a non-Russian organisation, thus avoiding the 'extremist' label stuck to its former iteration by the Russian state. His international advisers included his wife Yulia Navalnaya, the former Belgian Prime Minister Guy Verhofstadt, the historian Anne Applebaum and the futurologist and writer, Francis Fukuyama. The new foundation's start-up cash would be the $50,000 he won for the Sakharov Prize.

The 6,000 list was an even stronger poke in the crocodile's eye. Team Navalny set out the names of '6,000 bribe takers and warmongers' who it says enabled Russian President Vladimir Putin's illegal invasion of Ukraine. Volkov posted on Twitter that the 6,000 list unmasks: 'The ones who started the war. Those who helped Putin usurp power. Those who financed the war. The ones who stole' and 'those who repressed the dissenters' against the Kremlin.

The list categorises Putin's useful idiots in Russia under sections, some of which are headed: 'warmongers', 'propagandists', 'corrupt officials' and 'organizers of political repression'. Volkov added that the list's goal 'is to make Putin toxic'.

The Navalnyites saw that just picking on a handful of well-known oligarchs would not cut the mustard. To really challenge corruption, to stop the war, Volkov explained that 'it is important that we also list many middle-ranking criminals, those who are proud of their ability to operate below the radar. They thought their role in turning Putinism into a fascist dictatorship would go unnoticed. Well, they were wrong.'

If people on the list thought they had been wronged, all they had to do was renounce Satan, sorry, Putin. Navalny chipped in from his dog kennel prison cell: 'My space flight is taking a bit longer than expected. The ship is caught in a time loop.'

In November 2022, Navalny posted that he was now in permanent solitary confinement because of his repeated rule breaking. The rules he broke included 'not buttoning his collar', 'not cleaning the prison yard properly' and 'not addressing a prison official correctly' – an unbelievably harsh punishment for a mistake of no consequence.

The starvation diet, the throttling of privileges, the meanness of his concrete dog kennel home made him a sick man. In January 2023, it came out that Navalny was seriously ill with flu in solitary confinement and his lawyers were not allowed to give him basic medicine. More than four hundred doctors signed an open letter to Putin, calling on the president to 'stop the abuse' of the leader of the Russian opposition. A few weeks later, he was transferred to an isolated punishment cell: conditions, for him, got crueller and crueller.

In early August 2023, Navalny was tried in a closed-doors court, found guilty and sentenced to a further nineteen years in a 'special regime' colony on charges including publicly inciting extremist activity, financing extremist activity, and 'rehabilitating Nazi ideology'. On brand, Navalny posted that he had expected to get a 'Stalinist' sentence and wasn't taken aback by the fact that he would be freed in December 2038.

But throughout all of this time, very little of what was happening to Navalny was getting anything like the traction it would have received just a few years before. The war in Ukraine was the big story. And that summer, for the Russian audience at least, an even bigger story broke. The Wagner Army had been fighting furiously hard to 'liberate' the town of Bakhmut in Ukraine's east, most of its soldiers cannon fodder from Russia's prisons, seduced out of jail by Prigozhin himself. Fight on the front for six months, the country's murderers, rapists and thieves were told, and you would become a free man. For the most part, the convict-soldiers were used as mincemeat, thrown into battle to exhaust the Ukrainians' ammunition and, when the time was right, long-serving Wagner Army people would press home their advantage. As the war ground on, Prigozhin became increasingly furious that the Russian Ministry of Defence was corrupt, incompetent and not giving his Wagner soldiers the ammunition they desperately needed. He started attacking Defence Minister Sergei Shoigu and the Russian Chief of General Staff, Valery Gerasimov, in public, in his very pithy, very earthy slang. Unlike all the rest of Putin's creatures, Prigozhin was a master of Russian demotic and he became something of a cult figure, addressing nationalists and the war party in his camo uniform.

Unlike Shoigu and Gerasimov and, don't even whisper it, Putin himself, Prigozhin would go to the front line and be seen taking risks.

Prigozhin had a way of slagging off Shoigu that was quite something. In February 2023, he posted: 'I am not poking you in the eye with the fact that you sit down to breakfast, lunch and dinner, eating off gold plates, and send your daughters, granddaughters and dogs on holiday to Dubai. You're not embarrassed by anything. But, at a time when Russian soldiers are dying at the front, I'm just asking, "Give me ammunition!"'

In May 2023, he got ruder: 'Shoigu's son-in-law walks around, his buttocks a-quiver, and his daughter opens the Kronstadt forts. Did you make a killing out of these old forts? You spent money on forts? Spend it on fucking ammunition.' Prigozhin complained that 'the children of the elites smother themselves with creams and show this and that on Instagram, YouTube and so on, while ordinary people's kids return home torn apart in zinc-lined coffins.'

And ruder, posting a video beside a heap of dead Wagner Army soldiers: 'Now listen to me, bitches, these are somebody's fathers and somebody's sons. And those scum who don't hand over the ammo, bitches, will eat their guts in hell. We have a 70 per cent ammunition shortage. Shoigu, Gerasimov, where the fuck is the ammunition? Look at them, bitches.'

The holiest day in the Putinist Russian calendar is 9 May, marking the Soviet victory over Nazi Germany in 1945. On video, Prigozhin slagged off the Russian military high command and added: 'Happy Grandpa thinks he's happy. But what is the country to do if suddenly it turns out that grandpa is a complete asshole?' The Kremlin, the word was, did not like the stuff about 'Grandpa'. Meduza, an opposition website, mused: 'Of course, he can then say that this is about Shoigu or about an abstract layman, but people draw understandable conclusions.' And everyone knew that 'Grandpa in his bunker' was code for Vladimir Putin.

When Bakhmut fell, Prigozhin did not let up but let rip. His cult grew and that meant trouble, not just for Shoigu and Gerasimov, but for their master too. Furious that his demands were not being met, in late June he took his victorious army out of Ukraine and crossed the Rubicon into southern Russia. Rostov-on-Don, the biggest city in the region, fell to the mutiny without a murmur. His soldiers drove north, shooting Russian army helicopters out of the sky when, all of a sudden, one hundred miles south of Moscow, the mutiny stopped dead. At the time of writing there is still no good explanation as to why Prigozhin on a roll would give up. Attempting treason and then pulling out halfway through never looks good on your life insurance policy. Putin, it seems, was genuinely scared by the fall of Rostov and the march on Moscow. He went quiet and disappeared from view. It is possible that he suffered a 'Stalin moment', like the time in June 1941 when the Soviet dictator was caught napping by the Nazi invasion and feared execution. So why did Prigozhin stop dead? My working hypothesis is that the secret police got to Prigozhin's family. For example, if his grandchildren had been kidnapped, then that might well have forced him to call off his mutiny. In return, the word on the street was, Prigozhin and his lieutenants would be granted immunity because of their previous heroics. But would Putin honour his word?

On 23 August, Prigozhin and his intimates were flying in

a private jet from Moscow to St Petersburg when it turned into a ball of fire and fell to earth.

Putin's PR man, Dmitry Peskov, was greyhound-quick out of the gates: 'It is obvious that different versions are being considered, including the version, you know what we are talking about, let's say, a deliberate atrocity.' Then he went on to deny that the Kremlin had anything to do with it: 'an absolute lie'. It's his standard patter: ironically raise the possibility that the killings had something to do with his boss, then deny it, leaving both versions to drift like tumbleweed in the wind.

A Telegram channel linked to what was left of the Wagner Army claimed the private jet was shot down by Russian air defence missiles over Tver Oblast but it happened in broad daylight and no visible missile trails were photographed. US and other Western spooks put their money on a bomb on the plane, a theory that was coloured in some months later in December 2023 when the *Wall Street Journal* cited sources within Western and Russian intelligence agencies claiming that a bomb had been hidden under the wing during predeparture safety checks. The *Journal* said the hit had been orchestrated by Putin's right-hand man, Nikolai Patrushev, and that Putin had signed it off.

From his dog kennel prison, Navalny reflected on the death of the man who had tried to bankrupt him when he lay in a coma: 'Because of the terrorist attack that Putin arranged to kill his soldier Prigozhin, I would like to speak about decency, cunning and strategy. Just a few days ago I was writing to one person explaining what the secret of Prigozhin's survival is. Most likely, it's simple. Personal agreement and the dude's oath. Prigozhin promised Putin that he would fight for him and his war till the end. He would be his most reliable commander, who is ready to do anything to win. Putin, looking at the Defence Ministry's lack of enthusiasm, pretty much appreciated that.'

Quick point on translation: 'pretty much' technically means 'almost' but has developed over centuries of usage into a kind of negative, as in, 'have you finished writing the book yet?'

'Pretty much.'

Which really means: no. So, Navalny's translator should perhaps have written: 'Putin . . . very much appreciated that.'

Navalny noted Prigozhin's service to the master of the Kremlin, in particular getting thousands of prisoners out to the front line. He imagined the two men having a conversation. Once again, I have fiddled with the English to make it sound a little more natural:

Prigozhin: 'I will do anything for you, Vladimir Vladimirovich. Victory will be ours at any cost. However, please don't let me down and don't throw me to the dogs.'

Putin: 'Zhenya' – short-form for Evgeny – 'here's my hand and here's my word. Complete the task, and I'll be always by your side. Support is guaranteed.'

Navalny then sticks in the knife: 'How stupid I was to write this stuff. How naïve to assume that Putin can be characterized by any sort of decency: the decency of an officer or a dude or a gangster. There is nothing but lies for absolutely no reason.

'Lie, steal, kill, run away.

'And cunning. Here, it is worth laughing at those who believe in the ultra-sophistication of the intelligence services, that "If they want to kill, they know how to kill in such a way that no one will ever know." So here is the oh-so-brilliant work of Putin's assassins. They shoot down a passenger plane in Russia, in other words, they carried out a genuine terrorist attack, killing the pilot, the flight attendant and others who had absolutely nothing to do with it.

'Strategy. There are 50–60,000 former prisoners and veterans in Wagner uniforms all over the country. There are also several hundreds of thousands more fans of this cult . . . The point is that for some of the most aggressive supporters of the war against Ukraine, the history of this war has now become the saga of how Putin betrayed and killed his most loyal officers. These are the ingredients for the dish called "civil war". They created a gang. They armed the gang. Then they disbanded the gang and killed the leaders.'

Navalny concluded: 'the metaphor "spiders in a jar" is often applied to the Kremlin. However, another metaphor, "monkey with a grenade" is the better fit.'

In the short term, Navalny's prophecy that civil war would follow Prigozhin's assassination did not pan out. On the contrary, Vladimir Putin seemed to appear to be the great beneficiary of Prigozhin's failed mutiny. What few people in the West properly understood then, and still don't, to this day, is the extreme nervousness in the West Wing of the Biden White House that a Ukrainian victory in the war could lead to Russia becoming Iraq 2.0. Their number one neurosis is that a Ukrainian victory would lead to the fall of Putin and that, in turn, would end up with the breaking up of Russia liberating two dragons the Americans are very afraid of. The first dragon is an Islamist Chechnya getting hold of a nuke and holding the Western world to ransom while Donald Trump is on the stump. The second, more terrifying, dragon is of China seizing Siberia while Russia is in chaos. Overnight, China would become the biggest, most resource-rich country on earth. The grand strategy of the United States is thus reduced to *Jim*, a viciously dark comic poem by Hilaire Belloc:

> *There was a Boy whose name was Jim;*
> *His Friends were very good to him.*
> *They gave him Tea, and Cakes, and Jam,*
> *And slices of delicious Ham . . .*

Jim goes to the zoo, runs away from his nurse and is gobbled up by the lion:

> *His Father, who was self-controlled,*
> *Bade all the children round attend*
> *To James's miserable end,*
> *And always keep a-hold of Nurse*
> *For fear of finding something worse.*

The negative to promoting timidity as your number one strategy is that the other players in the game will notice and react aggressively, making the possibility of the things you fear the most coming true more likely than not. And there are three specific weaknesses: one, real Russian victory in Ukraine is a worse outcome than future possible Russian chaos; two, the break-up of the Russian Empire established by Peter the Great and Catherine is long overdue and trying to wallpaper over the Tsarist, Soviet and now Putinist cracks won't work; three, rewarding evil never ends well.

Foggy Bottom hasn't learned from its previous mistake in 1991 when it went out of its way to push the White House into supporting the continued existence of the Soviet Union when it was imploding. But Prigozhin's mutiny in 2023 scared the White House something rotten. After it was over, the White House's real – rather than its articulated – policy on Ukraine became easier to divine, that is, the United States will support Ukraine so that it survives but does not defeat the Russian army in Ukraine. The problem is that Biden has no pressure from the right to do better because Donald Trump gives every impression of being a Russian asset.

At the time of writing, in late April 2024, the word is that Putin's other tame psycho, Ramzan Kadyrov, the Chechen quisling, is mortally ill with pancreatic cancer. If Kadyrov dies, then the odds are high that civil war will break out in Chechnya, again, and Putin will be forced to strip soldiers from the war in Ukraine to put down an Islamist rebellion in Russia's troublesome south. We got a smell of how nasty this could be in October 2023, when a Jew-hating mob stormed into Makhachkala airport, in the majority Muslim republic of Dagestan, after hearing that a flight from Israel had arrived. One member of the would-be pogrom even popped his head inside a turbo-fan of a passenger jet, hunting Jews. Sadly, the engine was not switched on.

The chances of civil war are high because, after the Prigozhin fireball, everybody knows that any deal, any promise backed by the word of Vladimir Putin has no value. In the long run, Navalny's prophecy from his dog kennel, of civil war, of a catastrophic failure of the Russian state, are more likely to come true than not.

CHAPTER SEVENTEEN

'They Will Definitely Kill Me'

Navalny's longest-serving lawyer Olga Mikhailova spent much of her time after his return to Russia visiting her troublesome client in the penal colonies, where the authorities did their best to block face-to-face contact: 'We were very afraid for him. When he was arrested after returning from Berlin, we tried to go to see him every day; this was very important because we were afraid that he might be poisoned again. In the colonies he was starved, not allowed to sleep and put in punishment cells. In three years he changed a lot physically. But how much I didn't fully understand because when we visited him in the colonies, we communicated through plastic glass, which was quite scratched, and in several places covered with an opaque film. That is, it was quite problematic to see and hear anything. I could only see him face to face during court hearings, and when this happened for the first time in the summer [of 2023], I was horrified. He was very thin, his colour grey and standing next to him was this rosy-cheeked prison guard man. I burst out: "What did you do to him? Why does he look like that?"'

Lock somebody away from sunlight for three years and

they are starved of vitamin D. That lack weakens your immune system, making you all the more vulnerable to infection.

They came for his lawyers first, arresting Vadim Kobzev, Alexey Liptser and Igor Sergunin in October 2023. Thus far, Putin's prissy respect for the appearance — but not, of course, the substance – of the rule of law had stayed his hand from going for Navalny's legal representatives. The arrests were an omen and not a good one. Navalny railed against the Kremlin in a series of tweets: 'The trembling knees of Putin's crumbling system are on display. It attempts to project an image of strength and stability, but it is evident to all, including itself, that it lacks a solid foundation – the necessary support of the people. This is why these hysterical arrests are taking place. On Friday, I got to know from journalists covering the trial that my lawyers were being raided. Then on Monday, journalists at the court informed me that my defence lawyer Vadim Kobzev, along with two other defenders whom I had last worked with over a year ago – Alexey Liptser and Igor Sergunin – had been arrested.'

The three lawyers were charged with participating in an extremist group and locked up. The move was an attempt to 'completely isolate Navalny', Ivan Zhdanov, formerly the head of the now banned Anti-Corruption Foundation, said on social media. On top of that, it was announced that Navalny would be moved from IK-6 to the harshest category in the whole Russian prison system, a 'special security' penal colony. His PR Kira Yarmysh spelt it out: 'If he won't have access to lawyers, he will end up in complete isolation, the kind no one can really even imagine. Letters go through poorly and are being censored,' she said. With Navalny in the cooler nearly all the time, he was not allowed any phone calls and hardly any visits from anyone but his lawyers, she added 'and now it means he will be deprived of this, as well'.

Navalny said: 'Just like in Soviet times, not only political activists are being prosecuted and turned into political prisoners, but their lawyers, too.'

In early December, Navalny vanished, only to pop up in IK-3, nicknamed 'The Polar Wolf Colony', the cruellest gulag in the whole of Putin's archipelago, north of the Arctic Circle, near the one-reindeer town of Kharp, in the Yamal peninsula about 1,200 miles north-east of Moscow. The Kharp clink sits about twenty miles west of the mighty River Ob, about 100 miles before it flows into the Gulf of Ob which, in turn, flows into the Kara Sea, part of the Arctic Ocean. Yamal means 'end of the land' and is one of the grimmest places to exist on earth, a barren emptiness, snow-covered for much of the year, populated by half a million reindeer and very, very few people. Thanks to global warming, the permafrost is melting, releasing towers of methane gas that explode eighty feet high into the air and creating cryovolcanic sinkholes or 'pingo' 180 feet deep. In 2016, the big melt unfroze some Soviet-era mass graves full of corpses of zeks, slang for political prisoners, who had been infected with anthrax, leading to an outbreak amongst the reindeer and their human herders. Funnily enough, no Russian oligarchs park their super-yachts in Yamal.

Navalny described the climate of his new home in his trademark pithy, sardonic way when he arrived in December 2023: 'I am your new Father Frost. Well, I now have a sheepskin coat, an ushanka hat,' a fur hat with ear-flaps, 'and soon I will get valenki,' traditional Russian felt boots.

'It has not been colder than −32°C yet,' Navalny posted in

a blog in January 2024. 'Nothing quite invigorates you like a walk in Yamal at 6.30 in the morning. Even at this temperature, you can walk for more than half an hour only if you manage to grow a new nose, new ears and new fingers.'

Navalny referenced a scene in *The Revenant*, the 2015 movie in which Leonardo DiCaprio is ravaged by a grizzly bear and shelters from the extreme cold of the Dakotas inside the carcass of a horse.

'I don't think that would have worked here. A dead horse would freeze in fifteen minutes,' Navalny said. 'We need an elephant here, a hot elephant, a fried one.'

It is still something of a mystery how Navalny managed to get these posts out to the wider world, bearing in mind he was locked behind iron bars and ferocious coils of barbed wire in Russia's most secure prison at the far northern edge of the known world and three of his lawyers had been locked up. But do that he did. The whole point of Putin sending Navalny to Yamal was to break his spirit and within a month of arrival, he was cracking jokes about keeping warm in minus 32 degrees C inside the carcass of a hot, fried elephant. Once again, one is left thinking how much Putin must have hated him.

Navalny's last message to the outside world was a Valentine's Day note to Yulia: 'I feel that you are with me every second.'

The next day he joshed down the video link with the judge thinking about him giving him yet more jail time, to the open amusement of his jailers in the Polar Wolf colony standing next to him.

The day after he was dead.

On that grim day, Yulia was attending the Munich Security Conference. Still reeling from the reports that her husband had died, not knowing for sure whether they were true, she took to the stage in front of the presidents, prime ministers and generals and spoke for two minutes in Russian. It was clear that she was fighting hard to hold back the tears and that made her speech all the more gut-wrenching: 'I don't know whether to believe the news or not, the awful news that we receive only from government sources in Russia. We cannot believe Putin and Putin's government. They always lie. But if this is true, I want Putin and everyone around him, Putin's friends, his government, to know that they will bear responsibility for what they have done to our country, to my family and to my husband. And this day will come very soon. And I want to call on the world community, everyone in this room and people around the world to come together to defeat this evil, defeat this horrible regime that is now in Russia.'

The audience, which included US Vice President Kamala Harris, Secretary of State Antony J. Blinken and former House speaker Nancy Pelosi, gave her a standing ovation.

Later, Yulia posted a video address, vowing that Alexei's war against the tsar in blood was not over: 'I shouldn't have been in this place, I shouldn't be recording this video. There should have been another person in my place. But that person was killed by Vladimir Putin.'

Yulia hinted at the Team Navalny investigation into his death which we can all be sure is happening right now. She said that by killing Alexei, Putin had 'killed half of me, half of my heart and my soul. But I still have the other half, and it tells me that I have no right to give up. All these years I have been by Alexei's side. But today I want to be by your side, because I know that you have lost as much as I have. Putin killed the father of my children. Putin took away the most precious thing I had, the closest person to me, and the person I loved most in the world . . . I will continue Alexei Navalny's work . . . I want to live in a free Russia, I want to build a free Russia. I call on you to stand with me. To share not only grief and endless pain . . . I ask you to share with me the rage. The fury, anger, hatred for those who dare to kill our future.'

Nothing official in Russia is true, but the thugs who act as satraps for Putin are often morons who make stupid mistakes – Moscow4, Moscow4 – so the official version of Navalny's death merits examination.

At 2.19pm Moscow time, or 1119 GMT, the Federal Penitentiary Service of the Yamalo-Nenets Autonomous District on 16 February 2024 announced: 'On Feb. 16, 2024, in penal colony number 3, convict Navalny A.A. felt unwell after a walk, almost immediately losing consciousness. The medical staff of the institution arrived immediately, and an ambulance team was called. All necessary resuscitation measures were carried out, which did not give positive results. Doctors of the ambulance stated the death of the convict. The causes of death are being established.'

Navalny's 69-year-old mother, Lyudmila, lives in the Moscow time zone, two hours behind Yamal. The authorities gave her a death notice, Navalny's spokeswoman Kira Yarmysh said. The time of death in that notice was 2.17pm local, Yekaterinburg Time, or 0917 GMT. The timings are easier to understand if we go with GMT. Sorry for being British but it was our invention . . .

The Yamal authorities note the time of death as at 0917 GMT and make it public two hours later at 1119 GMT. Forgetting that Moscow and Yamal are in two different time zones led some reporters to note that the death announcement popped up two minutes after the official time of death. The thugs are better than that. But not that much better and the reporters were not wrong to be sceptical about the official version as it panned out.

'When Alexei's lawyer and mother arrived at the colony, they were told that the cause of Navalny's death was sudden death syndrome,' said Zhdanov.

'Sudden death syndrome' means, in plain English, something went wrong with the heart but we don't know exactly how the person has died. Then a source – not identified, of course – told Kremlin-controlled RT, Russia Today as was, that Navalny had died from a blood clot. One of the most common ways a clot can kill is when it moves up from the leg to block the blood vessels servicing the lungs or the heart.

Novaya Gazeta reported that the body showed signs of bruising consistent with some sort of seizure as well as traces of heart massage attempts. The newspaper said it was unclear why his heart had stopped.

This is classic Kremlin information poisoning: within hours of Navalny's death there are three competing, unsourced theories of how he had come to die naturally: some kind of heart attack; a blood clot; a seizure. Confusion is sown; the waters are muddied; the world moves on. The fog machine is working.

Intriguingly, reporters from *Novaya Gazeta* were able to track down an unidentified prisoner in the Polar Wolf colony who told them that a 'strange commotion' had erupted in the prison on the evening of 15 February, before the official time of death. The secret prisoner said that the guards had accelerated their evening checks of the prisoners and strengthened security. In the morning of the 16th there was a 'total shakedown' of the prison, with guards confiscating mobile phones and other items from prisoners. Soon after, a committee from the central office of the Federal Penitentiary Service arrived, the prisoner said. Word spread throughout the prison that Navalny was dead at 10am Yamal time, 8am Moscow time, 0500 GMT, more than four hours before the official time of death.

The prisoner passed on the gossip amongst the zeks – a far more reliable source of information than, say, Russia Today. The prisoner said that his guess was that Navalny had died on the evening of 15 February, that his death had caught the prison authorities by surprise.

Curious and curiouser.

In a democracy, the family would be given the body and they would have the right to do a thorough autopsy, to establish the cause of death. But Russia isn't like that. Instead, the regime started a game of hide the body, compounding the agony of Navalny's grieving mother, Lyudmila Navalnaya. The 69-year-old went from pillar to post, trying to find her son's corpse.

Navalny's body seems to have first been taken to Labytnangi, on the west bank of the Ob. Then live cam footage popped up, recording a four-vehicle prison service convoy travelling from Labytnangi across the river to Salekhard on the night of the 16th. One of the vehicles in the convoy was a van, suggesting that this was carrying Navalny's body. By the way, in 1907 Leon Trotsky was sentenced to exile in Salekhard, then known as Obdorsk, although he managed to escape on his journey there: proof that life for a political prisoner was so much easier under the tsars than it is in the twenty-first century under Putin.

On the morning of 19 February, Navalny's mother and

his lawyers went to the morgue in Salekhard to see if they could gain access to the body. They were told to go away. Officers from the Investigative Committee, detectives wholly under the thumb of the Kremlin, told his mother that his remains had been sent for a 'chemical examination' and would not be returned to the family for another fourteen days.

The reason for this disgusting charade by the authorities was that the longer they stalled handing over the corpse, the harder it would be for pathologists, for anyone, to find out how he had died. On 20 February, Navalny's mother posted a message to the Kremlin on YouTube from outside the Polar Wolf prison, the last place where Navalny had been known to be alive: 'For a fifth day I cannot see him, they aren't giving me his body and don't even tell me where he is. I appeal to you, Vladimir Putin. You alone can resolve this. Let me see my son. I demand that Alexei's body be released immediately so that I can bury him.'

Two days later, Navalny's mother gave up fighting the Kremlin and signed a death certificate that stated that her son had died of natural causes. That is the official lie.

So how did they murder him?

One hypothesis tallies with the prison authority press release that Navalny died after returning from a walk. The missing bit from the press release was that the temperature was minus 25 degrees C and, the hypothesis continues, that they made Navalny stomp around in the freezing cold inside the prison compound in jeans and a T-shirt so that his blood thickened and returned to the body's core.

In 2012, to illustrate a torture technique used by Putin's lapdog in Belarus, Alexander Lukashenko, I once stripped off in a frozen pea warehouse in North London in minus 25. I was shaking uncontrollably after three minutes. John

Oliver ran a clip of my naked bottom on his gag show recently without explaining the context of fascistic torture which led me to the conclusion that Oliver is a bit of an arse.

Navalny could have been made to walk around in the extreme cold until he was barely alive, then beaten up, causing heart failure or a lethal blood clot, his injuries passed off as those caused by the paramedics trying to save his life.

His widow, Yulia Navalnaya, and his great friend, the Bulgarian Sherlock Holmes, Christo Grozev, both suspected Novichok, the weapons grade nerve agent the Kremlin's goon squad had tried to kill Navalny with once already, back in August 2020. This time, in the Polar Wolf penal colony, there was no one to jab him with atropine.

'The KGB punch theory' was proposed by exiled Russian human rights defender Vladimir Osechkin, founder of the human rights group Gulagu.net which translates as 'No to the Gulag', and made it to the front page of *The Times*. Osechkin told Britain's journal of record that Navalny was likely to have been killed with a punch to the heart: 'I think that they first destroyed his body by keeping him out in the cold for a long time and slowing the blood circulation down to a minimum. And then it becomes very easy to kill someone, within seconds, if the operative has some experience in this. It is an old method of the KGB's special forces divisions. They trained their operatives to kill a man with one punch in the heart, in the centre of the body. It was a hallmark of the KGB.'

Thing is, after a few days, the corpse won't hold those secrets. Poison is the pathologist's friend because there is clear evidence of a foreign toxin in the blood. The KGB punch is the ultimate technique in invisible killing and that is Vladimir Putin oh-so-very-much on brand.

The bruising found on Navalny's body fits the KGB punch theory, according to Osechkin, now in exile: he told *The Times* that the Novichok theory is unlikely. 'When someone is under the control of the prison system there are many options as to how to kill them. Novichok would leave a trace in his body and would lead directly back to Putin, given he has tried it once before.'

To Osechkin, the KGB punch theory is the runner. There is only one problem with this hypothesis. In 2023, Osechkin was the subject of a long investigative piece by Roman Badanin in Proekt suggesting that, although his website had run some strong stories on the Russian prison system, his entrepreneurial endeavours sometimes get ahead of his ability to weigh evidence. 'Osechkin,' wrote Badanin, 'regularly produces stories that are sensational and absurd. For example, *Newsweek*, citing an Osechkin source "in the FSB", wrote that Russia was going to invade Japan in the summer of 2021. Osechkin's FSB source was called "Wind of Change".' Badanin continues: 'In another interview, the human rights defender, citing a "source in the FSO" [Russia's presidential security service], claimed that Yevgeny Prigozhin was preparing human meat for Putin. Another time, Osechkin quoted insights from an anonymous source, first saying that Russia was going to use nuclear weapons that night, and then reading out a popular Russian internet meme about "the father of an acquaintance who works in the FSB".' It later turned out that another internet activist may have pranked Osechkin. Badanin went on to allege that Osechkin is a 'human rights entrepreneur' who had been jailed for running a dodgy second-hand car dealership which defrauded its customers although, to be fair, Proekt reported his defence, that he was framed by corrupt local officials seeking protection money. Proekt went on to suggest that Osechkin may have over-dramatised his role in a number of former Russian soldiers being exfiltrated to the West and failed to back up his version of events with promised documents that never appeared. Osechkin retorted that Proekt reporters were 'working for the FSB' – something, knowing Badanin, I doubt. The KGB punch remains a possible cause of Navalny's death. Just because there are questions about what Osechkin has said in the past, does not rule out the theory.

A different version of the poison thesis had already been advanced by none other than Navalny himself to his lawyer, Olga Mikhailova. I had first seen her in the flesh in January 2018, in Strasbourg at the European Court of Human Rights: a feisty blonde who took no nonsense from the Kremlin's apparatchiks. After his murder, she told the independent Russian online news magazine, Meduza, the story that Navalny feared that he was being slowly and surreptitiously poisoned. Mikhailova had met her client Navalny in IK-6 Melekhovo in April 2023, before the move to the Polar Wolf colony. Navalny told her, 'Listen, I don't want to sound paranoid, but it seems that they're poisoning me here.' Mikhailova made the allegation public by posting it on a Twitter account used by Navalny's legal team, questioning the 'unknown illness' he was suffering from that had required an ambulance and caused him to lose about seventeen pounds in a period of around two weeks. His lawyers said at the time that the 'strange situation' surrounding his health was causing a deterioration that hadn't come about suddenly, but 'steadily' and 'gradually'.

The exact wording of the conversation hit the public domain when the Russian authorities released a wiretap of the theoretically legally privileged meeting long afterwards, when they charged Mikhailova and Navalny's other lawyers with extremism. Luckily, Mikhailova was out of the country at the time, on holiday in Jordan with her daughter. The other lawyers are behind bars.

Roman Borisovich, one of the original sponsors of the Anti-Corruption Foundation, suspects a simpler cause of death: 'It's possible that after three years of harsh treatment, of torture, of bad food and so little of it he lost so much weight, of hardly any sunlight so his face turned grey, that he died some kind of natural death, but only in the sense that they didn't actually kill him directly. The Kremlin turned an extraordinarily healthy man into a very sick man, old before his time. They killed him slowly, over time.'

That said, the suddenness of his death, the fact that he was laughing with his jailers one day and dead the next, makes me suspect that he was killed deliberately according to a plan. But whose plan? Who, exactly, gave the order to have Navalny killed?

Not long after his death, the story emerged that the West had been trying to trade Navalny with Putin's number one prisoner in the West, an FSB hitman, Vadim Krasikov, who had murdered Chechen dissident Zelimkhan Khangoshvili in Berlin. On 23 August 2019, at around midday, Khangoshvili was walking down a wooded path in the Kleiner Tiergarten park, on his way home from the mosque, when he was shot once in the shoulder and twice in the head by a Russian assassin on a pushbike with a suppressed Glock 26. The bike, a plastic bag with the Glock and a terrible wig Krasikov was wearing were dumped in the Spree and then fished out again. The word is that Putin is always keen on getting his killers out of western jails because it sends a message to the others: 'Don't worry if something goes wrong. We will have your back. We will get you out.'

But Team Navalny was also working on getting their hero out. Shortly after Navalny's return to Russia, Christo Grozev, CNN reported, had approached Hillary Clinton at some bash in the States and she had passed on the contact to Jake Sullivan, Old Man Biden's National Security Adviser. The trade was tricky. Navalny to be swapped for Krasikov required a German sign-off. Then the Americans wanted to add two more wholly innocent US citizens locked up in Russia, *Wall Street Journal* reporter Evan Gershkovich and former US marine Paul Whelan, both of whom have been banged up on rubbish evidence of spying.

Was Navalny killed by a Kremlin insider in order to stop the trade?

Paul Joyal thinks exactly that. Joyal is the former US intelligence analyst who, you may recall, was shot by two unknown would-be assassins a few days after he told an American NBC *Dateline* programme that he believed that Putin was responsible for the killing of Litvinenko and shared a story implying that Putin might not be quite as macho as his propaganda suggested. Thankfully, Joyal survived. He told me: 'You must look at what has happened since. Nikolai Patrushev has suffered a brutal and humiliating demotion, from head of the National Security Council to an adviser on maritime affairs. Why? Patrushev, I believe, is close to being a paranoid schizophrenic. He believes this nonsense that the Americans are creating bio-weapons targeting the Russian genome. And he's a player. He will act on his own, outside the lines. I believe that he did that in the Moscow apartment bombings that brought Putin to power.'

Joyal believes that the trade was on and had heard that

Navalny was due to be moved to Moscow, prior to his release to the West, on the very day he was killed: 'My working hypothesis is that Patrushev had Navalny killed without getting the OK from Putin because he hated Navalny. Remember when Navalny tricked the poisoner Konstantin Kudryavtsev, he pretended to be an aide to Patrushev? That was his death sentence. Patrushev believed that Navalny was the CIA's creature. He wanted to stop the trade at all costs and so had Navalny murdered. After the dust settled, Putin sacked him.'

So, in this version, it was not Putin, but Putin's number one guard dog that had Navalny killed. The owner is, of course, responsible for the actions of a killer dog.

In late April 2024, the *Wall Street Journal* published a funny peculiar story headlined: 'Putin Didn't Directly Order Alexei Navalny's February Death, US Spy Agencies Find'. As ever with the CIA, the sourcing was opaque, the paper citing 'unnamed people familiar with the matter'. The US assessment was based on some classified intelligence, an analysis of public facts – including the timing of Navalny's death and how it overshadowed Putin's re-election in March – and had been 'broadly accepted within the intelligence community and shared by several agencies, including the Central Intelligence Agency, the Office of the Director of National Intelligence, and the State Department's intelligence unit.' The key finding was: 'the assessment doesn't dispute Putin's culpability for Navalny's death, but rather finds he probably didn't order it at that moment.'

Readers should by now, I hope, be fully aware of how difficult it is to establish the exact truth of a murder when it has been sponsored by the Kremlin. But there is one last hypothesis on who commissioned the killing of Alexei

Navalny and how it happened – poison – and this is the one I give the most weight to.

For this book, I reached out to someone with established, well-placed and reliable sources inside the Russian power vertical. Their primary source says that Putin himself gave the boss of the FSB, Aleksandr Bortnikov, actual but not minuted 'approval' for Navalny to be poisoned using a sophisticated technique back in December 2023. You may recall from the Navalny documentary that in the *Beautiful Mind*-style diagram of the Poison Squad, Bortnikov sits directly below Putin. So commanded, the source says, Bortnikov then designated the FSB team involved and personally managed the murder operation overall. Sources were confident of this, despite the fact that no formal orders had been given. This was the same modus operandi as had been employed in August 2020, when another FSB operational team had poisoned Navalny with Novichok. The same FSB institute, NII-2, Scientific Research Institute No.2, was involved in the 2024 Navalny poisoning, but orders were carried out by a wholly different team of 'specialists'.

The primary source said that at the time of writing there had been no leaks of any minutes of secret meetings or talks between Putin and Bortnikov immediately prior to Navalny's death. But that is not at all surprising. The two men always took the highest security precautions when discussing the most secret and sensitive issues, amongst which Navalny was one. They often met alone in special secured facilities known as 'bubbles' or 'capsules'. Even then they talked very discreetly, rarely using context-specific words or names.

A second source said that other top-level Russian officials did not know about the plan to kill Navalny in advance.

The senior Kremlin official reported that no actual Navalny killing operational plan had ever been officially discussed and/or approved at any state level. But poison him they did, and the man behind it was Putin himself.

Navalny knew the Russian dark state better than anyone. When they met in IK-6 he told his lawyer that he feared they were slowly poisoning him. I buy that. After all, at the very moment of his greatest triumph, when he pranked one of the Poison Squad into coughing up exactly how they had administered the Novichok, thus fixing Vladimir Putin in history as the Underpants Poisoner, he said, with a smile on his lips: 'They will definitely kill me.'

And so they did.

CHAPTER EIGHTEEN

'I'll Be Back'

The other great Russian spirit who died on the same day as Navalny was Dmitry 'Dima' Markov, the photographer who took the iconic photograph in the Moscow nick of the armour-clad goon in the balaclava glaring at the young Navalny supporters with Putin looking on from behind a frame. This picture, as Howard Amos wrote, 'became a symbol of the brutality of the Russian regime, its crackdown on dissent and – because the police officer was hiding his face – the Kremlin's fear of its own people.'

The photo is an icon of Russian fascism. It went viral on social media, becoming a source of dozens of memes. The only signed author's print of the photograph was sold at a charity auction for two million roubles, Markov giving the money to human rights groups. Markov explained the chemistry behind the shot: 'To get a full idea, it would be great to see the people who were sitting in front of that riot policeman. There were young people, some around twenty-five years old, and the [police officer] is obviously close to fifty. And he is ashamed, he is afraid to show his face, he is wearing a balaclava indoors even though it was very hot in there.'

Check out Markov's Instagram to see his extraordinary eye capture another Russia, the one which Vladimir Putin and his naff, murderous gang with their fancy watches and yachts and corgi-carrying private jets despise, the Russia that Alexei Navalny loved and fought so hard to make better. A heroin addict at eighteen, Markov spent two decades fighting his addictions. Photography saved him and in return he captured the real Russia. People making do inside Russia's eternal Soviet apartment blocks, kids mucking about in the river, two sisters in wellington boots standing underneath storm clouds in Karelia, a fat man tending his fat pig in the snow, orphans, junkies, conscripts. He was a 'Russian Cartier-Bresson', said Kirill Serebrennikov, a leading Russian theatre director: 'He was able to capture the soul of the people, their DNA. If you want to understand Russians, you should look at Dima Markov's photos. A lot of people live in the Russia that Dima Markov photographed. But they don't see it like he saw it. They see it as something terrible, something shameful, and something that should be forgotten. Dima looked at it and was able to see beauty.'

To me, from afar, Dmitry Markov was Caravaggio with a mobile phone and an Instagram account.

One simple yardstick of someone's life, of the good or bad they have done, is how many people turn up for their funeral. In Navalny's case, there was an extra dimension knowing that the likely consequences of turning up to say a last goodbye could include getting sacked, arrested, a clubbing by the police or worse.

The Kremlin commanded something quiet and out of the way. Navalny's family and friends wanted a very public funeral. The Kremlin didn't want to express their will out loud so, instead, every time Team Navalny approached a firm of funeral directors, they said no because the word had already been spread by the secret police. Navalny's PR woman, Kira Yarmysh, tweeted on 27 February 2024: 'We have called the majority of private and state funeral agencies, commercial entities and funeral halls. Some say the premises are booked, some refuse to talk after they hear Navalny's name. At one place, they directly said to us that they had been ordered not to collaborate with us.'

The preconditioning described by Soldatov to me as we circled the grey toad of the Lubyanka held solid: 'We are still in fear of Stalin's secret police.' Everyone knew that if they took a risk and helped Navalny's mother bury her son, then things would not go well for them in the future. That was true from the very top of Russian society all the way down to the gravediggers.

And the Kremlin went out of its way to jog people's memories. On the same day that Navalny's friends could not find anyone willing to bury the corpse, Vasily Dubkov, a lawyer who had kept Lyudmila Navalnaya company when she was haring around the Yamal peninsula trying to find her son's body, was arrested in Moscow on charges of 'violating public order'.

The funeral had originally been scheduled for 29 February but there was an unexpected clash. Zhdanov, the former director of the Anti-Corruption Foundation, explained that no venue would hold it on that day because it coincided with Putin's annual Presidential Address to the Federal Assembly. It did take place a day later on 1 March at the Church of the Icon of the Mother of God in Moscow's Maryino District, where Navalny had lived. The police arrived early and in force and blocked off an area directly in front of the church the size of a parade ground with crowd control barriers, reminding everybody that this was no ordinary funeral. Peskov rammed the message home, saying: 'Any unauthorised gatherings will be in violation of the law and those who participate in them will be held accountable.'

But still they came, thousands, then tens of thousands, moving slowly through the snow, the queue stretching back a kilometre past the phalanxes of riot police in balaclavas. People chanted 'Russia will be free!' 'Putin's a murderer!' 'No to the War!' and, again and again, simply: 'Navalny'. The funeral was streamed live on YouTube and is very moving. It is a church service to a victim of a fascist state carried out inside that fascist state. Navalny lay in an open casket, his face exposed but with a white band covering his eyes. When the service was over, mourners tried to take photographs on their mobile phones, but the undertakers hurried to get on with the job, causing an unseemly melee. It was as if the undertakers were not working for the family but were operating under instruction from someone else.

Yulia Navalnaya and their two children were safe, out of Russia. The Kremlin denied them their proper right to grieve. They could not go back and it must have been extraordinarily painful for them to attend the funeral remotely, via YouTube, watching their husband and father lie face up in a coffin from thousands of miles away, knowing that for the foreseeable future they cannot visit his grave. They could not kiss him goodbye, they could not leave flowers on his grave, they could not mourn with his mother and father. It is hard to imagine a crueller form of psychological torture.

Pretty much all the famous names from the Russian opposition were not present because they were either in exile or in jail or dead. The American, French and German ambassadors turned up, plus other Western diplomats, two disqualified opposition presidential candidates, Boris Nadezhdin and Yekaterina Duntsova, and the former mayor of Yekaterinburg, Yevgeny Roizman.

At Borisovskoye cemetery, Navalny's body was lowered into the ground to the tune of 'My Way' by Frank Sinatra and then the theme music from *Terminator 2: Judgment Day*.

Across Russia, human rights groups said that 128 people were arrested in nineteen cities for participating in memorial events on the day of his funeral, most commonly for trying to lay flowers at monuments to victims of Soviet repression. One video clip showed two giant OMON cops in balaclavas and full-armour riot gear taking a youth across the road to a line of police vans, the boy's arms twisted so high up his back that he had to walk with his back arched forward, his face almost in his knees. Mourners kept on coming for three days, leaving so many flowers and wreaths on Navalny's grave that they became a small mountain until council binmen moved in to demolish the makeshift shrine.

Father Dmitry Safronov, the priest who officiated at the service, and, according to the Orthodox tradition, a follow-up service forty days after Navalny's death, was suspended in April from leading church services and ordered to serve three years of 'penance'. The Moscow diocese of the Russian Orthodox Church said Safronov would be demoted to psalm reader, forbidden from wearing a cassock and sent to another Moscow-region church where he would serve his 'penance'. If he failed, he would be defrocked. The *Guardian* reported that no formal reason was given for the punishment. 'In the absence of official information, the ban can be linked only with the memorial service that Father Dmitry did for Alexei Navalny,' wrote Ioann Burdin, a priest who was fined and then defrocked after criticising the war in Ukraine. Yulia Navalnaya called for supporters to give donations to Safronov's family. 'I am very grateful to him,' she wrote. 'Let's help him and his family.'

The Make America Great Again wing of the US Republican Party has been highly critical of Ukrainian attempts to police the Kremlin-controlled Russian Orthodox Church, also known as the Moscow Patriarchate, not perhaps realising that its head, Patriarch Kirill, was an active KGB agent in Soviet times, has been mired in a cigarette smuggling scandal and is reckoned to be worth $4 billion. For the avoidance of doubt, Kirill has called Putin's presidency 'a miracle of God'. Praise be, some say.

Ilya Yashin is a Russian opposition politician and a close ally of Alexei Navalny, now in jail for eight years for spreading 'false information' about the Russian military's war crimes in Bucha, Ukraine. Yashin's 'false information' was, of course, entirely true. The Russian army committed war crimes in Bucha. I went to Bucha myself in early April 2022, and saw with my own eyes the mass grave full of bodies murdered by the Russians. Off the main street, I stumbled across two civilians, one shot in the back of the head, the other between the eyes.

After Navalny was killed, Yashin blogged a noble piece from his prison cell about the contrast between Putin and the man who tried so hard to evict him from the Kremlin: 'Putin speaks often, and at length, about conservative values. Europe and the US want to impose their debauched and godless ways on us, he tells Russians, to frighten them and to justify a stand-off against "the collective West". On the subject of the war, he expounds that only the Russian army can save Ukrainian schoolchildren from "gender-neutral toilets". His electoral manifesto places a heavy emphasis on the family as the basis of Russian society, and on his commitment to tradition and religious belief. All this rhetoric is pure hypocrisy. Conservative discourse is, for Putin, no more than a political tool for manipulating the consciousness of the populace. The reality is that the Russian president leads an immoral life, wholly contrary to the values he purports to embody. Putin claims to be a man of faith who partakes in Christian rituals. The reality is that he has started a bloody war in Eastern Europe, a war in which Christians are killing other Christians. He claims to be the defender of family life. In reality, he is a man who has publicly distanced himself from his own daughters, and when he mentions them to the press, it's as "those women". Putin's hypocrisy is obvious; next to him, Alexei Navalny appeared as a much more holistic, balanced person . . . I knew Alexei for twenty-three years; we were friends, and I know his family well. I can attest that he truly was a man of faith, for whom the commandments "Thou shalt not kill" and "Thou shalt not steal", and the ethical precepts of the Sermon on the Mount, were not the mere trappings of religion, but became a lodestar for his life and his politics. I can say with certainty that unlike Putin, Alexei was a true family man, too: a loving son, husband and father. His family life, based on love and mutual respect, was always for me a source of admiration.'

Yashin went into detail about the pressure the Kremlin placed on Navalny's family: his family home routinely searched; also, the home of his parents; his brother, Oleg, effectively held hostage for three and a half years in jail; his children spied on, his daughter, Dasha, regularly followed on the way to school by plain-clothes officers of the FSB.

Yashin concluded: 'His family remains Alexei's source of strength even now that he has perished in prison. Yulia never had independent aspirations, nor intended a political career for herself. But by killing Alexei, Putin left her no choice – and she has seized the banner of struggle. I suspect that Putin is prone to chauvinism and will hardly take a woman seriously as an opponent. But he doesn't know Yulia very well, and soon, I'm sure, he will realise his mistake. As for me, I wish Yulia Navalnaya every success, and will be rooting for her, if only from behind bars.'

Navalny had one last poke in the eye for the Kremlin crocodile from beyond the grave. On 17 March 2024, Russia came out to vote in the presidential election, sorry, re-coronation. There was, as always, only one candidate who had any chance of winning because the competition were straw men or dead. But people started to notice that great crowds had begun to gather at noon at the polling stations. Welcome to 'Noon against Putin', a phrase which is sweetly alliterative in Russian: Полдень против Путина, roman-ised: Polden protiv Putina, although in English-English it might better be translated as 'High Noon for Putin'. In January 2024, Navalny backed the protest before he was killed, but the original idea came from Maxim Reznik, a former councillor in St Petersburg: 'This is not an election, this is a "special election operation". Why does Putin need to do it? To prove the union between Fuhrer and nation: Putin and Russia are the same.'

Reznik, by the way, is now living in exile. You can't call Putin a Fuhrer and stay alive for long in Russia. He con-tinued: 'It is important for him to confirm this thesis, once again, which many people already believe in. Our task is to demonstrate exactly the opposite . . . Therefore, it is important for us to show to ourselves and to the world that there are many of us. So, this noon we should be everywhere: in Kaliningrad, Vladivostok, St Petersburg, in the Nile Valley and on the top of Everest. Our high noon will demonstrate what Russians think about Putin.'

And they did: huge queues everywhere at the polling stations at noon. It was a great single finger raised at the authorities who had very little traction to stop it. If they started arresting people en masse, that would be like 'Russian democracy' was itself something of a sham. The cops did move in against some of the protesters, barging into polling booths, harassing voters. It did not look good. The Kremlin was snookered.

Dictators fuck things up, big time. They destroy the chance of peaceful political change so that when, eventually, they die in their sleep or blow their brains out or are stabbed repeatedly in the anus – the respective ends of Stalin, Hitler, Gaddafi – chaos reigns. At best, for him, old age will come to Vladimir Putin and then the only end of age and the Russia he created will fall apart. At worst, Alexei Navalny's prediction after the fireball that did for Evgeny Prigozhin that creating, then destroying, armed gangs is a recipe for civil war will come true sooner than Putin thinks.

And then, perhaps, Russia will descend into *Mad Max* with snow on its boots, cast out of the pale by the Western world, hated by the Islamists in its south and east, its Siberian riches eyed by the Chinese dragon.

Time, then, for Navalny, like *Terminator 2*, to be brought back to change the future. But that's silly old science fiction and the science fact is that he's dead and his nemesis, the lizard king, is doing what he does best, a-killing. Navalny, had he ever been allowed to stand in a fair and square election, could have won, and if he had done so, he had the charisma and the love of life to bring fresh energy to build the beautiful Russia of the future.

But Russia blew it.

So did the West. The Anti-Corruption Foundation did an extraordinarily good job of investigating the Russian crooks around Putin. None of them were greatly inconvenienced until the big war started because, it seems, people in the West prefer the rule of money to the rule of law. And when it really mattered, when Navalny was being tortured in the gulag, Western liberals at Amnesty International and on the Nobel Peace Prize Committee put their own moral ease above his life.

Full of flaws, unbelievably arrogant, a man who did flirt with the far right, but, over the course of the last ten years, the boy from Chernobyl stood up for the idea of another Russia, a country not defined by grotesque corruption, cruelty and a stupid war, but by honesty, courage and great good humour. That secures his place in history. When all hope was lost, and Russia turned, yet again, back to darkness, then along came a knight in dented armour, tilting at evil windmills.

Alexei Navalny was bold and good.

Alexei Navalny kept the red eye of Russia's soul alive and one day it will start blink-blink-blinking again as it stomps, like *Terminator 2*, towards the machinery of greed that controls the Kremlin.

Alexei Navalny is dead, but what he stood for will be back.

Acknowledgements

Teachers defeat tyrants. So, hats off to the late Norman Levitt, who taught us Russian at Barton Peveril Grammar School in Eastleigh all those years ago by opening all the classroom windows one freezing morning and saying, 'Свежий' or 'fresh'. Mr Levitt was from the north-east and had no proper understanding of the cold. Still, his methods worked. But, of course, if I have got any re-translations wrong in this book, that's my fault for not paying proper attention because of the shivering.

The people who opened my eyes to the threat from Vladimir Putin were the bold and good Chechens who smuggled me into their country, twice, in 2000 when I saw evidence of Russian army war crimes with my own eyes.

Down the years, dozens of Russians and Ukrainians have helped me understand the nature of Russian power and what it costs to stand up to it. What drove me to write this book telling the story of Alexei Navalny is that he is not the first but the fourth great Russian I had the honour to meet who challenged Putin and was then killed. The first three were Anna Politkovskaya, Natalia Estemirova and Boris Nemtsov, respectively: poisoned, then shot; shot; shot.

My old colleagues at BBC *Panorama*, staff and freelance, got me in a position to doorstep Putin in 2014. Above all, Nick Sturdee waved his magic wand and filmed it. In 2018, BBC *Panorama* worked out a way for me to interview Navalny in Moscow for our film *Taking on Putin*. Special thanks to the whole gang, but in particular Jon Coffey, Seamas McCracken, Andrew Head and Zagit for their grace under pressure. One supporter and two members of Team Navalny who talked to me then stand out: street cleaner Vladimir Ivanyutenko, election campaign manager Nikolai Lyaskin and human rights activist Dinar Idrisov, respectively: tasered, then stabbed; hit over the head with an iron bar; beaten senseless.

For this book, I must thank my fixer in Ukraine, Sasha Aleksandrenko, who went to New Zalyssia and tracked down people who knew the boy Navalny when they lived under Chernobyl's shadow, my Russian-speaking Ukrainian translator Mariia Chepa and my Ukrainian pal and adviser, Jenny Klochko. I am acutely conscious that many Ukrainians take a dim view of Navalny. I understand their reasoning but, with respect, I disagree. To me, Navalny is a flawed hero.

Roman Borisovich was a staunch supporter of Navalny's Anti-Corruption Foundation and a great help for this book; special thanks to Andrew Duncan, Paul Joyal, Arthur Snell and Chris Steele for their wit and common sense; to Daniel Roher and everyone who worked on the brilliant *Navalny* documentary; to Roman Badanin and team at Proekt; to everyone at Team Navalny; to Catherine Belton, Ben Noble and Andrew Roth. Special thanks to Clarissa Ward of CNN for her thoughts on Navalny and her account of a truly great doorstep; thanks also to Marvin Rees, former mayor of Bristol, for sharing his memories of his old friend at Yale.

My agent Humfrey Hunter has played the usual blinder; thanks to my publisher, Martin Redfern, at Headline, to Ellie Harris and all the gang there. For a grim book, it was great fun working on it.

My neighbours, friends and wonderful dysfunctional family have looked after me as I recovered from my broken knee and wrote and wrote: thanks to Jeremy and Margaret, Maria and Yeva, Luisa, Alessio, Anne, Tomiko, Molly, Sam, Lou and Shilah.

To Mike Lambert, my physio who caused me a lot of pain and then went off to paddle his canoe around Britain, where I hope he will get gobbled up by a stray salt-water crocodile.

Ordinary people in Britain and around the world have no proper idea of how cruel Russian power can be. I have written this book in memory of a brave and singular man who tried to warn us, to prepare, before it is too late.

John Sweeney, London, May 2024

Shortlist of Putin Critics, Adversaries Killed, When, Why and How

Anatoly Levin-Utkin: 1998; was Putin corrupt?; beaten to death.

Artyom Borovik: 2000; was Putin a paedophile?; plane crash.

Antonio Russo: 2000; was Putin a paedophile?; crushed to death.

Nikolay Palenniy: 2002; protested corruption; strangled?

Sergei Yushenkov: 2003; investigating September 1999 bombs; shot.

Yuri Shchekochikhin: 2003; investigating September 1999 bombs; poisoned.

Roman Tsepov: 2004; was Putin corrupt?; poisoned.

Lecha Islamov: 2004; investigating war crimes; poisoned.

Anna Politkovskaya: 2006; investigating war crimes; poisoned, then shot.

Alexander Litvinenko: 2006; was Putin a paedophile?; poisoned.

Stanislav Markelov: 2009; investigating neo-Nazi links to Kremlin; shot.

Anastasia Baburova: 2009; investigating neo-Nazi links to Kremlin; shot.

Natalia Estemirova: 2009; investigating war crimes; shot.

Boris Berezovsky: 2013; an irritant; hanged?

Sergei Tsapok: 2014; an embarrassing murderer; poisoned?

Boris Nemtsov: 2015; political opponent; shot.

Dawn Sturgess: 2018; Salisbury lass who got in the way; poisoned.

Max Borodin: 2018; investigating Wagner Army deaths in Syria; 'fell out of a window'.

Dr Sergei Maksimishin: 2021; saved Navalny's life; 'heart attack'.

Dr Rustam Agishev: 2021; saved Navalny's life; 'stroke'.

Evgeny Prigozhin: 2023; mutiny; fireball.

Alexei Navalny: 2024; political opponent; murdered, method unknown.

Notes on Sources

Books

Dollbaum, Jan Matti, Morvan Lallouet and Ben Noble, *Navalny: Putin's Nemesis, Russia's Future?* 2021.

Herszenhorn, David, *The Dissident: Alexey Navalny: Profile of a Political Prisoner*, 2023.

Michnik, Adam, *Opposing Forces: Plotting the New Russia*, 2015.

Sweeney, John, *Killer in the Kremlin: The Explosive Account of Vladimir Putin's Reign of Terror*, 2022.

Voronkov, Konstantin, *Threat to Crooks and Thieves*, 2012.

Epigraph

Amelina, Victoria, 'Sirens', first published in *Invasion: Ukrainian Poems about the War*, ed. Tony Kitt, SurVision Books, Dublin, 2022.

Introduction

Terminator 2 *music*
https://www.bbc.co.uk/news/av/world-europe-68445602

Navalny wrong on Ukraine
https://www.washingtonpost.com/world/2023/10/27/navalny-ukraine-putin-russia/

Tucker Carlson soft, suggests Putin
https://www.politico.eu/article/vladimir-putin-
    tucker-carlson-soft-interview/

Tucker Carlson talks to Andrew Cuomo about his Putin interview
https://www.youtube.com/watch?v=o9Y15fiTIuw

Chapter One: The Boy from Chernobyl

Chernobyl childhood
https://galka-galkina.livejournal.com/875989.html

Navalny speaks to Russian Esquire *magazine*
https://www.mk.ru/politics/2011/11/24/646636-esquire-teper-s-
    navalnyim.html

Young Navalny
Dollbaum, Jan Matti, Morvan Lallouet, Ben Noble, *Navalny:
    Putin's Nemesis, Russia's Future?*, 2021
Herszenhorn, David, *The Dissident: Alexey Navalny: Profile of a
    Political Prisoner*, 2023

Putin's media wrestles with the truth about Chernobyl
https://www.themoscowtimes.com/2019/06/04/putins-media-
    struggle-to-deal-with-hbos-chernobyl-a65866

Navalny cousin killed in 2012
https://www.themoscowtimes.com/2022/04/19/navalny-
    relative-killed-in-ukraines-bucha-reports-a77404
https://www.amnesty.org/en/wp-content/uploads/2022/05/
    EUR5055612022ENGLISH.pdf

Chapter Two: Biting the Apple

The Wild East
http://www.bulvar.com.ua/gazeta/archive/s28_64799/6968.html

Yavlinsky's son maimed
https://www.themoscowtimes.com/archive/rybkin-affair-is-
no-laughing-matter

Yeltsin circles over Shannon
https://www.independent.ie/life/just-plane-rude-the-day-boris-
yeltsin-overslept/30615643.html

Not afraid of Mayor Luzhkov
https://www.kommersant.ru/doc/482159

Chapter Three: Bit of a Fascist?

'People for the legalization of weapons' Navalny video
https://www.youtube.com/watch?v=oVNJiO10SWw

'Become a Nationalist' Navalny video
https://www.youtube.com/watch?v=ICoc2VmGdfw

The evolution of Alexei Navalny's nationalism
https://www.newyorker.com/news/our-columnists/the-
evolution-of-alexey-navalnys-nationalism?_sp=
db2a5f41-889e-42b3-bcf5-66f94ed71bcd.1710845665630

Navalny defends himself against the charge of nationalism
Navalny, Alexei and Adam Michnik, *Opposing Forces: Plotting the
new Russia*, Egret Press, 2016, p. 63

Marvin Rees on his Yale pal
Conversation with the author

Navalny investigation into Transneft
https://www.bbc.co.uk/news/world-europe-11779154

Oleg Kashin beaten up
https://www.theguardian.com/world/2010/nov/07/nationalist-
thugs-attack-russian-journalist

Navalny corruption target gives money to Tory MPs
https://www.bbc.co.uk/news/world-58791274

Chapter Four: Jailhouse Rocker

Navalny's private emails leaked
https://www.themoscowtimes.com/2011/10/26/navalnys-
    private-e-mails-leaked-a10439

Navalny's blog mocking the 2011 Duma election rigging
https://navalny-en.livejournal.com/1560.html

Navalny on 5 December 2012
https://navalny-en.livejournal.com/2012/12/07/

Navalny's address from prison: 'We are not cattle or slaves'
https://navalny-en.livejournal.com/3039.html

Navalny's speech on 24 December 2011
https://navalny-en.livejournal.com/4410.html
https://www.theguardian.com/world/2011/dec/24/russia-
    europe-news

Navalny arrested on 6 May 2012: 'you're breaking my arm'
https://youtu.be/RupZW2Zcfwg?si=HaNWZCiZZxXPAXbW

Chapter Five: One Russia, Two Tsars

Navalny not being afraid
https://globalvoices.org/2010/10/27/russia-blogger-alexey-
    navalny-on-fighting-regime/

Putin threatens to castrate journalist
https://www.telegraph.co.uk/news/worldnews/europe/
    russia/1413083/Putin-suggests-castration-for-journalist.html

Navalny moves from investor to activist
https://www.kommersant.ru/doc/1197604

Navalny's blog on 'How They Saw at Gazprom'
https://navalny.livejournal.com/342311.html

Borisovich sponsors the Anti-Corruption Foundation
Conversations with the author

Chapter Six: The Man Who Stole a Forest

Taking on Putin *podcast*
https://open.spotify.com/show/0rwlMXKNQK0a7ug2p4oX1D

Stalin's library
https://www.theguardian.com/books/2022/feb/16/stalins-
library-by-geoffrey-roberts-review-the-marks-of-a-leader

Putin's gangster mentor
Sweeney, John, *Killer in the Kremlin*, Penguin, 2022.

Putin the plagiarist
https://www.brookings.edu/wp-content/uploads/2012/09/
Putin-Dissertation-Event-remarks-with-slides.pdf

A very Russian massacre
https://www.bbc.co.uk/news/world-europe-11736312

Bastrykin the kidnapper
https://web.archive.org/web/20130118124158/http://www.
novayagazeta.ru/columns/53061.html?print=1

Bastrykin the plagiarist
https://www.newyorker.com/news/news-desk/heckling-
russias-j-edgar-hoover

Bastrykin an ape
https://navalny-en.livejournal.com/26788.html

Bastrykin owned estates in Czechia
https://navalny-en.livejournal.com/28761.html

Chapter Seven: Schrödinger's Mayor

Mayor Sobyanin the plagiarist
https://wiki.dissernet.org/wsave/SSS.html

Navalny's speech to the Kirovles trial, July 2013
https://www.nytimes.com/2013/07/06/world/europe/text-of-
    navalnys-closing-remarks-in-russian-court.html?
    pagewanted=all&_r=3&
https://www.youtube.com/watch?v=VQGpcEjezqQ

The mayor's daughter has a nice flat
https://www.themoscowtimes.com/2013/08/11/
    sobyanin-daughters-apartment-triggers-controversy-a26693

The door was sawn by Navalny's daughter
https://navalny-en.livejournal.com/101866.html

Chapter Eight: Is This a Sausage Sandwich I See Before Me?

Navalny blogs on Crimea
https://navalny.livejournal.com/914090.html?fbclid=IwAR33u
    Dqii3ax0gVU8BbwHU8eZMxTExb_vA7aSKI1LQmHVciu
    kzeb7JSvG4s_aem_AcUu1UpzzZEANcA2nkCdkjrwwi
    XZ2nPYzrFUUJjnxijG35TtblKekXA0AsXT7dOkSdBHzA4-
    Ds3gMNbWKqicek7I

Navalny would not give back Ukraine
https://www.themoscowtimes.com/2014/10/16/navalny-
    wouldnt-return-crimea-considers-immigration-bigger-issue-
    than-ukraine-a40477

Chapter Nine: Thieves R Us

Udaltsov jailed
https://www.nytimes.com/2014/07/25/world/europe/russia-2-
    activists-sent-to-prison-colony.html

Razvozzhayev kidnapped
https://www.nytimes.com/2012/10/23/world/europe/leonid-
    razvozzhayev-russian-opposition-figure-says-he-was-
    kidnapped-and-tortured.html
https://navalny-en.livejournal.com/40640.html
https://navalny-en.livejournal.com/73570.html

The administrative torture of Udaltsov
https://navalny-en.livejournal.com/54915.html

Locking up Navalny's brother
https://www.theguardian.com/world/2014/dec/30/
    kremlin-critic-navalny-given-suspended-sentence-brother-
    jailed

Abramovich's Closeness to Putin
In the following link, Team Navalny called for thirty-five
oligarchs to be sanctioned. Roman Abramovich sits at number 1.
https://en.wikipedia.org/wiki/Navalny_35

BBC Newsnight *on Prosecutor General Chaika*
https://www.youtube.com/watch?v=qU2AVcyUgGU

Navalny's film on Chaika
https://www.youtube.com/watch?v=3eO8ZHfV4fk

The Observer *on Chaika film*
https://www.theguardian.com/world/2015/dec/13/alexei-
    navalny-yuri-chaika

Parliamentary evidence on Chaika
https://committees.parliament.uk/writtenevidence/63782/html/

Vladimir Medinsky on Russia's extra chromosome
http://rusk.ru/st.php?idar=58000

Vladimir Medinsky accused of plagiarism
https://www.rferl.org/a/russia-profile-culture-minister-vladimir-
    medinsky/24602133.html

Nemtsov's mother feared he would be killed
https://sobesednik.ru/politika/20150210-boris-nemcov-boyus-togo-
    chto-putin-menya-ubet

Kasyanov falls victim to zugzwang
https://www.themoscowtimes.com/2016/04/22/former-prime-
    minister-kasyanov-stifled-by-both-kremlin-and-allies-a52631

Chapter Ten: Fighting the Lizard King

'Taking on Putin', Panorama, *2018*
https://www.bbc.co.uk/programmes/b09w85tc

Blinding Navalny
https://www.rferl.org/a/russian-authorities-launch-criminal-
    inquiry-navalny-assault-green-antiseptic/28469160.html

SERB threw shit
https://www.rferl.org/a/thugs-attack-volunteers-guarding-
    nemtsov-memorial-in-moscow/29478626.html

Putin a war criminal
https://www.theguardian.com/world/2000/mar/05/russia.chechnya

Putin blew up Russia
https://www.theguardian.com/world/2000/mar/12/chechnya.
    johnsweeney

Russians' use of torture in Chechnya
https://www.theguardian.com/world/2000/oct/15/russia.chechnya

Blair got Putin wrong
https://www.theneweuropean.co.uk/alastair-campbells-diary-
    vladimir-putins-belligerence-must-not-be-underestimated/

Idrisov attacked
https://meduza.io/en/news/2018/01/29/things-turned-
    violent-for-this-human-rights-activist-at-sunday-s-voters-
    boycott-rally-in-st-petersburg

Framing the man who wore the Putin mask
https://meduza.io/en/feature/2019/03/26/st-petersburg-activist-
    investigated-for-trying-to-kill-putin-s-chef-is-now-under-
    arrest-for-trafficking-bombs

The Navalny aid who paid for himself to be hit over the head
with an iron bar
https://meduza.io/en/feature/2017/09/22/an-ex-con-bashed-
    navalny-s-moscow-campaign-chief-over-the-head-with-a-
    pipe-police-think-he-hired-his-own-attacker*

Chapter Eleven: The Man Who Rose from the Dead

Unlikely messiah
CNN documentary, Navalny, 2022, directed by Daniel Roher

Pilots ignored bomb alert at Omsk airport to save Navalny
https://www.thetimes.co.uk/article/pilots-ignored-bomb-
    alert-to-save-alexei-navalny-gqp6rjlgm

Doctors who treated Navalny die
https://www.rferl.org/a/russia-navalny-omsk-another-doctor-
    dies/31174637.html
https://edition.cnn.com/2021/02/04/europe/russia-navalny-
    doctor-maximishin-dies-intl/index.html#

Boss Omsk doctor vanishes, reappears
https://www.themoscowtimes.com/2021/05/10/
    russian-police-find-missing-ex-head-of-siberian-hospital-that-
    treated-navalny-a73845

Bellingcat investigation into Navalny poisoning
https://www.bellingcat.com/news/uk-and-europe/2020/12/14/
    fsb-team-of-chemical-weapon-experts-implicated-in-alexey-
    navalny-novichok-poisoning/

Chapter Twelve: Moscow4, Moscow4

How Navalny pranked his poisoner
CNN documentary, *Navalny*, 2022, directed by Daniel Roher
https://edition.cnn.com/2020/12/21/europe/russia-navalny-
poisoning-underpants-ward/index.html

Clarissa Ward doorsteps one of the Poison Squad
https://www.youtube.com/watch?v=ODcuEE799r4

Putin pooh-poohs the poisoning
https://www.theguardian.com/world/2020/dec/17/putin-
questions-navalny-poisoning-covid-crisis-annual-press-
conference-russian-president-kremlin

Chapter Thirteen: The Temple to Cupid Stunt

Navalny returns to Moscow
https://www.theguardian.com/world/2021/jan/17/alexei-
navalny-detained-at-airport-on-return-to-russia

Matthew Parris on politicians and risk
https://www.thetimes.co.uk/article/politics-is-a-magnet-for-
the-rash-and-reckless-sxrwfp80x

Putin's Palace
https://palace.navalny.com/
https://www.youtube.com/watch?v=T_tFSWZXKN0

Inside Putin's Palace
https://www.thetimes.co.uk/article/vladimir-putins-1bn-palace-
built-with-illicit-funds-says-alexei-navalny-from-prison-cell-
plflch3ft
https://www.theguardian.com/world/2022/jan/21/russian-activists-
publish-leaked-photos-of-putin-linked-palace

Chapter Fourteen: A Brave but Terrible Mistake

Team Navalny gets locked up
https://www.rfi.fr/en/russia-detains-navalny-allies-after-apartment-raids

Navalny's speech from the dock, 2021
https://theins.ru/politika/239043

Trump's links to the Mob
https://www.youtube.com/watch?v=-k3B-tw2sB0

Chapter Fifteen: 'The Cook Likes It Spicy'

Prigozhin threatens to ruin comatose Navalny
https://www.themoscowtimes.com/2020/08/26/kremlin-linked-businessman-prigozhin-vows-to-ruin-navalny-a71246

Prigozhin sues Navalny
https://punchng.com/court-fines-russian-opposition-leader-1-4m-for-defamation/

Sobol investigates Prigozhin
https://navalny.com/p/5086/

Proekt investigates Prigozhin
https://www.proekt.media/en/portrait-en/evgeny-prigozhin/

Navalny investigates Prigozhin
https://navalny.com/p/5382/

Prigozhin's goon confesses, kind of
https://www.occrp.org/en/investigations/9038-operative-for-putin-s-chef-shares-secrets-vanishes-then-reappears-and-retracts

Prigozhin's men in Syria
https://www.occrp.org/en/other-articles/9039-prigozhin-s-men-in-syria

The street cleaner recognises the man who stabbed him
https://meduza.io/en/feature/2019/03/26/st-petersburg-activist-
  investigated-for-trying-to-kill-putin-s-chef-is-now-under-
  arrest-for-trafficking-bombs

Chapter Sixteen: Big War, Little Clout

Putin's boring essay
http://en.kremlin.ru/events/president/news/66181

Navalny's battle cry against corruption
https://www.theguardian.com/commentisfree/2021/aug/19/
  action-against-corruption-russian-sanctions-oligarchs-alexei-
  navalny

Not being an Amnesty Prisoner of Conscience
https://www.bbc.co.uk/news/world-europe-56181084

Not winning the Nobel
https://www.nytimes.com/2021/10/08/world/europe/russian-
  laureate-.html

Navalny denounces big war
https://www.rferl.org/a/navalny-condemns-russia-attack-
  ukraine/31720484.html

Prosecution witness denounces big war
https://www.svoboda.org/a/na-sude-nad-navaljnym-svidetelj-
  obvineniya-otkazalsya-davatj-pokazaniya/31714818.html

Torture at IK-6
https://novayagazeta.ru/articles/2018/07/26/77289-promochil-
  nogi-v-kartsere-i-umer-ot-pnevmonii

Navalny goes to the cooler, again
https://www.themoscowtimes.com/2022/09/07/navalny-put-
  in-solitary-confinement-for-fourth-time-in-month-a78737

Team Navalny publishes the 6,000 list
https://www.occrp.org/en/daily/16253-navalny-s-foundation-
  lists-putin-s-6-000-bribe-takers-and-warmongers

Navalny on Prigozhin's murder
https://x.com/navalny/status/1694742307810013541

Anti-Jewish mob in southern Russia
https://www.telegraph.co.uk/world-news/2023/10/29/
  anti-israel-mob-airport-plane-dagestan-russia-makhachkala/#

Chapter Seventeen: 'They Will Definitely Kill Me'

Navalny's lawyers arrested
https://www.theguardian.com/world/2023/oct/14/russia-detains-
  lawyers-acting-for-opposition-leader-alexei-navalny

Navalny's lawyer hears his fear of being slowly poisoned
https://www.thedailybeast.com/navalny-told-lawyer-he-thought-
  he-was-being-slowly-poisoned

Arctic Wolf Penal Colony
https://www.reuters.com/world/europe/russias-navalny-describes-
  harsh-reality-polar-wolf-arctic-prison-2023-12-26/

Effective torture
https://novayagazeta.ru/articles/2024/02/16/vy-liudi-voobshche

Navalny's death
https://www.reuters.com/world/europe/alexei-navalnys-death-
  what-do-we-know-2024-02-18/

'KGB punch' theory
https://www.thetimes.co.uk/article/alexei-navalny-killed-
  punch-death-cause-russia-putin-x86g6jcdx

Navalny trade
https://edition.cnn.com/2024/03/08/europe/navalny-prisoner-
    swap-deal-abramovich-intl/index.html

The Times *quotes Osechkin*
https://www.thetimes.com/world/russia-ukraine-war/article/
    alexei-navalny-killed-punch-death-cause-russia-putin-x86g6jcdx

Proekt investigate Osechkin
https://www.proekt.media/en/portrait-en/vladimir-osechkin-en/

Osechkin's FSB source said Russia to invade Japan
https://www.newsweek.com/russia-planned-attack-
    japan-2021-fsb-letters-1762133

US intelligence believes Putin didn't order Navalny's death
https://www.reuters.com/world/europe/us-intelligence-
    believes-putin-probably-didnt-order-navalny-be-killed-wsj-
    2024-04-27/

Chapter Eighteen: 'I'll Be Back'

https://www.theguardian.com/artanddesign/2024/feb/26/dmitry-
    markov-russia-cartier-bresson-photographer

About the Author

John Sweeney is a writer and journalist who has challenged dictators, despots, cult leaders, con artists and crooked businessmen for almost half a century. As a reporter, first for the *Observer* and then for the BBC, he has covered wars in around 100 countries and has been undercover in the danger zones of Chechnya, North Korea and Zimbabwe. The author of 16 books, including the *Sunday Times* bestseller *Killer in the Kremlin*, he has challenged both Donald Trump and Vladimir Putin face-to-face. He regularly appears on *Good Morning Britain* to report on life in Kyiv, where he has lived on and off since the Russian invasion.